QUEEN'S

COURT

Queen's Court

JUDICIAL POWER IN THE

REHNQUIST ERA   Nancy Maveety

 UNIVERSITY PRESS OF KANSAS

Published by the

University Press of Kansas

(Lawrence, Kansas

66045), which was

organized by the Kansas

Board of Regents and is

operated and funded by

Emporia State University,

Fort Hays State University,

Kansas State University,

Pittsburg State University,

the University of Kansas,

and Wichita State

University

Library of Congress Cataloging-in-Publication Data

Maveety, Nancy.

 Queen's court : judicial power in the Rehnquist era /
Nancy Maveety.

 p. cm.

 Includes bibliographical references and index.

 ISBN 978-0-7006-1610-7 (cloth : alk. paper)

 1. United States. Supreme Court—History. 2. Judicial
process—United States—History. 3. Concurring
opinions—United States—History. 4. Rehnquist, William
H., 1924–2005. 5. O'Connor, Sandra Day, 1930– I. Title.

 KF8742.M287 2008

 347.73'26—dc22   2008015522

British Library Cataloguing-in-Publication Data is available.

Printed in the United States of America

10 9 8 7 6 5 4 3 2 1

The paper used in this publication is recycled and contains
30 percent postconsumer waste. It is acid free and meets
the minimum requirements of the American National
Standard for Permanence of Paper for Printed Library
Materials z39.48–1992.

CONTENTS

PREFACE AND ACKNOWLEDGMENTS

This book for me will always be the one punctuated by my exile from my university and city because of the ravages of Hurricane Katrina. But it has been my good fortune to find sponsorship and support through all stages of this project. My deepest gratitude goes to my colleagues and friends at the Princeton University Program in Law and Public Affairs and especially to its director, Kim Lane Scheppele, who took me into their community as an academic refugee and made me a "Katrina Fellow" during that uncertain fall of 2005. Although I was a woefully poorly prepared evacuee, I did manage to flee the New Orleans floodwaters with file copies of the draft chapters of my manuscript in progress. One of these I had the opportunity to present to the Law and Public Affairs seminar, and what is now Chapter 4 was improved greatly by the thoughtful and incisive commentary provided by the seminar participants.

The archival research with the Harry A. Blackmun Papers, which undergirds the arguments presented in Chapter 1, was accomplished with the support of a National Science Foundation Small Grant for Exploratory Research. I thank the two program officers with whom I worked in securing and then extending this grant—again, in the professionally destabilizing aftermath of Hurricane Katrina (or "post-K," as we New Orleanians now and forever after will speak of the period since the storm). My appreciation goes to Chris Zorn for his original sponsorship, and to Isaac Unah for his flexibility and understanding of the difficulties of my situation. The summer weeks of 2004 that I first spent at the Library of Congress Manuscript Division and the follow-up visits made later contributed to my understanding of the interjudicial decision-making processes on the early Rehnquist Court.

An earlier version of Chapter 2 appeared in a 2005 special issue of the journal *Judicature* as "The Era of the Choral Court." My thanks go to that issue editor, Thomas Marshall, for his beneficial suggested revisions, which improved the article and helped shape the chapter for this book. The approach taken and the inferences drawn from the aggregate data available on the Rehnquist Court depend directly on collaborative work with my two fine coauthors, Lori Beth Way and Charley Turner. Our shared interest in—some might say fixation on—concurring behavior on multimember courts has fueled my attention to the Rehnquist Court's legacy, a chief part of which has been its identity as the Court-as-chorus. In our work together we are a "choral" author, and I would be a lesser scholar of judicial decision making without the accompanying voices of my dedicated and creative collaborators.

Finally, I am indebted to my editor at the University Press of Kansas, Fred Woodward, for his unflinching support, encouragement, and personal faith in me and my work. He secured the services of the two reviewers of my manuscript, whose attentive reading and constructive criticism challenged and inspired me to craft my arguments more carefully and conduct my analysis more thoroughly. I especially thank Shep Melnick for reading and critiquing the manuscript with more care and precision than its author sometimes did. I trust that both reviewers will see ample evidence of the dialogue their input inspired, even as those shortcomings that remain are my fault, not theirs.

Final revisions to and copyediting of the manuscript occurred during my Fulbright lectureship at Shandong University, in Jinan, China. To my colleague there, Wang Jianmin—my "Ge Ge"—I am grateful for his sponsorship and friendship during my visiting appointment, for his provision of excellent work space and resources to complete this project, and for his promise to make the first international purchase of the new book.

This study of the Rehnquist era is both the continuation of a topic that has long interested me and a prelude to the study of a phenomenon that both includes and transcends the Rehnquist Court. My 1996 book, *Justice Sandra Day O'Connor: Strategist on the Supreme Court*, was an examination of the patterns of behavioral and jurisprudential accommodation O'Connor exhibited from the time of her appointment to the Burger Court that prefigured her influence as a judicial decision maker. In that study, I also identified her use of the concurring opinion as a strategic and substantive device to influence both public and legal audiences. This study of judicial power in the Rehnquist era obviously draws on my conclusions about O'Connor, but extends the analysis to the institutional level. I suspect we will be feeling the effects of the Rehnquist Court, and not only jurisprudentially, for quite some time in the American political and constitutional systems. By wielding an infrequently used tool of separate opinion writing, this "supremely individualist" Court stressed the power of individual judicial judgment in, and the contributions of individual jurists to, the collegial doctrinal promulgation project. What Justice O'Connor had done in a somewhat isolated fashion during her early years on the bench became a hallmark of the associate justices and members of majority coalitions during the Supreme Court of the 1990s and early 2000s. This is the "continuation of a topic" mentioned above, and the reason for this book's evocative title, Queen's Court.

It is perhaps premature to speak of the "prelude" that this study constitutes. Still, studying the ascendance of multivocal judicial decision making in the post-Marshall period of univocal normalcy naturally raises the question of whether such a golden age of institutional unanimity ever existed. Majority opinions bracketed by concurrences that clarify, explain, extend, or limit—or, at times, challenge concurring and dissenting in part—have become much more typical of Supreme Court doctrinal pronouncements. If the Rehnquist Court was the period of maturation of this tactic, then the periods of its inception, growth, and development await and merit future research. I hope this book is a catalyst for my own and for others' judicial scholarship.

Supreme Court scholars specialize in reflection on a moving target, and are shaped by the political times in which they write. It is undoubtedly wrong, Martin Shapiro once remarked, to confuse what the Supreme Court does with what the commentators say about what it does. Sage though that advice is, I am unable to follow it completely, for much of the importance of the Rehnquist Court, and its legacy, lies, I think, in court commentators' reactions to it. But in the same essay, Shapiro offered this additional rumination: "This generation of commentators," he observed, referring to the deeply dissatisfied critics of the Burger Court, "is no happier with the present Court than its predecessor was with the preceding one . . . no doubt in part because of the tension that always exists between critic and playwright" (1983, 236). Metaphors abound in the study of the American judiciary, from robes to crowns; some illuminate, others obfuscate. But there is a sense in which the Court's "performance" never lives up to either our idealized or scholarly image of its role. In that distance between what we expect and what we observe is located my reading of the Rehnquist years, which is an accommodation to the ineluctable disappointment Shapiro predicts for those who study their contemporary Supreme Court.

New Orleans, Louisiana, and Jinan, China
November 2007

QUEEN'S

COURT

The Rehnquist Court had come to seem like the Supreme Court that would never end, its identity as fixed as its personnel. For its final years, from 1994 through 2005, with no change of justices, the Court ossified into its predictably unpredictable decision-making habits by two blocs of "stalwarts" and several central "swingers." Legal commentators, who had the luxury of an enduring Court period to contemplate, ruminated over its defining actors but seldom its definitive characteristics.

Stasis engendered less reasoned reflection than overheated speculation from Rehnquist-era court watchers. In the years that followed the 2000 presidential election, forecasting the next vacancy on the bench and projecting its likely impact on the Court's decisional configurations took center stage in academic and journalistic commentary. Illness and the advanced age of several justices lent a macabre tone to some of this forecasting—a tone that (finally) acquired a discomforting reality during the summer of 2005, when Chief Justice Rehnquist died and Associate Justice Sandra Day O'Connor announced her retirement. Despite Rehnquist's long illness, his death seemed somewhat sudden, and his passing, his ultimate replacement by the renominated John Roberts, and O'Connor's extended service as an announced retiree contributed to the feeling of a lingering withering of a Court era, of a labored transition from something that had not been conclusively defined.

The Rehnquist period of 1986 to 2005 usually has been summarized in terms of its conservative activism, its ideological divisiveness, or some inconclusive mixture of the two. Each new grand narrative joins a conversation well under way (Siegel 2006, 1099 and n. 1). Yet despite the extended period for taking stock of an era as it drew to a close, judicial scholars who have written about this Court share a profound difficulty in naming the Court era. A 2005 symposium in the newsletter of the Law and Courts Section of the American Political Science Association confronted this difficulty head-on. Eminent scholars of the judicial institution explained the divided Court as a product of divided government, verified with sophisticated statistical techniques the shifting center of the Court—even during the period of personnel constancy from 1994 to 2005—and struggled to label "the mixed bag that we may remember fondly as the Rehnquist Court" (Brigham 2005, 26). "Mixed bag" of course reprises the theme of a Court divided and thus hard to characterize in terms of ideology or policy-making contributions. The phrase "that we may remember fondly as the Rehnquist Court" suggests that the Court during this period had something for everyone, that its style and outputs of compromises prevented further political polarization of society. Yet to acknowledge this is to admit that of the Court's many faces and many voices, few belonged to Chief Justice Rehnquist.

Was the "Rehnquist" Court's lack of eponymous identity the fault of its chief and his lack of leadership ability? Not according to many accounts, which praised his administrative skills and personal aplomb and identified him as one of the most all-around successful chiefs (Bradley 2005; Rosen 2005b, 80). Rehnquist's virtues as a chief seem particularly noteworthy if we recall the Burger Court, whose "rootless" activism (Blasi 1983) is forever identified with the various infirmities of its leader, Chief Justice Warren Burger. Neither does subsuming the period from Burger through Rehnquist under the label "the Republican Court era" create an accurate frame for the Court decisions of the 1990s and the new millennium. The adjective "Republican" is over- and underinclusive to describe the Court's late twentieth- and early twenty-first century activities. For the author of the best-selling screed *Men in Black: How the Supreme Court Is Destroying America*, GOP appointees like Justices Anthony Kennedy and Sandra Day O'Connor were the worst sort of apostates (Levin 2005); for other court watchers, the intellectual influence of idiosyncratic moderates such as John Paul Stevens and pragmatists such as Stephen Breyer tempered the impact of conservative ideology on constitutional law making. The presence of both kinds of justices on the contemporary Court has yielded more debate than declaration.

The judicial version of this debate as to the identity of the institution both characterized and distinguished the Rehnquist era. This debate took the form of "multivocality," or many separate judicial voices raised in opinion to constitute Court decisions. Over the past two decades, the notion of the individual judicial voice apart from that of the Supreme Court as an institution gained a presence in the literature about the Court and stature on the Court itself. The emerging legitimacy of the individual judicial voice in Court decision making fueled a profound increase in separate opinion writing, particularly concurrences, and cultivation of separate judicial identities. "Rehnquist's" was an individualist's Court, staffed by nine separate sovereignties, each "concerned with building up and maintaining a separate identity, ideology, and body of opinions" (Friedman 2002, 145). This is why there was at once no Rehnquist Court and, also, a distinctively Rehnquist-era Court chorus. Rehnquist's Court was individualistic in another systemic sense: its decisions showed that it was jealously protective of its place vis-à-vis the other powers in the separated system of government. Even former solicitor general Kenneth Starr (2002), in his contemporaneous book on the Court intended for a popular audience, unabashedly characterized the place of the Rehnquist judicial branch as "first among equals."

Was there one judicial individual on the Rehnquist Court who acted as choir director, the "first among equals" in the Court chorus? The leading contender has been none other than movement conservatives' favorite apostate, Reagan appointee and Court centrist Justice O'Connor—or "Queen Sandra," as movement blogs, columnists, and websites unflatteringly branded her.[1] Less ideologically inflamed commentary also singled out the first female associate justice for status elevation: "Why the Chief Justice Isn't the Chief Justice," Washington Post reporter Charles Lane opined in a piece on O'Connor's importance for the 2004 Pledge of Allegiance case; "Queen of the Center" affirmed a Newsweek article at the time of her retirement announcement in July 2004. "It's the O'Connor Court," one 2004 law review article titled itself, evoking a commonplace understanding among legal academics as well as journalistic pundits (Rappaport 2004).

The basis for these invectives and accolades was O'Connor's critical role as a decisional pivot, as a centrist conservative justice on a sharply divided and jurisprudentially polarized Supreme Court. For years, she functioned as "a Court of one," in the words of court watcher Jeffrey Rosen (2001); she was the deciding vote across a range of legal issues coming before the justices, and her doctrinal and policy positions determined many minimally winning majorities. The Rehnquist Court was really the O'Connor Court, reporter Jeffrey Toobin (2007) wrote in his behind-the-scenes look at the Supreme Court.

O'Connor was clearly Toobin's most important source, alleged a *New York Times* review of the book, noting that "she's also—readers can decide if it's coincidental—his hero: the justice, he argues, who through her pragmatic, seat-of-the-pants jurisprudence single-handedly kept the Court close to the American mainstream, particularly on matters like reproductive freedom and affirmative action" (Margolis 2007).

Because of her centrality to the legacy of the Rehnquist Court, O'Connor was perceived as the institution's first woman chief justice in all but name. Fair or unfair this characterization, Associate Justice Sandra Day O'Connor was more influential in the Court majorities than any of her associate colleagues, and left more of a mark on the Court jurisprudence than its chief. But she was no usurper, despite the intimations of some tell-all accounts of "her" Court. The Court on which she served was the "queen's Court" in this sense: she was, as an individual associate justice, *the crucial contributor* to each of the several legacies of the Supreme Court during the Rehnquist era. In remembering the Rehnquist Court, then, it is impossible not to mark the presence of its other Arizonan.

This book aspires not only to assign a definitive meaning to the "Rehnquist Court," but to identify its historical importance for the constitutional order and the conception of judicial power within it. My argument is that to do both requires placing O'Connor where she long sat, figuratively if not literally: at the center. In this introduction I catalog the legacies the Rehnquist Court leaves, focusing on what attributes demarcate it from its predecessors and threaten to shadow (or condition a response from) its successor. Subsequent chapters illustrating and analyzing these attributes explain how O'Connor's actions were essential in establishing them. My goal is to offer a systematic argument as to why the Supreme Court best remembered for its judicial individualism and presumptive theory of judicial power should be remembered legitimately as Justice O'Connor's, and to identify the real difficulties—jurisprudential and systemic—of the "judicial O'Connorism" that colors our recollection of that Court era.

The years of O'Connor's tenure were distinctively formative for the U.S. Supreme Court. Although her appointment predated Rehnquist's as chief, her five years of service under Chief Justice Burger offered indications of her emerging importance as an accommodationist on a divided bench where

neither the conservative nor liberal bloc held the balance of power and a centrist justice could broker compromise (Maveety 1996). Still, with the onset
of the Rehnquist era, the Court developed more entrenched patterns of both
polarization and identifiable response—attributes that are found in or linked
to O'Connor's decision making. These attributes, moreover, constitute the
multiple legacies of the supremely individualist Rehnquist Court. The attributes may be grouped as follows: the individuated behaviors of the justices
during this Court era, the Court's rule-of-thumb jurisprudence—a "rule" that
was context-determined and oriented toward the individual judgment of the
reviewing justices—and the impact of both on the court commentary industry and its view of the Supreme Court as an institution.

"COLLEGIAL" BEHAVIORS

Although the congressional maxim "to get along, go along" may never have
applied fully to the judicial institution (if, indeed, it ever applied fully to Sam
Rayburn's House of Representatives), a consensual norm, or expectation of
collegial behavior, did govern Supreme Courts of the past. The contemporary Court and its members have been a decidedly less unified, self-sacrificing
lot. This departure from past convention was illustrated indirectly by the new
Chief Justice John Roberts's remarks at the 2006 Georgetown University Law
School graduation: "Division should not be artificially suppressed," he commented, "but the rule of law benefits from a broader agreement" (Yen 2006).
"Broader agreement than under the previous chief justice," he might have
added, and such a thought hovered unsaid behind the current chief justice's
statement.

Chapter 1, "Policy Leadership on the Early Rehnquist Court," argues that
individuated judicial behavior defined the Rehnquist Court even though its
personality and membership were still in flux. What the early Rehnquist years
imply is that "policy leadership" on the High Court was principally a matter of influence over legal policy outputs (O'Brien 2005, 252), and that such
influence was highly variable and situational. During the period from 1986 to
1994, which predated the seating of Justice Breyer and the longest period of
stable membership in recent Supreme Court history, a changing cast of associate justices on the Rehnquist bench fulfilled leadership roles in conjunction
with that of the chief.

Although some might claim policy leadership on the Rehnquist Court
never resided in its chief but largely in its most strategic centrist, Justice

O'Connor, Chapter 1 offers a more nuanced understanding of the Rehnquist-era leadership legacy. It explains why various court watchers have spoken, at different times, about several different Courts and Court leaders: the "first" and "second" Rehnquist Courts (Garrow 2002, 276) and the "Scalia factor" in creating the latter (Merrill 2003, 570–571, nn. 7–9), a less sure-handed "third Rehnquist Court" of its twilight years (Greenhouse 2005), a "Brennan Court" continuation (Irons 1994; Richey 2004; Tushnet 1993, 33), Kennedy as the "most dangerous justice" (Edelman and Chen 1996, 2001; but see Baker 1996), and, last but not least, the "O'Connor Court" (Rosen 2001). Policy leadership on the Rehnquist bench was subdivided and issue-sensitive among the justices, and this convention was well established by the time of the most important institutional turning point of the Rehnquist era in 1994.

Chapter 2, "The Choral Court of Separate Voices," addresses a second type of individualistic behavior: the emerging predominance of separate, concurring opinion writing by the justices during the Rehnquist era and its substantive and procedural influence. Like diffused leadership, increasing concurrence was a phenomenon already apparent in the earlier, Burger Court era. Indeed, one of its most prevalent and effective practitioners on that Court and throughout the Rehnquist years was Justice O'Connor (Maveety 2003). But just as she was a participant in and not the sole perpetrator of decentralized policy leadership, she contributed to but (by definition) could not be solely responsible for the Rehnquist Court's decisional multivocality.

Separate opinion writing, and separate opinions that bracketed majority and plurality opinions of the Court, acquired new decisional significance and led to new institutional implications during the Rehnquist years, such that it now makes sense to speak of "the era of a choral Court" (Maveety 2005). Again, the words of Chief Justice Roberts are illustrative in their reaction to the lack of agreement in the rulings by his predecessor Supreme Court. "Broader agreement among the justices"—univocality where possible—is the new chief justice's goal, to be achieved by deciding cases on "the narrowest possible grounds" (Yen 2006), therefore avoiding opportunities for the separately filed, multipart harmonies in which the Rehnquist justices indulged.

Taken together, my two chapters that document these judicial behaviors on the Rehnquist Court employ a mixed methodology to describe the manifestation of judicial individualism: qualitative assessment of empirical measures generated from archived case records, and quantitative analysis of aggregated decisional data. Two data sources are principally referenced: for Chapter 1, the archived judicial papers of Justice Harry A. Blackmun covering the Supreme Court period of Rehnquist's chief justiceship from 1986 to 1994, and for Chapter 2 the Benesh-Spaeth Supreme Court Database of decisions from the Burger and Rehnquist Courts. From the Blackmun records of intra-Court memos and opinion drafts, I reconstruct the individual justices' input into the decisional process for a subset of cases from the early Rehnquist period, using these qualitative measures of influence to validate the claim that policy leadership was fragmented and accepted as such. From the database, which distills the Court record into an aggregation of observations about the characteristics of cases, votes, and opinions, I draw inferences about behavioral tendencies from aggregate patterns of decision making by the Rehnquist justices in order to test claims about the prevalence and the salience of separate opinions and multiple juridical voices.

The purpose of Chapters 1 and 2 is to describe the way intra-Court dialogue took place on the Rehnquist Court. The duration and impact of both diffused leadership activity and separate opinion writing during the Rehnquist era are evidence that the judicial individualism of the period altered the procedural, collegial conventions of the Supreme Court. Whether temporary or more entrenched, that the alterations seem targeted for dismantling by Chief Justice Roberts suggests the reality of their operation. The multivocality of the Rehnquist bench was a product of its members' take on the Court's institutional norms or customary practices. Significantly, these now-extant norms and customs are those into which subsequent judicial appointees will be inaugurated, and from which they may have to be discouraged by a new High Court leader.

JURISPRUDENTIAL ARROGANCE OR MODESTY?

Two eminent scholars of the Court, in books written for a general audience, stressed that the Rehnquist era was a divisive one, both ideologically and jurisprudentially. Mark Tushnet's *A Court Divided* and Cass Sunstein's *Radicals in Robes* appeared in 2005 at the close of the Rehnquist Court. Both attributed the divisions among the mostly Republican justices of the Court to the intra-party tensions of the current political regime, and respectively took comfort in the bland jurisprudence that resulted as evidence that the judicial institution influences national politics only at the margins (Tushnet 2005), or stressed that the dominant pragmatic conservatives left an appropriately minimalist jurisprudential record—although one endangered by a GOP variant of judicial fundamentalism (Sunstein 2005).

Both scholars can be interpreted as agreeing that the lack of decisional unity on the Rehnquist Court, however it should be described and analyzed, had a singular jurisprudential consequence: rule-of-thumb balancing approaches prevailed over bright-line, ideologically driven rules for deciding cases and adjudicating legal issues. This was true even for the issue areas in which the chief justice was said to be leading his Court, such as federalism, and even for the most politically charged rulings where the Republican judge coalition prevailed, as in *Bush v. Gore* (2000) and *Hamdi v. Rumsfeld* (2004). It was clearly the case for those rulings recognized and lauded as compromise decisions on polarizing questions: *Planned Parenthood v. Casey*, the University of Michigan affirmative action cases, *Shaw v. Reno* and its progeny, and the 2005 Ten Commandments display cases. What is not so clear is whether this doctrinal output is a legacy that will last, or should.

Chapter 3, "Associates' Justice," provides a summary of the doctrinal contributions of the Supreme Court during the Rehnquist era, characterizing them as rule-of-thumb jurisprudence, generally leaning toward conservative balancing. In so doing, the chapter identifies which of the Court's most noteworthy doctrinal contributions—its balancing tests intended to cover litigation of various issue questions—were the product of its centrist jurists. The answer is all of them; furthermore, the most prolific centrist was moderate conservative Justice O'Connor. This is no revelation. Thomas Keck (2004) isolates O'Connor as the pivotal justice who endorsed both the conservative activist and the progressive activist strands of legal policy making by the Rehnquist Court. But O'Connor, by her actions, also established a *practice of power* by individual associate justices that characterized both the process and the product of the Rehnquist Court. The subsequent jurisprudence was, as a result and in conjunction with the decisional trends discussed in Chapters 1 and 2, a *rule-of-thumbs* approach, heavily dependent on singular judgment calls by individual justices in case-by-case adjudication. So in identifying O'Connor as the jurist who chiefly spoke for the Rehnquist Court, jurisprudentially, we also need to ask two questions about this constitutional legacy. First, are there conditions under which the rule-of-thumb balancing approach to constitutional policy making persists? Does its use, in other words, depend on associate justice empowerment or just judicial moderates in the balance of power? Second, are O'Connor's balancing tests likely to endure, then, as precedent?

Persistence of O'Connor's legacy aside, it is also interesting to note that court scholars differ as to the institutional-role message of judicial balancing and fact-based decision-making approaches in general. Scholars differ, in other words, as to whether fact-based judicial balancing *should* endure. Deciding one case at a time, limiting the reach of judicial pronouncements, has the effect of saving other, bigger questions for another day—or another lawsuit. Where some see in this deferring of judgment judicial humility, appropriate minimalism, and institutional restraint, others see Court-centric arrogance and presumptive claims of judicial competence, with judges using cryptic formulations in order to retain the last word over all policy deliberation. If the real legacy of O'Connor-style jurisprudence is arrogance cloaked as humility, then the successor Roberts Court inherits a double-edged sword, juridically speaking. A new Supreme Court using the Rehnquist-era precedents to guide its own decisional directions could suggest the substantive influence of O'Connor-fashioned balancing doctrines. But it could also suggest an overall institutional influence: the unconstraining effect of the Rehnquist-era arrogations of judicial power that authorize all manner of judicial declarations as consistent with existing doctrinal standards.

CATALYST TO COURT COMMENTARY

In another way, the institutional-role meaning of Rehnquist-era jurisprudential legacy is already clear and firmly in the hands of the court commentary industry. Not surprisingly but perhaps disproportionately compared to some of its predecessors (Friedman 2004), the Rehnquist era inspired a series of scholarly reflections on and reassessments of the Supreme Court's role as a constitutional court. Keck (2004) built a convincing case that this was the most activist Supreme Court in U.S. history; following from this, this Court's "juricentric" decision making (Post and Siegel 2003) produced a sea change in the theory of judicial review and the constitutional role of the Supreme Court. This theoretical literature alternatively predicts or preaches judicial caution and was profoundly animated by the Rehnquist era.

Chapter 4, "The Commentators' Court and the Return to Judicial Restraint," first traces the efforts of Rehnquist Court commentators to back away from the legal liberalism and progressive contexts of judicial activism central to the construction of the Supreme Court's role in constitutional democracy since the Warren era. Cass Sunstein's (1999) praise for judicial minimalism, Mark Tushnet's (2003) identification of a new constitutional order, and Sanford Levinson's (2006) many and various calls for a truly democratic constitutionalism were all strategic efforts to back away from judicial activism. In place of the traditional systemic acceptance of judicial countermajoritarianism as the defense of minority rights, legal scholars ascribed a new role to a new Court, convincingly reviving and reinvigorating theories of judicial restraint and regime-based majoritarianism (Graber 1993; Sunstein 2005) thought long discarded or discredited. Collectively, these writings show how the Rehnquist era shaped legal theorizing about the Supreme Court as powerfully as did the Warren era.

The Rehnquist Court's "legal impact" thus can be construed in terms of intellectual impact. Its record precipitated significant alterations in judicial scholarship and, ultimately, in public understandings of the Court as an institution. "Public understandings" include journalistic interpretations, as these were frequently reactive to the arguments of academics. Examination of these various sources suggests that Rehnquist Court commentators found in that Court material to inspire an influential but sobering revision of the theory of judicial review in constitutional governance.

Crucial in that Court material, and to the commentary on its legacy, was Justice O'Connor herself, who seemed to exhibit antipathy for Warren Court constitutional perfectionism, although she exhorted the public to depend on her judicial guidance. She became the vehicle in several studies for examination of the particular judicial hubris of the Rehnquist Court era, though she was never the only exemplar of it.

THE FINAL INSTALLMENT

The real impact of the Rehnquist era and its judicial practices will be felt in the decisions of the next Supreme Court (Tushnet 2005, 12), because powerful legacies will press upon the Roberts Court. O'Connor herself supplied an intriguing parable for this notion by her continued service on the bench, almost like a queen regent, as the nation awaited the confirmation of her replacement through fall 2005 and winter 2006. Chapter 5, "The Queen Regent's Court in the Roberts Transition," argues somewhat irreverently that the Rehnquist Court era symbolically ended with O'Connor's July 2005 resignation statement, and effectively ended only with her final departure from the Court on January 31, 2006. As a postscript to the study of the Rehnquist era, the chapter examines the events that transpired from her resignation announcement through the confirmation hearings to consider the replacement for "the model Supreme Court justice," as Senator Patrick Leahy first described the "O'Connor template" against which her successor should be measured.[2] The focus of this penultimate chapter, however, is the portion of the October 2005 term in which O'Connor participated, and the chief concern of the chapter is to assess which Rehnquist Court legacies persisted in the early days of the Roberts transition, especially in those cases decided with O'Connor as a voting member of the Court.

The concluding chapter, "Long Live the Queen's Court?" considers the implications of naming, blaming, and remembering the "O'Connor" judicial era. Was "her" Supreme Court typical, interesting, or somehow formative, in that it changed the institution and conceptions of its power? And what was Associate Justice O'Connor's role in effecting any or all of that? My stance is that the importance of the Rehnquist years extends from the substance of constitutional law to the institutional operation of Court decision making, and that O'Connor the justice was vital to those important changes.

Still, for certain commentators, the most important legacy of the Rehnquist era was the judicial triumphalism that profoundly affected the ways in which the polity thinks about constitutional democracy. Objecting members of the Court's public no longer "feel constrained to passively accept the Court's rulings while waiting for justices to die or retire in the hope that they will be replaced by others with more sympathetic views" (Kramer 2004). There has been revisiting of the meaning and narrowing of the scope of judicial action in the modern political order, from the constitution-in-exile believers (Barnett 2005) to the political regime theorists (Graber 2005; Lovell 2003; Whittington 2005) to the advocates for term limits for federal judges (Cramton and Carrington 2006; Levinson 2006). At the center of this Supreme Court revisionism is the political nature and role of the judicial institution—what it has been, and what it should be, and what it was during the O'Connor judicial era.

Theorizing about judicial review, even and especially when spurred by contemplation of the Rehnquist Court record, has nevertheless begged the empirical question of the Rehnquist Court's actual manifestation of judicial power. If O'Connor was central to its exercise of judicial power, and if the O'Connor-style approach to institutional norms and jurisprudential balancing was a form of judicial aggrandizement, then how can some court commentators seriously embrace her judicial "minimalism" as model "restraint"? The only possible answer is that certain court scholars have misunderstood "O'Connorism," and mistaken the kind of political Court it creates for the politically aware, politically strategic, but politically cautious Supreme Court they desire. Such desire perhaps unintentionally is fueled by contemporary political study of law and courts, which posits that courts and their judges must be understood as goal-seeking actors whose goals include policy outcomes *and* institutional presence. Fundamental to this view that courts are political in nature is the acknowledgment that judges—particularly Supreme Court justices—care about the power and the legitimacy of the judicial institution in the American political system, and reach only as far as they think is strategically rational and likely to be successful. Strategic models of intra-Court behavior (Maltzman et al. 2000), too, stress and cannot help but pay tribute to politically savvy courts composed of supremely individualist, competitive, but ultimately cooperative judicial players. This expectation was largely fulfilled by the power plays of individual associate justices on the Rehnquist bench.

Such political, strategic courts are admired for being practical. If such a Court had a "queen," she could only have been the associate justice who was the consummate strategist. This O'Connor was on the Rehnquist Court. She contributed to the recent Supreme Court's sense of institutional prominence and notion of the individual justice's creative preeminence, yet observed the limits of each. But her legacy, for her Court and as a politically powerful justice, is not one of judicial restraint so much as the power that lies in judicial pragmatism. The strategic judicial action that fashioned this pragmatism fascinated students of judicial politics—even as court commentators' memory of it, and of the Rehnquist years, distorted the potentially detrimental impact of judicial pragmatism for the Court as an institution and for the Court's function of doctrinal promulgation.

In her behavior and her understanding of judicial power, O'Connor was the "political scientists' justice"—despite her insistence on being remembered only as "a good judge."[3] Indeed, she was the last former politician to sit during this political Court era. By most accounts, she showed considerable interest in cultivating her public persona, as reflected in her public appearances and television interviews, books for a mass audience, and statements on the record indicating that she cared about public opinion—both about her and her Court's decisions (Baum 2006, 69). But she was not a political scientists' justice in the sense of overtly and reliably performing as the attitudinalists' ideological jurist (Segal and Spaeth 2002), or in actively courting a specific policy audience's approval (Baum 2006) as a political jurist.[4]

As a retired justice from the Court, O'Connor has been functioning more as an apolitical queen dowager might, as the figure symbolizing a bygone era whose symbolic power is especially pronounced given that the chief justice of the Court has passed away. Of course, in O'Connor's case, she also personified and personifies a judicial role, a "lofty desire to save the country from its most divisive debates" (Rosen 2005a, R4). Queenly though this sounds, the O'Connor Court with this role orientation was less regal than openly politically involved, enacting those divisive debates in its opinions, within its decision-making processes, and among its justices. The consequences of this O'Connoresque kind of decisional and doctrinal judicial individualism are more troubling than the O'Connor admirers—such as Senator Leahy and the neorestraintist law professors—would admit. But few would deny that this judicial individualism has left a telling mark on the High Court and its practices, and likely marks its future as well.

As prescriptive or predicted path, "Long Live O'Connorism" is not an unmitigated blessing. As Toobin (2007, 226) charges, "it is a scary prospect to consider what other justices in the Court's history, including some of her contemporaries, would have done with the power that O'Connor arrogated to herself" in deciding cases and setting quasilegislative policy standards.[5] Still, it remains striking that in remembering O'Connor we recall an entire Court era, which suggests her essential connection to that era's legacies. But lest she become a vehicle for romanticizing or distorting a juridical past, we must carefully and accurately detail and then assess those legacies—of the power of the accommodating associate and her pragmatic jurisprudence, of "chiefless" but juricentric justice, and of the supremely individualist Court of the Rehnquist years.

I

The Rehnquist Court, that "mixed bag," inspired a unique lack of consensus about two important aspects of its legacy: whether it was a disappointment to political conservatives, and whether the Court should be labeled "Rehnquist's" at all. Thus the convention of naming becomes a proposition to test in terms of policy leadership by the conservative chief justice. Policy leadership refers to which justice—chief or associate, conservative, liberal, or other—controls or fashions the Court's legal policy outputs.[1] A look at policy leadership leads to several questions that shape the analysis of this first chapter. What institutional or operational changes did Chief Justice Rehnquist promote, and did these changes affect his exercise of leadership on the High Court? Did Rehnquist facilitate or happen to preside over an emerging norm of judicial individualism? And did the accommodationist conservative Justice O'Connor simply take advantage of such a norm or did she actively help to establish it (Maveety 1996)?

Two things we know from simple observation and from credible reports by members of the high bench regarding institutional and operational changes during the Rehnquist era. First, the Rehnquist period occasioned a steep decrease in the number of cases accepted for review and formally decided, from a Burger Court high of more than 150 to a low of just under 80 (Epstein et al. 2003, 83–85). Second, Rehnquist personally inaugurated a truncated and nondeliberative conference period among the justices (Davis 1999, 145; Peretti 1999, 110). Consequently there were, at the same time, fewer decisions to talk about and less time devoted to talking about them collectively on this Supreme Court.

Examining the correlation between these two developments and the exercise of leadership on the Court is a more interpretive than scientific enterprise. Systematic study of judicial leadership by law and court scholars has been hampered by a methodological difficulty: few of the empirically observable and/or objectively measurable behavioral indicators amenable to aggregate-pattern analysis and hypothesis-testing protocols are agreed upon as fitting a definition of "leadership." Danelski's (1960) typology of conference leadership as the roles of task leader and social leader emphasized individual intellectualism, interpersonal skills, and personality—attributes difficult to evaluate other than subjectively or intuitively. The studies that offer direct comparisons of justices across operationalizable indicators of performance tend to focus on discrete behaviors, such as opinion assignment tactics, which nevertheless "provide only a partial view of the wide panorama of leadership" (Davis 1999, 150). Thus, the most promising approaches to the study of judicial leadership are now institutionalist-informed, addressing "which past practices have affected the development of institutional norms" and "how changing norms shape the dimensions of the power of the Chief Justice" (Davis 1999, 150–151).

I argue in this chapter that what began as a practice became an institutional norm on the Rehnquist Court: decentralized policy leadership among the justices reified the individuated judicial behavior that defined that Court. The process could be described in this way: uncertainty surrounding the scope of a norm, ambiguity regarding the practice of policy leadership, and the willingness of the Court's political actors to engage in "norm entrepreneurship" by decentralizing policy leadership created a context in which the development of a new norm of judicial individualism was possible (Gerhardt 2001). Norms, it should be acknowledged, are troublesome concepts to many political scientists, for their presence can only be inferred from the exhibition of certain behaviors. Their independent operation on actors' behaviors is never proven; indeed, to posit it involves circular logic, given the inferential identification of the norms themselves. (The only other way to "know" that a norm is in operation is if subjects say so, a method of verification that raises its own problems of veracity.) Still, despite the opaque quality of norms, inquiring into the Court's conventions of collective operation is a promising approach to exploring policy leadership on the Rehnquist Court because of two plausible assumptions I discuss in the following paragraphs.

First, because justices care about the Court's legal policy outcomes (Baum 1999; Hansford and Spriggs 2006), they will use whatever forums and tactics exist for exerting influence over the Court's collective output. Some forums, like conference discussions, may be ineffectual, especially if their availability is limited. The restriction of the deliberative forum may reflect the conference leader's view that minds are not likely to be changed (or coalition-inducing influence exerted) in that context—as seems to have been the case with Chief Justice Rehnquist (Rosen 2005b, 80–81). Indeed, a contemporary journalistic account of the Rehnquist-O'Connor Court period characterized the Rehnquist-led conference this way: "Rehnquist lets anyone speak—in turn, of course. After discussion, Rehnquist announces what he perceives to be the final vote. Often, he will say that there are some issues that need to be worked out 'in the writing.' That gives the justice to whom he assigns the task of writing the Court's opinion enormous latitude and enormous responsibility" (McFeatters 2005, 90). So, if certain forums and tactics for exerting influence over the group are of diminished value, justices more frequently seek and use other options or methods to influence Court outcomes.[2]

Second, the conventions of Court decision making and the outcomes produced expose the types of collegial behavior in operation. If decentralized policy leadership characterized the Rehnquist Court's customary practice, then this convention as governing the Court task of legal policy making suggests the acceptance of some level of individuated judicial behavior. Moreover, decisions, opinions, and bargaining expressions as outcomes of this convention are the visible residue of the collegial body's institutional norms. Indeed, the justices' alternative methods of influencing the Court's decision making—methods of exerting policy leadership outside of conference—may result in reconstituting Court *outcomes*. This latter phenomenon is something that can be observed if, for instance, the Court's rulings come to be constituted by more collective than unitary (opinion) statements.

Given the above assumptions, I recommend attention to (1) the opinion draft circulation and coalition formation phases of the Court's decision making and (2) a comparative examination of the influence-exertion behaviors of the chief and the associate justices during that phase. Previous research establishes that the content of opinions matters to the justices, and they frequently make concerted efforts to shape the final opinion of the Court because "justices care about the development of the law, rather than merely a case disposition" (Maltzman, Spriggs, and Wahlbeck 2000, 124). The ability of certain justices to set the parameters of and marshal support for the Court's judicial doctrines is a mark of leadership, or at least influence.

Thus, the story of the exercise of policy leadership on the Rehnquist Court lies in the behind-the-scenes decision-making process and the parts certain justices played there. That story can be developed by examining policy leadership as judicial input into the majority opinion that results in accommodation/change by its author, or judicial input into the Court majority's legal policy making in the form of a concurring opinion. Identifying evidence of the first type of policy leadership exertion involves tracking who sent "conditional join" memos to whom and what impact the memos had on the final opinions for the Court. Conditional join memos are signals of possible support sent by one justice to another, containing conditions for that support. They are, in short, leverage tools wielded by putative majority coalition members, and they necessitate a response from the majority opinion author—either full accommodation, partial or purely decorative accommodation, or no accommodation. The memo writer then chooses the countervailing response, which may be to unfurl his/her legal message—and thus contribute to legal policy making—in an official, separate writing.

Memos are indicators of who is attempting to exert influence during the coalition-formation/opinion-drafting process. Other indicators are circulations of concurring opinion drafts, whether withdrawn or released. Filing a concurring opinion also must be taken as an act of policy leadership—both in the sense of exerting leverage upon the intra-Court bargaining process (by making good on the putative threat of conditional joining) (Murphy 1964, 54) and, equally importantly, in the sense of attempting to affect a Court majority's legal policy output from *outside* the intra-Court bargaining process. The prevalence of such artifacts of judicial influence indicates acknowledgment that "Court" policy outputs include individual statements by majority coalition members. Because on a divided Court these individual opinion statements are functionally equivalent to the Court policy output, they exhibit policy leadership.

Comparing Rehnquist's circulation, accommodation, and concurring behaviors with those of his judicial associates during the early period of his chief justiceship will expose (1) whether influence over legal policy making, as measured by leveraging majority opinion content, was dispersed among the justices, and (2) whether policy leadership was decentralized, with certain justices (other than the chief) assuming an individual role of policy issue leader. Whereas condition (1) has been a part of collegial decision making since the early twentieth-century advent of opinion draft circulation, condition (2) following upon condition (1) during the early Rehnquist Court strongly suggests judicial individualism as a broadly operating Court norm. Although the institutional opinion-writing process on the Supreme Court is a collaborative enterprise by definition (Epstein and Knight 1998), and all justices presumably strategize for individual influence within it, a Court on which policy leadership is exercised by several different associate justices—in addition to or instead of the chief justice—is arguably a Court whose conventions empower its individual members.

In order to study policy leadership during the early Rehnquist Court years, I selected three terms for analysis: 1986, 1991, and 1993, landmark terms for which internal Court memoranda are available. These terms mark Chief Justice Rehnquist's leadership ascent: 1986 was his first term as chief and serves as a starting point or baseline, 1991 was the term when the chief's conservative voting bloc gained the reliable fifth vote of Justice Clarence Thomas and presumably the decisional upper hand, and 1993 was the last term before the final membership change of this Court era and is the most recent Rehnquist Court period open to scrutiny. The October 1993 term was Justice Harry Blackmun's last term of service on the high bench—significant because his judicial papers, held at the Madison Manuscript Archive of the Library of Congress, are the source for the record of interjustice opinion draft circulations and memo exchanges on the Rehnquist Court from 1986 to 1994.

There are limits, of course, to a study of circulation practices and internal Court bargaining behavior that uses the memoranda record of a single justice. But Blackmun's papers are nonetheless a useful window into policy leadership processes on the Rehnquist Court. His collection of memoranda and opinion drafts is currently the only available "inside look" at the recent Court period; moreover, it is an astonishingly voluminous collection because of Blackmun's propensity to save even the most casually scrawled personal memos. Second, although Blackmun's papers may not include all memos and correspondence between majority opinion authors and justices in the majority opinion coalition for those cases in which Blackmun himself was not with the majority, his papers do include other memos and correspondence not circulated to all of the justices. Thus, any lack of inclusiveness with respect to the policy leadership and influence-wielding record in the Blackmun memoranda archive is compensated by an especially rich record for those justices and that coalition with which Blackmun regularly interacted during his Rehnquist-era tenure. One of these justices was, of course, William Brennan, who arguably continued to exert significant policy influence on the Court even after Rehnquist's elevation to chief. The coalitional peculiarities of Blackmun's record of memos and correspondence potentially reveal this Brennan influence. Finally, Blackmun's papers include a comprehensive record of (his) clerks' memos, which contain informal bargaining information and shed light on interjudicial leveraging behaviors.

Review of these various internal memoranda does not reveal a Court whose outcomes or even deliberative processes were dominated by its chief justice. Rather, all of the justices on the early Rehnquist Court, with the possible exception of Clarence Thomas, engaged in influence-exertion behavior. Moreover, the chief justice was no more active and, compared with associates like John Paul Stevens, Antonin Scalia, David Souter, and, of course, Sandra Day O'Connor, substantially less active in terms of memo circulation behaviors, and less successful in exerting policy influence. Rehnquist was frequently pressured to accommodate to retain a Court majority for his opinions, caught as he was between the cross-pressures from the centrists and the conservatives on his bench. Finally, it is plausible to claim that "the combative and confrontational style of Justices Scalia and Thomas" drove O'Connor and Kennedy into departures from the Rehnquist Court's conservative bloc (Smith and Hensley 1994, 1129), as this more aggressive style governed their approach to memo and draft circulation. Thus, the failure of Scalia and Thomas "to participate in persuasion and compromise" (Smith and Beuger 1993, 126), or in effective bargaining for policy output influence, partially explains why at least the early Rehnquist Court was not as consistently conservative as its chief justice, and how the "O'Connor Court" gained a foothold.

INFLUENCING JUSTICES: WHAT THE BLACKMUN PAPERS REVEAL

Interjudicial influence has been a subject of study by political scientist judicial scholars for decades. From Walter Murphy's classic *Elements of Judicial Strategy* (1964) to Harold Spaeth and Michael Altfeld's (1984, 1985) attitudinalist-informed analyses of judicial influence relationships to more contemporary research on "crafting law" on the Supreme Court (Maltzman, Spriggs, and Wahlbeck 2000), scholars agree that certain regularly occurring patterns of behavior constitute judicial influence and contribute to policy leadership. Those practices include appealing for support and joining in support. One recent study of bargaining and accommodation on the Supreme Court affirmed, for instance, that the number of bargaining statements affects the likelihood of accommodation by the majority opinion author (Corley 2007). Given that an individual is less likely to be accommodated than a phalanx, the justice who does shape the content of a majority opinion successfully should be considered an influential jurist in terms of policy leadership on the Court—at least on that case. In addition, discerning the true level of bargaining and accommodation on the Court, this same study continued, requires analyzing the content of bargaining memos to see, specifically, what the justices are bargaining about (Corley 2007). The assumption is that minor modifications are more easily accommodated but are less indicative of significant exertion of influence, presumably because minor modifications carry little to no policy import. Although ideological distance or heterogeneity in a putative majority coalition increases the likelihood that the opinion author will accommodate a bargainer (Maltzman, Spriggs, and Wahlbeck 2000), a bargainer's attainment of accommodation to more than minor modification cannot be presumed and is therefore a noteworthy achievement.

Cognizant that not all bargaining memos and their responses are created equal, my examination of circulation and accommodation practices on the Rehnquist Court during the 1986, 1991, and 1993 terms opted for a weighted sampling of cases from each term, using those cases in which a record of circulation of at least one substantive memo or concurrence existed. A substantive memo is one that expressed conditionality with respect to joining the circulating majority opinion. Circulating a concurrence, even if it is ultimately withdrawn, is likewise an unambiguous assertion of conditional support. I examine this specific sample of cases from each selected term in order to focus on manifestations of policy leadership. No doubt the majority opinions in cases without such an explicit conditional bargaining record were the product of various policy leadership efforts, either in conference or during the drafting of the majority opinion itself. But without clear evidence, such attribution would be speculative.

Occurrences of policy leadership were identified in the selected terms, summarized, and then assessed qualitatively. For the 1986 and 1991 terms, a random sample was drawn from those cases with a record of circulation of at least one substantive memo or concurrence, resulting in twenty-eight and twenty-seven case records, respectively. For the 1993 term, all cases with a record of circulation of at least one substantive memo or concurrence were identified and examined, a total of sixty cases. This term could be thought of as the cusp of the "mature" Rehnquist Court period—that period of membership stability beginning with the appointment of Justice Stephen Breyer. Thus, its practices arguably shaped or at least prefigured the balance of that Court era.

Of the eighty-five cases decided by a full opinion for the Court during the 1993 term, then, almost three-fourths were resolved by opinions reflecting some amount of judicial bargaining over content.[3] The significance of the figure is this: the influence of other justices and the dynamics of collegial decision making can lead a justice to abandon or subordinate his/her personal policy values as a primary decision-making guide. Thus, the numerical dominance of any ideologically similar group of justices is no guarantee of its policy output dominance. With respect to the Rehnquist Court, bargaining over opinion content evidenced policy leadership (or at least influence) by justices outside of or at the margin of the numerically dominant ideological bloc—the conservatives—which neutralized their policy output dominance. The upshot was that the conservative chief justice was not the leader or shaper of his Court.

The bargaining patterns of the different terms can be seen by analyzing each sampled case record with regard to the following attributes: the majority opinion author, substantive memoranda[4] authors, the response to the memos (whether the suggestions were accommodated, in part, or not), the response of memo authors (from joining opinions to filing some separate ones), and any other (non–memo writing) concurring opinion authors.[5] Cataloguing this information allows for tallying the number of policy leadership exertions in the sample cases from each term, and by whom this influence was exerted. "Exertion" is defined as bargaining that produces accommodation or filing a concurring policy statement either with or without bargaining. Concurrence is especially relevant for gauging judicial individualism in the practice of policy leadership. Of course, there is also an important element of policy leadership in the ability of a majority opinion author to avert defection from the opinion coalition, especially without having to compromise, that is, modify the majority opinion policy goal. This behavior, too, and by whom it is practiced, should be noted. Clearly, there can be multiple exertions in any given case decision; influence over policy outputs is not a zero-sum game. But the prevalence of such multiple and at times competing exertions suggests the condition of judicial individualism.

Table 1.1 reports the number of cases with multiple exertions of policy leadership per term. Cases decided after multiple judicial exertions of policy leadership, or through various types of policy leadership, were not rare on the early Rehnquist Court. Although the number of cases examined is not sufficient for definitive conclusions, the ratio of multiple-exertion cases appears to show a steady increase across the terms: from one-half to two-thirds of all cases with a record of circulation of at least one substantive memo or concurrence. Overall, "the collective product of several individuals" describes the legal policy outputs of the Court during these three terms. But how broadly dispersed among the justices was the formation of this collective product?

Table 1.2 shows policy leadership exertions by justice per term. The findings presented in Table 1.2 strongly suggest that influence over legal policy making, as measured by leveraging or framing majority opinion content, was dispersed among the justices in all three terms examined. The frequency of exertion varied somewhat across the terms, with O'Connor, Scalia, Stevens, and Powell dominant in the 1986 term sample; Blackmun, Stevens, Kennedy, and Scalia more active in the 1991 term sample; and Scalia, Souter, and Stevens having the highest policy leadership exertion scores in the 1993 term cases, followed closely by O'Connor and Ginsburg. I hesitate to label such exertions as "success," since majority opinion content is the product of multiple inputs—including its author's—and because my understanding of policy leadership exertion includes concurring opinion writing, which some judicial scholars would not see as a straightforward success either. Suffice it to say that several different justices were involved in influencing the Court's legal policy outputs during this Court period; most but not all were centrist justices on their respective natural Courts; and in no term was Chief Justice Rehnquist among the most active in policy leadership exertion as conceptualized here.

Previous studies of intra-Court strategic action emphasize that coalition size, along with the number of justices who have already joined an opinion, condition both successful bargaining and accommodation decisions; my study does not challenge the operation of such strength in numbers, but does question the completeness of such an analysis of policy leadership during the early Rehnquist years. Exploring more qualitatively the content of bargaining and dynamics of influence in early Rehnquist Court decision making addresses this matter, necessitating some further probing of various features of the sampled cases. For instance, did a copious memo record follow from minimal conference discussion? This might suggest that Chief Justice

Table 1.1. Cases Decided after Multiple Policy Leadership Exertions

TERM	1986	1991	1993
Number of Cases	14	17	40
Cases Sampled	28	27	60

Rehnquist's curtailing of conference deliberation produced an alternative outlet. Did clerks play an informal role in the interjudicial bargaining process by passing information to their justices and receiving it from other clerks about their justices? This too suggests new methods of judicial communication, supplementing diminishing face-to-face dialogue.

Exploration of these two descriptive characteristics of the case memo record yields mixed results. First, there is little to no relationship between the extensiveness of conference discussion and the fulsomeness of the interjudicial memo record. Two salient cases from the 1991 term stand out as having little record of an extensive conference discussion but copious use of memo and opinion-draft circulations to hammer out some sort of consensus: *Burson v. Freeman*, a plurality judgment authored by Blackmun, and *Planned Parenthood v. Casey*, which featured the infamous joint opinion for the Court by O'Connor, Kennedy, and Souter. *Burson*, a First Amendment political speech and solicitation case, was particularly interesting. Blackmun's papers reveal that several memos to and from the putative majority opinion author were not circulated to the entire conference: Blackmun appealed privately to Rehnquist, Stevens, and Kennedy; and Stevens, Scalia, and Souter communicated conditionality messages to Blackmun in private memos only. *Casey*, the most important abortion precedent since *Roe v. Wade*, was the product of serious behind-the-scenes efforts by Stevens to broker a compromise with Blackmun and the joint opinion authors; Kennedy's private consultation with Blackmun was also instrumental in creating consensus around portions of the joint opinion and reducing Rehnquist's original majority opinion to a concurrence in the judgment in part and partial dissent. Conversely, in the same term, *Lee v. Weisman* and *R.A.V. v. City of St. Paul*, which concerned First Amendment religious establishment and First Amendment speech rights, respectively, showed both heavy memo traffic and an extensive conference discussion record—information about the latter came from Blackmun's conference

Table 1.2. Policy Leadership Exertions in Sampled Cases, by Justice

1986 Term

Justice	Bargaining	Concurring	Not Accommodating	Total Exertions
Rehnquist	2		2	
Brennan	3	3		6
White		4	1	5
Marshall		2	1	3
Blackmun	3	1		4
Powell	3	2	3	8
Stevens	1	7		8
O'Connor	1	9		10
Scalia	5	6	1	12
	18	34	8	56

1991 Term

Justice	Bargaining	Concurring	Not Accommodating	Total Exertions
Rehnquist	2	1		3
White	2	2		4
Blackmun	5	8		13
Stevens	5	7	1	13
O'Connor		3		3
Scalia	1	8		9
Kennedy	5	5		10
Souter	3	6		9
Thomas	1	2		3
	24	42	1	67

1993 Term

Justice	Bargaining	Concurring	Not Accommodating	Total Exertions
Rehnquist	4	1		5
Blackmun	6	7		13
Stevens	7	14	1	22
O'Connor	9	11		20
Scalia	11	19		30
Kennedy	7	6		13
Souter	9	14		23
Thomas		4	1	5
Ginsburg	9	11		20
	62	87	2	151

notes. Thin conference discussion, then, was just as likely to generate multiple conditional join memos and bargaining activity.

The same pattern—or lack thereof—holds for the cases examined from the 1986 term. Only one case memo record provides special insight into the relationship between Rehnquist's supposedly expedited conference proceedings and the Court's decision-making process. In the Title VII racial discrimination case of *Goodman v. Lukens Steel Co.*, majority opinion writer White's accommodation of Scalia's conditional join statement set off a chain reaction of conditional join memos and a flurry of separate opinions. Blackmun's conference notes suggest that some discussion of the statutory aspects took place, but more revealing is a memo to Blackmun from his clerk commenting on the White opinion draft. "Once again," the clerk writes on April 26, 1987, "the Chief's policy of encouraging those who write quickly has brought forth a rather perverse fruit—the sort of opinion that one would expect to see from a busy district judge, not from a Member [sic] of this Court" (Box 474, Folder 2). This comment suggests that early on, Chief Justice Rehnquist consigned various case issues "to be worked out in the writing"—and such responsibility falling to the justice assigned the task of writing the Court's opinion was not always fulfilled.

The 1993 term produced case memo records that begin to suggest the breakdown of the utility of conference and reveal evidence of frustration with the intra-Court bargaining process in general. In several cases judicial fluidity occurred, necessitating opinion reassignment. In *Holder v. Hall*, a voting rights case, three different majority opinion authors circulated drafts, and multiple concurrences were ultimately filed; as the decision-making process ground to a close, Rehnquist seemed to acknowledge his disappointment in a June 21, 1994, memo to the conference: "This late in the Term, there does not seem to be any possibility of getting a Court opinion for the position [to reverse]. But one opinion must be the lead opinion which states the facts and announces the judgment of the Court" (Box 631, Folder 9). He went on to assign its preparation to Kennedy. Kennedy was again central to an unstable coalition scenario in *Central Bank of Denver v. First Interstate Bank*, in which he had been assigned by Blackmun to write the majority opinion for a five-to-four Court, then switched his vote to the other side even as he retained majority opinion authorship. Thomas changed his vote from conference in *U.S. v. Granderson* and *Turner Broadcasting v. FCC*; only the latter case featured a record of extensive conference discussion in which tentative views were aired.

O'Connor switched sides in the course of drafting the majority opinion for *Davis v. U.S.*, and was reassigned to write for the Court by Rehnquist; the chief himself switched sides after reading O'Connor's draft opinion for the majority in *PUD No. 1 of Jefferson County v. Washington Department of Ecology*; neither case contained a record of extensive conference discussion. Blackmun abandoned the majority opinion he himself assigned to Thomas in *Thomas Jefferson University v. Shalala*, and never did circulate the majority opinion he assigned to himself in *Board of Education of Kiryas Joel v. Grumet*; his first draft appeared as a concurrence to Souter's already circulated majority opinion draft. Although fluidity is not in and of itself a sign of a Court in disarray, its occurrence during the 1993 term suggested that Rehnquist's practice of allowing case issues to work themselves out in the writing was not an effective management decision if the goal was to streamline the decision-making process.

The memo record in the 1994 decision *Turner Broadcasting v. FCC*, a First Amendment challenge to the "must carry" provisions of the Cable Act, demonstrates the problem of judicial fluidity. A case in which Thomas exhibited voting fluidity, *Turner* contained a record of extensive but inconclusive initial conference discussion, with both the chief and the senior associate, Blackmun, passing on their votes. There was heavy memo traffic and circulation of multiple and separate opinion drafts. At one point early in the decision-making process, both Ginsburg and O'Connor urged more discussion at a subsequent conference, as the case was not "working itself out." "Perhaps we should discuss this case again," O'Connor recommended to Rehnquist in a January 20, 1994, memo copied to the conference; "maybe it will 'come out in the writing,'" she offered—unconvinced and unconvincingly. Reliance on policy leadership exerted during the drafting phase also doomed the Rehnquist majority opinion in the Base Closing Commission case of *Dalton v. Specter*, in which, when the chief's draft extended the limits on judicial review over claims that the president had violated his statutory authority, he lost the support of the moderate justices in his coalition for the opinion. And in the government workers' First Amendment speech rights case of *Waters v. Churchill*, the chief's exasperation with the memo and draft circulation phase of the decision-making process was apparent. As O'Connor jockeyed between Scalia and Souter, she struggled to maintain the support of Rehnquist. Finally, her accommodation of the more moderate justice had gone too far for the chief: in a memo to the conference of March 2, 1994, he communicated his displeasure, saying "the changes you have made . . . move the opinion in a direction which I do not care for . . . the change on page 17 . . . seems to me inconsistent with the other parts of the opinion, and if that is retained I *will come down in favor of recasting the entire opinion*" (Box 638, Folder 1 [emphasis added]). Blackmun's conference notes on *Waters* reveal that few major differences were aired among the majority coalition; Stevens, who ultimately dissented but apparently said he "could go along" during the conference, was the only justice who contributed more than one or two points to the discussion. Once again, Rehnquist's approach to case issue management invited copious and lengthy bargaining through individual memo writing.

With respect to the involvement of clerks in the interjudicial bargaining process, one caveat is in order about the evidence used for this study. It comes exclusively from Blackmun's papers and clerk-justice memo record, and Blackmun and his clerks may or may not have been representative of Court behavior as a whole. Still, even if Blackmun's clerks were atypical proxies for their justice, if their reports to him about the activities of other justices' clerks are to be believed, gathering intelligence on other chambers and communicating the intentions of their justices are regular behaviors of contemporary Supreme Court clerks. Such actions are corroborated by other recent studies of the Court's clerks (Lazarus 1999; Ward and Weiden 2006).

There were certainly many occasions, in cases in each of the three terms examined, in which justices' decisions to circulate a separate opinion or requests for changes to a circulating draft were conveyed entirely via clerks in the respective chambers. However, it would not be accurate to say that clerks are surrogates who entirely replace other forms of interjudicial communication. Clerks' informational communiqués—such as Blackmun's clerk's message that "several justices" felt Thomas's circulated majority opinion in *Wright v. West* disobeyed the instructions he was given at conference (Memo of May 27, 1992, Box 600, Folder 6)—supplemented but did not supplant less mediated forms of interjudicial bargaining. Although some scholars conclude that an increase in the number of law clerks, and their increasingly active role in patterns of interaction with their justices, are related to an increase in the frequency of nonconsensual opinion writing (Best 2002), a resource is not necessarily a reason for writing separately or exerting policy leadership through memo writing. The availability of support staff for drafting additional opinions could very well "alter the justices' willingness to engage in the time-consuming search for the type of consensus that yields institutional opinions" (Best 2002, 227), and one study specifically linked changes in the number of law clerks assigned to the justices to the frequency of memo writing by the justices prior to final votes on the merits (Wood 1998, 11). True, all of the justices have multiple clerks, facilitating their use of memo circulation as an exertion of policy leadership and, with this behavior, the dispersal of policy leadership on the Court. But clerks alone cannot account for the early Rehnquist Court's legal policy outputs as the *collective product of several individuals* who lobbied and leveraged policy influence in various ways: through conditional join circulations, through conference discussion (still), using the conduit of the clerks, and even through limited use of the old-fashioned, personally handwritten note.[6]

To conclude, nothing in the terms' memo record of circulation and accommodation, or in this section's findings regarding policy leadership exertion on the early Rehnquist Court, was inconsistent with the establishment of judicial individualism as the Court's new norm of collegiality. Policy leadership came from multiple sources in cases and was dispersed across justices; conference discussion, although diminished, still supplemented interjudicial bargaining, and clerks apparently did, too. Although many of these phenomena prefigured the new norm, the Rehnquist justices themselves seemed keyed into their own individualistic tendencies. For instance, an unusually active (albeit successfully consensual) bargaining process in a case decided by a Kennedy per curiam inspired this tongue-in-cheek comment from Ginsburg in her rejoin memo to the conference: "Glad to see collegiality working so well" (Memo of April 21, 1994, Box 647, Folder 8).[7]

THE REHNQUIST COURT LEADER: VIEWS FROM THE BENCH

The significance of the dispersion of policy influence notwithstanding, the decentralization of policy leadership on the early Rehnquist Court is a better marker of the emergence of judicial individualism as a Court norm. There is no perfect measure for such decentralization, but qualitative answers to certain questions shed light on its existence. For instance, what did the interjudicial memo record and bargaining process for those decisions authored by the chief justice suggest about his execution of policy leadership on the Court? We already know that he was not terribly active in comparison with his associates on the indicators for policy leadership exertion shown in Table 1.2. Was he also an accommodator, allowing decentralization of policy influence over "his" decisions? And in those especially divisive cases—in which the justices struggled for control of the Court's policy output—which Court members played important individual roles? We already know that policy leadership exertion was dispersed among the Rehnquist justices, but individual associate justices' contribution to the Court's legal policy making—especially contribution to the resolution of those contested case situations—is putative evidence of decentralized leadership practices on the early Rehnquist Court. Regular contributions of this kind by various individual justices suggest the emergence of a norm of individualized decision-making behavior—or at least signal continuing conflict or uncertainty about the status of the preexisting norm of unitary Court leadership of a titular leader (the chief justice) or a de facto one. It is in such conditions of flux or instability that norm entrepreneurship—individuals fostering new institutional norms by deviating from prior ones—becomes possible. Such theoretical possibilities lead to consideration of O'Connor's importance to the legacy of individualistic policy leadership and to consideration of the point at which a "queen's Court" began in the Rehnquist era.

With respect to the chief's own record as a case manager, across the terms examined, Rehnquist was generally an accommodating opinion author. In the cases sampled from the 1986 term, of four majorities led by the chief, he accommodated other justices in every instance but one—the exception was Stevens, who then filed a partial concurrence/partial dissent in response. In the cases sampled from the 1991 term, there were again four majorities led by the chief—he lost a fifth majority opinion coalition in *Planned Parenthood v. Casey*, and one of his original majority opinion circulations (in *INS v. Doherty*) was reduced to a plurality as a result of an especially persuasive partial concurrence in the judgment filed by Scalia and joined by Stevens and Souter. Another case from this term, *International Society for Krishna Consciousness v. Lee*, merits some extended commentary. The case, which concerned solicitation and distribution restrictions in an airport and the related question of whether the latter was a public forum for First Amendment purposes, produced a fractured vote at conference and a proliferation of views. The chief assigned the majority opinion to himself, but styled the petition and cross-petition as separate cases, dissenting from the Court in the latter. A memo by Blackmun's clerk on the circulating opinions recounts some additional details about the chief's behavior: "He has also opined that, as to [the cross-petition], in which he dissents, he thinks 'Sandra is the logical person to write it or to assign it.'. . . Since he is dissenting, he has no business expressing any view as to who should write the Court's opinion in that case or who should assign it. In response to my surprisingly delicate inquiry, his clerk told me that he dictated the memo as he was leaving for the airport on Friday. I suppose that he simply made a mistake (although such an obvious one as to raise some questions for me)," the thought concludes, ominously (Memo of May 4, 1992, Box 598, Folder 2). The same clerk's memo also continues with some observations of Rehnquist's management of interjudicial dialogue: "At conference, your notes (and the Chief's notes) indicate that [O'Connor] thought the regulation was unreasonable. Apparently, she changed her mind and wrote a postconference memo to the Chief. I didn't get a copy of that memo, nor did any clerk other than the CJ's, so far as I have discovered. This strikes me as bad practice, but it's possible that there is an entirely innocent explanation."

Accusatory editorializing aside, this clerk's memo is interesting for what it reveals about Rehnquist's nonaccommodating side. His seeming heavy-handedness in opinion assignment backfired as "communication among the Court's members . . . broke down"—as the clerk's June 4, 1992, follow-up memo characterized the process. The concurring opinions, the varying jurisprudential standards issued by O'Connor, Kennedy, and Souter, and the dissenting opinion of Stevens, which partially joined Kennedy's opinion and made it the Court's judgment in part, were testimony to the decentralization of policy leadership that occurred in this Rehnquist-"led" decision.

The cases sampled from the 1993 term show Rehnquist both accommodating other justices and presiding over poorly orchestrated policy leadership. Of nine cases where Rehnquist was the majority opinion author, he declined to accommodate in three—spurring Thomas to concur in one, Stevens to dissent in another, and Stevens to withdraw his concurrence in the third case only to join Souter's concurrence in the judgment, which was itself a response to no accommodation. The decision-making process in this latter case of *Dalton v. Specter* was an unfortunate advertisement for the fragmentation of policy leadership on the early Rehnquist Court, featuring aggressively competitive bargaining along the majority coalition's Stevens-Souter-Blackmun axis. Tellingly, the chief played no part in these negotiations.

Another decision from the 1993 term in which Rehnquist's accommodative efforts bore decentralized leadership fruit was *Madsen v. Women's Health Center*. This time, the chief made more constructive use of the differences among the justices in the case, which concerned the effect on abortion protesters' First Amendment rights of a state court's injunctive creation of clinic buffer zones. Rehnquist wrote an opinion for the Court of which the "moderate tone" appealed to judicial centrists (Memo from Justice Ginsburg to the Conference, June 6, 1994, Box 646, Folder 6) and of which the content was clearly shaped by substantive input from Ginsburg, O'Connor, Souter, and Blackmun, as their memos to the chief and his replies indicate. The price of such coordination was the partial alienation of the more extreme and opposing Justices Stevens and Scalia: the former withdrew his join and filed a partial concurrence/partial dissent, and the latter filed a concurrence in part and in the judgment. Souter, too, ultimately filed a concurring statement to clarify his position. The strong intra-Court differences were evident at conference and expressed in discussion there, but the justices were basically in agreement that the injunction should be upheld. The heavy memo traffic turned on the inquiry for determining a content-neutral restriction on speech, along with the standard governing review of generally applicable legislation versus that for challenges to judicial remedies for proven wrongdoing, as had occurred in *Madsen*. Perhaps there was no way for Rehnquist to have averted the multiple separate filings that conveyed justices' different analytical approaches to the case problems, for he made a concerted effort to appease the associate justices he needed for the majority. Indeed, as he conceded in a memo to Stevens that explained his inability to accede to the latter's suggestions prompted by objections to Rehnquist's previously made revisions, "'you have to go hunting where the ducks are.'"[8] By self-assigning the opinion, Rehnquist retained some influence on policy output for himself, but the decentralized process that produced the *Madsen* opinion—combined with Rehnquist's allegorical admission in his memo to Stevens—revealed several associate justices with policy leadership power equal to the actual opinion author's.

Of course, Rehnquist looked no worse in *Madsen* than O'Connor did in *Williamson v. U.S.*, another case from the 1993 term with disparate views expressed at conference and heavy memo traffic during the opinion circulation phase of decision making. As majority opinion author, O'Connor seemed quite less willing than Rehnquist had been to accommodate others. "Perhaps getting a Court for any position will prove impossible," she observed in a memo to Stevens: "I do take issue with some of what you say. . . . I would not rely much on the academics' views," she retorted to Kennedy's memorandum (Memos of May 31, 1994, and June 10, 1994, respectively, Box 647, Folder 4). The case, which concerned the hearsay exception under the Federal Rules of Evidence, produced a fractured majority coalition and, in the end, a partial plurality judgment. What was interesting about the decision making was that, once again, a group of associate justices exercised the policy leadership that shaped the Court's legal output—Ginsburg was instrumental in facilitating a compromise with her separate opinion circulation, as was Blackmun, who had originally assigned the opinion to O'Connor but found himself in the awkward position of being reluctant to join it.[9] Also noteworthy was Rehnquist's ancillary status in the collegial conversation: he was a silent joiner to Kennedy's concurrence in the judgment, which itself prompted Scalia's concurrence in reply.

It is true that divisive cases, by definition, are cases in which the justices are contentious actors; it is also possible that the issue areas likely to produce fractured coalitions in which policy influence is dispersed are likely to accentuate the policy leadership potential of centrist justices and thus falsely highlight the chief's policy leadership incapacity. Both scenarios suggest that an analytical focus on divisive cases risks oversampling and overemphasizing cases of decentralized policy leadership—cases that may be neither representative nor illustrative of the Rehnquist period in question. But although divisive cases do encourage fragmented judicial decision making, we are not using such case examples to measure whether or how often fragmentation exists—such would be rather circular reasoning. Instead, we are using such cases only to identify which justice or justices were policy leaders under such conditions. Moreover, there is no reason to suspect that issue areas that divided the justices and/or fractured majority coalitions would disproportionately stress case situations showing Rehnquist's incapacity as a Court leader; these are simply cases where policy leadership is needed for legal policy promulgation, for the case is neither easily unanimous nor stably polarizing along predictable ideological lines. The question is, then, which justice or justices made these efforts at wielding individual influence in the collaborative decision-making enterprise?

If we examine the divisive cases in which justices struggled for control of the Court's policy output, and if we identify Court members who played important individual policy-making roles, we find further evidence of decentralized policy leadership on the early Rehnquist Court, but no particular evidence of O'Connor's emergence as a singular Court leader. Review of the early Rehnquist Court's contentious or divisive cases in the case samples from three terms shows that several associate justices constituted the regular contingent of policy "dispute resolution" leaders on the bench. Of course, to be fair, these justices also caused policy disputes by putting forth their individual legal policy preferences in memos or separate opinion circulations. But the main point is that Rehnquist was not among these justices, nor was Thomas—the conservative bloc's supposed fifth vote to make majorities. Instead, Blackmun and Stevens from the left of center, Kennedy's pressure from the right, and Souter's and O'Connor's influence in the middle were regularly observable and dispositive to the Court's legal policy outputs in contentious or divisive cases. Such were the leadership conditions, in which individual justices were empowered by circumstances and recurring behavioral patterns, into which Ginsburg and soon Breyer would step.

So what was O'Connor's importance to this legacy of individualistic policy leadership? One study of the justice offered this relevant comment: "One reason O'Connor is respected among her peers is that instead of broadly philosophical opinions, she tended to write on narrow issues of fact, which made their *job* of dissenting *or concurring* much easier" (McFeatters 2005, 95 [emphasis added]). Whether this statement about O'Connor as a facilitator is empirically valid is testable, of course. But what is arresting is the author's presupposition that concurring opinion writing—policy influence exertion, perhaps—is a judicial duty, and was considered so, during the era of O'Connor's service.

O'Connor herself seemed to echo such a view in a memo she wrote to Chief Justice Rehnquist in June 1993, cosigned by Kennedy and Thomas, titled "Statement of Understanding about Release of Court Working Papers." The memo was of course precipitated by retiring Justice Blackmun's decision to leave his papers to the Library of Congress for immediate public scrutiny. O'Connor and her colleagues worried about the harm to the Court's vital and creative processes from premature disclosure, commenting that "a free and open exchange of tentative views is itself part of the creative and disciplined process by which Justices shape their understanding of the law. A system that encourages tentative or exploratory statements is essential to the judicial process" (Blackmun Papers, "Agenda Items," Box 627, Folder 3).

Whether "tentative or exploratory statements" are the same as separate opinions, certainly O'Connor and her colleagues behaved as if the circulation of conditional join memos and concurrence drafts was the duty of all justices in their individual performance of policy leadership exertion. The 1987 Fifth Amendment takings case of *Hodel v. Irving* is a good illustration of this along with individual associates' roles in policy dispute resolution on the early Rehnquist Court. A collaborative effort among Stevens, Scalia, and O'Connor, the decision in *Hodel* was the product of a long period of opinion draft circulation and separate opinion circulations in response. In the end, O'Connor's characterization of the legal issue carried the Court, but she made this acknowledgment in a memo to the conference: "Credit for the discussion of the facts goes to John, and for much of the standing analysis to Nino. They each graciously consented to the 'appropriation' of their efforts in these areas" (Memo of April 21, 1987, Box 465, Folder 3).[10]

Compare this rather placid example of decentralized policy leadership with the more pointed illustrations of judicial individualism from the 1991 term. In the 1992 capital sentencing case of *Sochor v. Florida*, Justice Souter, assigned the opinion by senior associate Blackmun, had to be "goaded"—these were Souter's words, in his memo of May 7, 1992—by Stevens and O'Connor to make revisions to allow their and Kennedy's joins. O'Connor's goading came in the form of a circulated dissent, which she later modified into a concurrence. And an individuated approach to collaboration could rise to no higher level than it did in the term's 1992 decision of *Planned Parenthood v. Casey* with the jointly written opinion of O'Connor, Kennedy, and Souter, the so-called troika. The same case featured individual maneuvering by Stevens and awareness of such entrepreneurship by Court personnel, as Blackmun's clerk reported in her June 18, 1992, memo: "JPS is going to call you to discuss the possibility of getting the troika to make some modifications that would allow us to join the first three sections of the opinion . . . you should probably act surprised when he calls" (Box 602, Folder 4). Both 1992 cases showed O'Connor was a policy leader among several on the bench.

A last illustrative case from the 1993 term is the collective, disunited product in *Holder v. Hall*. This racial vote dilution case was difficult for the Court, and was distinctive in that almost every justice—every justice if we include its companion voting rights case of *Johnson v. DeGrandy*—played a vocal or otherwise constitutive role in deciding it. Scalia was originally assigned the majority opinion as a result of the five-to-four conference vote with the chief, O'Connor, Kennedy, Scalia, and Thomas in the majority. But O'Connor was crucial to recasting the ruling from Scalia's narrow construction of vote dilution under Section 2 of the Voting Rights Act, as the entries for *Holder* on Blackmun's opinion log sheets indicate (Box 630, Folder 8). The interjustice bargaining also suggested the beginnings of the breach that would open between the more centrist and the more ideological conservative justices. Blackmun's clerk's memoranda are particularly candid in reporting O'Connor's position-taking and stratagems for influence as gained from her conversations with O'Connor's clerk: "[Justice O'Connor] feels considerable personal discomfort in taking on Scalia . . . she fears that Scalia will simply throw her own language back in her face . . . her opinion now takes on Scalia as directly as she is willing to do" (Memo of December 1, 1993, Box 632, Folder 5). Later, the clerk wrote and also advised her justice: "[O'Connor's] breaking ranks with AS [Antonin Scalia] was a big—and in some ways, hard—step for her to take, and I would like to see her rewarded for it (and perhaps encouraged to take similar steps in the future)" (Memo of February 17, 1994). Finally, she commented on O'Connor's strategic success: "[SOC] has withstood tremendous pressure to join AMK [Anthony Kennedy] on this one. Indeed, she has stood firm in the position she adopted in her original concurring opinion. . . . When AS first switched his vote, giving you the majority, SOC graciously withdrew her opinion and invited you to use as much of it as you would like. Because she had done such a good job, we adopted much of her language verbatim" (Memo of June 27, 1994).

Although O'Connor was pivotal in *Holder*, Blackmun played an important role as peacemaker in reaching out to her, and Kennedy actively brokered the compromise between O'Connor and Scalia. The *Johnson* case, with only a slightly less extensive conference discussion record, was more of a face-off between Scalia and Souter, who lobbed dueling "Ninograms" and DHS rejoinders at each other throughout the drafting process. Relatively late in the proceedings, however, O'Connor sent a conditional join memo to Souter that would solidify both her and the chief's support. "I have inserted the substance of the cautionary statement Sandra requested," Souter reported in a memo on March 11, 1994 (Box 632, Folder 8).

Are the cases I discussed in this chapter adequate evidence of ongoing conflict or uncertainty about the status of a preexisting norm of unitary Court leadership, of the titular leader the chief justice, or a de facto one? More observations would be necessary before definitively concluding that conditions of flux or instability had facilitated norm entrepreneurship. But in reviewing the case records, one can make a plausible argument that decentralized policy leadership was no rare event on the early Rehnquist Court—that conditions ripe for the development or maturation of judicial individualism existed under Chief Justice Rehnquist from 1986 to 1994.

The opening paragraph of this chapter asked whether the accommodationist conservative Justice O'Connor simply took advantage of an emergent norm of judicial individualism or actually helped to establish it. The answer is probably the latter, for although O'Connor derived no special benefit from dispersed policy influence and individuated decision making, she was an active practitioner—along with several other associate colleagues—of memo writing and opinion circulation that fostered individual judicial significance and identity. She was less a solo "norm entrepreneur" than one of several powerful associate justices who shaped the policy outcomes of their chief justice's Court. Whereas certain justices were the political centrists who might be expected to have influence on any polarized bench (O'Connor, Kennedy), others were more distant from the conservative pole of the chief, but still regularly exerted influence on policy outputs from his Court (Blackmun, Stevens). Still others displayed what can only be described as intellectual independence and disregard for coalition-building—indeed, Scalia as the illustrative justice here seemed to relish coalition-busting. A relative newcomer was also a visible policy leader (Souter), and a first-year justice seemed poised to step right into active involvement in policy leadership (Ginsburg).

Whether Rehnquist facilitated or simply presided over a period of emerging judicial individualism is more difficult to answer. But whatever his culpability, his Court was more his colleagues' than his own in terms of influence over legal policy outputs. Thus, this chapter's analysis provides a powerful rationale for conceptualizing the Supreme Court period from 1986 to 2005 as something other than "Rehnquist's Court." To wit, policy leadership in the early Rehnquist years was at best diffuse, at worst, out of the chief justice's hands entirely. This was partly because of the associate justices' predilection to add their individual commentaries to the Court's majority opinions—those commentaries being separate concurrences. As Chapter 2 shows, on the Rehnquist Court, those commentaries came to function as satellite opinions for the Court—complete with their own joiners and directions for court watchers to follow.

2

Instructing his clerks in a memo of September 1976, Justice Lewis Powell of the Burger Court observed, "A concurring opinion almost always awaits the circulation of the Court opinion, as one hopes he may be able to join it without writing separately."[1] Contrast this somewhat circumspect view of concurrence with this May 1992 caution from a Rehnquist Court clerk to his boss, Justice Harry Blackmun: "[Justice Stevens] is surreptitiously reworking his concurrence in an attempt to split up the majority. . . . I should warn you that the CJ may try to push you on getting your [concurring] statement out. I think he's concerned that he may lose his majority" (Blackmun Papers, Box 604, Folder 6). Whatever this clerk's comment might reveal about Chief Justice Rehnquist's coalition management skills, it suggests a more aggressive, proactive use of concurring opinion writing on his Court than on its predecessor.[2]

One of the lesser-noted aspects of the Rehnquist era was that Court's propensity for judicial chorality—the issuance of separate concurring opinions—often including joiners—that bracketed the opinion of the Court and collectively made up the Court's decision-making "chorus." The justices' intracoalition exchanges and differences—perhaps once saved for conference or suppressed altogether—were aired publicly, with little concern that such candor (or cacophony) would harm the role of the institution. Indeed, at times the Rehnquist justices created the impression that such separate opinion-writing behavior *was* the institution's role. This development and its implications for the Court's decisions and decision-making practices are potentially the most significant of any legacy—doctrinal or behavioral—the Rehnquist Court leaves. It is significant whether it continues because it is entrenched or whether it is overturned by subsequent justices' reactions because they fear it is entrenched.

But was the Rehnquist Court distinctively "choral"? The rising number of separate opinions and the decline of unanimity as an intra-Court norm of course did not begin with the Rehnquist Court, but during this era the practice of writing concurrences became regularized if not institutionalized. Empirical studies reveal increased incidence of concurrence on the contemporary Supreme Court (Epstein, Walker, and Dixon 1988). Since the late 1960s, the proportion of cases with at least one concurring opinion has held steady at roughly 40 percent, and has occasionally exceeded this rate according to figures on the Supreme Court's opinion, decision, and outcome trends reported in the *Supreme Court Compendium*.[3] Prior to this period, the proportion of cases with at least one concurring opinion was negligible, 10 percent or less; indeed, 1941 was the first Court year in which 10 percent of such cases occurred. Two studies elaborate (if indirectly) on the relationship between concurrence and dissensus generally. Caldeira and Zorn (1998) point to the 1940s as a key period in the emergence of a Court culture of dissensus. Haynie (1992) identifies key changes in behavioral expectations as first occurring under Chief Justice Hughes. Viewing these findings in conjunction with the steady rise of dissenting opinions since the 1940s, we must conclude that individualistic judicial behavior was hardly unknown on the Supreme Court prior to the Rehnquist era.

But judicial individualism still tended to be suppressed through institutional norms. Epstein, Segal, and Spaeth's (2001) study of the Waite Court dockets revealed a norm of consensus manifested through public unanimity despite private conference disagreement. Justices of the early Supreme Court often saw their task as a unitary one—voting on the case outcome—and left the legal reasoning to the opinion of the Court. This primacy of institutional focus during the Marshall era explains why the majority opinions sometimes suggest a lack of agreement, and even dissent, in cases where no written opinions to accompany these differing views exist (Maveety, Turner, and Way 2007). Not surprisingly, concurrence was almost nonexistent, and those few opinions that did exist seldom contained language of jurisprudential and/or institutional significance (ibid.). Most scholars agree that the era of the norm of public unanimity and self-effacing justices continued into the twentieth century. Even the tradition of exchange between the opinion of the Court and a dissent was not well established as late as the Taft era, with written dissents issued in an average of just 9 percent of its cases each year, and concurrences in only 1 percent (Way, Turner, and Maveety 2007). Taft's concern as chief justice was to forge judicial autonomy, which meant conceptualizing the judiciary as a "team" whereby federal judges would surrender a substantial portion of their individual autonomy in exchange for enhanced institutional autonomy (Crowe 2007, 81, n. 43). Dissenting distractions—the give and take of free discussions in print—were clearly anathema to his agenda as Court leader.

Taft was the last chief to strangle judicial disagreement. The Roosevelt-era Courts and the Warren era enshrined, if not lionized, the voice of dissent as the voice of legitimate legal conscience. Yet even during this period of great dissenters and their great dissenting opinions, speaking separately within the Court's decisional coalition remained more rare and less salubrious—though it certainly did occur. Justices Douglas, Frankfurter, and Harlan II are among the non-Rehnquist-era justices to have filed more than one hundred concurring opinions during their tenure, with 154, 132, and 204 respectively, according to statistics assembled in the *Supreme Court Compendium*. The same source highlights the active concurring performance of several Warren/Burger-era justices: Powell, Stewart, and White, with 186, 173, and 236 concurring opinions filed respectively. "Transitional" justices Blackmun and Brennan, whose tenure of service spanned into the early years of the Rehnquist Court, topped these rates, with 256 and 258 concurring opinions, respectively, during their long careers on the Court. Still, concurrence remained specific to certain individuals rather than a widespread, individualistic practice. In the midcentury age of the great battles between conservatives and liberals on the bench, the concurring option was muted by comparison and its purpose poorly articulated or sketched out in practice.

During the Rehnquist era, the trend toward concurring opinion issuance continued unabated, but the Rehnquist justices did more than simply carry on a dissensual trend. A qualitative study of the use of concurrence during the first terms of the Rehnquist Court observed that the more expansive minority opinions were moving the Court "closer to a form of decision making that prolongs debate by incorporating divergent views" (Ray 1990, 780) and "moderat[ing] the Court's polarization into the two sharply defined blocs of 'winner' and 'loser'" (830 [emphasis added]). That kind of concurring "moderation," and that level of individual judicial contribution to the Court's collective output, represented a qualitatively different use of concurrence than in the past. Concurring opinions on the Rehnquist Court expanded "the conventional *dialogue* of majority and dissent to a *choral conversation*" (Ray 1990, 780 [emphasis added]) of individual voices and sections of voices. As I show in this chapter, the rise in concurring coalitions, as opposed to individuals discreetly disagreeing with the majority opinion coalition, suggests a Court of individually inspired jurists who found purpose in concurrence and perfected this device for sounding their discernable notes within the institutional refrain.

As with the decentralized policy leadership discussed in the previous chapter, this Rehnquist Court attribute was also the product of actions by Associate Justice Sandra Day O'Connor. Her behavior as a frequent and frequently influential concurring justice began with her service on the Burger Court from 1981 to 1986, and she continued to exhibit this characteristic under the successor chief justice. But she was joined and/or copied in such behavior by several other associate justices. As a result, Rehnquist's was the era of the "choral Court" in which doctrinal rules and policy outcomes were less the result of majority opinion directives than interpretation of those directives by concurring justices (Maveety 2005). A chorus of judicial voices not necessarily singing in harmony made the rulings of the Court. Single-authored majority opinions speaking for the Court, unadorned by concurring commentary, became more infrequent, particularly in decisions with constitutional policy-making implications. This development, along with the increase in the sheer number of concurring voices, distinguished the Rehnquist period of judicial individualism even from its immediate predecessor—and the Burger Court was no stranger to individual fractiousness.

How this happened, why it happened with the mix of justices who served on the Rehnquist Court, and what the trend means for constitutional jurisprudence and the Supreme Court's institutional role require some discussion of the history and logic of concurring opinions and the appeal of their use. This chapter, then, continues with an empirical analysis of such practices on the Rehnquist bench, arguing that concurring opinions served a rule-making function that enhanced the authority of individual justices to promulgate doctrine.

WHY CONCURRENCE?

A noted advocate of the collegial court philosophy, at least in her off-the-bench writings (Ginsburg 1990, 1992), Associate Justice Ruth Bader Ginsburg has spoken of "the competing tugs of collegiality and individuality" that affect judges on multimember courts (Barnhart and Zalesne 2004, 293, n. 128). Although the role of a justice may well be "to nurture collaboration through restraint" (Barnhart and Zalesne 2004, 292), individual judges are also understood to enjoy the prerogative to express their differing views in opinions separate from the majority. But unlike dissent, which is viewed as "a cherished part of the common law tradition" (Murphy, Pritchett, and Epstein 2002, 622), concurrence receives a less warm reception from scholars and jurists alike. Not only is it more destructive of institutional integrity and more invidious with respect to legal clarity, it seems difficult to understand as anything other than judicial egoism. Why undermine the institutional policy voice of a majority one supports by filing a concurrence unless one is incorrigibly persnickety?

Whereas Justice Ginsburg's critical view of such separate opinions is well known, other Rehnquist justices presented more nuanced or fully positive opinions of the practice of concurrence. Justice Scalia, not surprisingly, was candid in his contrarian praise of "be[ing] able to write an opinion solely for oneself, without the need to accommodate, to any degree whatever, the more-or-less differing views of one's colleagues . . . [as] an unparalleled pleasure" (Scalia 1994, 42). Both Justices Stevens and O'Connor, however, suggested a more instrumental purpose for writing concurring opinions. For Stevens, their appeal is "great institutional interest in the forthrightness of different justices' views"; to O'Connor, unanimity, "recorded at the expense of strong, conflicting views, is not desirable in a court of last resort" (O'Brien 2005b, 300; O'Connor 2003, 120). The pressure to join an opinion with which one does not fully agree, she continued, "does not overwhelm our other goals" (O'Connor 2003, 118). What Stevens's "institutional interest" in the state of the Court's collective mind, or O'Connor's "other goals," might be is answered, again, by Justice Scalia, who observed that the Supreme Court's position "in the forefront of intellectual development of the law" means that the Court "is center stage for significant legal debate."

Political scientists who study law and courts generally eschew such judicial rationalizations in favor of a simpler explanation of a concurrence as a vote indicative of a more or less strongly held ideological policy preference by a member of a majority coalition. Yet even these scholars have admitted that there is no good explanation for the observed increase in opinions concurring in the judgment, in proportion to dissenting opinions, from the Burger to the Rehnquist Court. "Is there something about conservatives," one study mused, "that causes them to haggle about the details of opinions that support conservatively decided outcomes?" (Segal and Spaeth 1993, 282). Apparently, there is, or was.

Scholars of the Supreme Court who take a more historical developmental view would argue that concurrence on the Rehnquist Court was a product of both judicial role orientations and political ideology. The Rehnquist conservatives were a fragmented bloc, divided as to the jurisprudence that should inform their judicial activism (Keck 2004). They were divided, too, over the very meaning of judicial conservatism, with Justices Kennedy and O'Connor unwilling to support broad, bright-line articulations of conservative doctrinal rules.[4] Instead, they filed concurring opinions, limiting the reach of doctrinal promulgation of Scalia's or Thomas's majority opinion. Or, the more right-of-center justices concurred in an otherwise moderately conservative result they found too accommodationist in its outcome or too legislative in its crafting of fact-sensitive standards for an issue area.

Were this ideological account the whole story of the Rehnquist Court's chorality, that story would mean little in terms of the institutional legacy of this Court era. But just as interesting as the divisions among the conservative justices were the concurring tendencies exhibited by the more left-leaning personnel of the Rehnquist Court. Indeed, no justice has a lifetime record of writing separately more frequently than Justice Stevens, a Burger Court veteran and senior associate justice who came to lead the liberal wing of the Rehnquist Court (Rosen 2007b). More recent appointees, including concurring critic Justice Ginsburg, who has in fact written more concurrences than dissents in her tenure on the bench (Ray 2003, 673),[5] have embraced the concurring option as a way of adding "something left unsaid" by a majority opinion—as Justice Breyer framed his own cautionary concurring commentary in the otherwise unanimous *Clinton v. Jones* (1997). Currently held notions of judicial intellectual integrity, it would seem, demand a revised understanding of judicial institutional integrity, for concurring voices, in spite of their potential to fracture majorities, produce the legal debate that furthers the intellectual development of the law on the Supreme Court. Whether this approach to the job of justice results from the appointment of more academics or more appellate court judges to the high bench, recent appointees arguably derive a great deal of "satisfaction" from ruling on questions of legal policy and have "perspectives that cause them to give the Court's outputs a very heavy priority" (Baum 1999, 211). Apparently, then, the Rehnquist justices conceptualized both the "Court's outputs" and their contribution to them in a more individualistic fashion than the cohorts of justices who served in past eras.

TRENDS AND PERSONAL BESTS IN CONCURRENCE

In terms of both aggregate patterns and individual justices' exhibition of concurring opinion writing, the practice became fully established if not durably institutionalized during the Rehnquist era. Some comparative, descriptive statistics illustrate this.

The decline in an operative norm of consensus for majority coalitions predates the Rehnquist Court (Epstein, Walker, and Dixon 1988); indeed, for both the Rehnquist Court and its immediate predecessor, the Burger Court, 41 percent of cases had at least one concurrence filed.[6] The ratio of regular to special concurrence, too, was fairly constant throughout the two Court eras, although tremendous fluctuation in that ratio existed: in the 1969 term, 60 percent of Burger Court concurrences filed were regular, but by the 1991 term of the Rehnquist Court, 77 percent of concurrences filed were special.

Regular concurrences could be thought of as "me, too" concurring opinions: they join both the majority holding and the majority opinion reasoning but supply additional reasoning or commentary. A good example of this kind of annotation on a majority opinion was Stevens's brief concurrence to the 2005 ruling against the juvenile death penalty in *Roper v. Simmons*. Joined by Justice Ginsburg, Justice Stevens offered a one-paragraph comment that included this telling statement: "Perhaps more important than our specific holding today is our reaffirmation of the basic principle that informs the Court's interpretation of the Eighth Amendment . . . that our understanding of the Constitution does change from time to time has been settled since John Marshall breathed life into its text." Stevens's *Roper* effort illustrates that even brief regular concurrences can be quite revealing of a justice's (or, in this case, justices') take on the majority opinion, even when the specific content of the concurrence seems somewhat superfluous. Special concurrences, however, are more like "me instead" concurring opinions: they join only the majority's result in terms of case disposition, but provide their own distinctive reasoning for that result. A good example was O'Connor's concurrence in the judgment of the 2003 *Lawrence v. Texas* ruling overturning the state statute criminalizing homosexual sodomy. Whereas Kennedy's majority opinion relied on privacy rights and substantive due process under the Fourteenth Amendment, O'Connor based her argument on a narrower, equal-protection-of-the-law violation. Neither did her approach require the Court to overturn its prior ruling of *Bowers v. Hardwick* from 1986—illustrating just how different and dissonant from a majority opinion a concurror's reasoning can be.

Although special concurrences depart more significantly than regular ones from the opinion of the Court, both types of concurring opinions increase a decision's multivocality by offering more perspectives on the doctrinal promulgation of the decision. Generally speaking, there was a rough increase in the use of special concurrence on the Supreme Court from the beginning of the Burger era through the early 1990s, followed by a decrease over the last decade. Increasing levels of regular concurrence made up the difference in proportion during the later Rehnquist years.

Still, figures tallying the overall frequency of concurrence for both recent Courts conceal as much as they reveal. More salient as a measure of the choral nature of the Rehnquist Court was how many separate justices joined the concurring opinions filed. In other words, how often did the Rehnquist justices create concurring coalitions?

During the Burger Court era, 73 percent of all concurrences filed were sole-authored, but on the Rehnquist Court, 64 percent of all concurrences were sole-authored. By that Court term, there was a steadily increasing trend in the number of joiners. Figure 2.1 shows the mean number of individuals (opinion writers plus joiners) taking part in concurrence over time and illustrates that a greater number of justices have been speaking through authoring and joining concurring opinions, particularly during the Rehnquist era.

Although the Rehnquist justices arguably were continuing a dissensual trend that began long ago on the Supreme Court, their particular expression of the decline in consensus seemed to be unique. Accordingly, even when a Rehnquist Court justice did not write a concurring opinion, she or he appeared more likely to join a concurrence than did members of the Burger Court.

Did certain issues trigger concurrence on the Rehnquist Court? Table 2.1 displays the "top ten" most multivocal decisions of the Rehnquist era as captured by the Benesh-Spaeth Database. Multivocal decisions are ranked in terms of highest number of voices per decision (concurring opinions plus

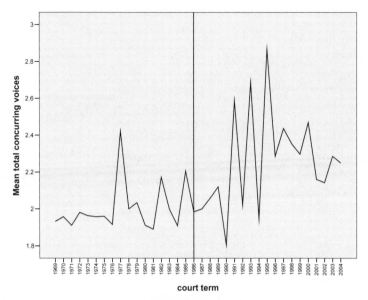

Figure 2.1. Concurring Voices, Burger through Rehnquist Court 2004 Term

Source: Maveety, Turner, and Way (forthcoming), Graph 5.

joiners) and, following this, highest number of concurring opinions per deci-sion. The "voices" measure is a true indicator of chorality in decision mak-ing, and the concurring opinions measure reveals the multivocal content of the decision. Some decisions rank high in both categories, resulting in eight noteworthy, illustrative cases.

Only two of the cases displayed in Table 2.1 qualify as high-salience cases in terms of the issues they address: the 1992 First Amendment hate speech case of R.A.V. v. St. Paul and the 1997 decision upholding the state assisted-suicide ban in Washington v. Glucksburg. Clearly, it was not only cases of great policy or constitutional legal significance that produced multivocal decisions during the Rehnquist period, nor did the justices save their individual concur-ring voices for cases of special importance to the court-watching public.[7]

Did certain justices' opinions account for a large proportion of these con-currences, suggesting that the Rehnquist Court's multivocality was fueled by disagreements among its judicial conservatives? Aggregate figures are in-structive, but not dispositive. Whereas on the Burger Court, majority opinion authors were clearly more conservative than concurring writers,[8] by the Rehn-quist era the ideological difference between majority and concurring opinion

Table 2.1. Most Multivocal Decisions of the Rehnquist Era, 1986–2001 Terms

Case Name	Date	Issue	Number of Voices	Number of Concurrences
Nevada v. Hicks	2001	Tribal court jurisdiction of civil claims	9	4
Penzoil v. Texaco	1987	Federal injunction against state trial judgment	8	5
Sacramento v. Lewis	1998	Wrongful death and substantive due process	8	5
Steel Co. v. Citizens for a Better Environment	1997	Standing to sue under federal statute	8	4
Hodel v. Irving	1987	Tribal land allotment and Fifth Amendment taking	8	3 or fewer
R.A.V. v. St. Paul	1992	Hate speech and First Amendment	8	3 or fewer
Williamson v. United States	1994	Federal rules of evidence	8	3 or fewer
Washington v. Glucksburg	1997	Assisted suicide ban and substantive due process	5	5

Source: Benesh-Spaeth Supreme Court Justice–Centered Judicial Database, 1953–2004 Terms. Thanks to Charles Turner for his assistance with identification of these cases.

writers dissipated. Though the concurring justices on the Rehnquist Court were as likely to be to the left as to the right of the majority opinion author, the presence of more conservative justices on this Court made it statistically more probable that judicial conservatives were responsible for the growing amount of majority coalition bickering. This inference is in keeping with observations by court scholars such as Tom Keck (2004) and Mark Tushnet (2005), who found the Rehnquist Court "a Court divided"—especially within its Republican ideological bloc.

Yet individual concurring patterns belie that only the Rehnquist conservatives were driving the rise in choral decision making on their Court. Although no one can deny the prolific concurrences of Justice Scalia with an average of ten per term (compared with a Court average that fluctuates from four to six per term), Chief Justice Rehnquist was his Court's least prolific; indeed, there were four terms in which he filed no concurrences. Clearly, institutional factors such as the demands of chief justiceship could have been depressing Rehnquist's previously noted tendency as an associate justice to speak his mind individually (though usually in dissent on the Burger Court) as to his conservative judicial philosophy. Justice Stevens was the most prolific career concurror, which was partly a function of his longer record of service than the other Rehnquist justices. But Stevens also maintains a proportion of concurrences slightly higher than his career proportion of opinions for the Court, and is distinctive in this ratio from all of his colleagues on the bench but Scalia.[9]

Examining and ranking individual justices' concurrence rates by term also indicates that concurring behavior was widespread and approaching entrenchment on the Rehnquist Court. For the natural Court that began with the 1994 term and ended in summer 2005, the top three filers of concurring opinions per term came from across the ideological spectrum (see Table 2.2).

Not surprisingly, Scalia and Stevens were regularly among the top three concurring opinion writers. But several other justices contended for the top spots, including centrists O'Connor and Kennedy, the very conservative and thus inclined to speak separately Thomas, and the left coalition member Breyer, whose individual vocality was especially pronounced in the final Rehnquist Court term. For each term of the natural Court, Chief Justice Rehnquist was the least frequent author of concurring opinions, filing from zero in the 1995 term to just three in the 1998 term. Justices Ginsburg and Souter routinely but not consistently filed the fewest concurrences during the natural Court period, but this seemed partly a feature of their low number of opinions per term generally.

Another interesting composite statistic suggests that separate opinion writing was not obviously a function of membership in an ideological bloc. The top-scoring justices for total number of opinions written from 1994 to 2003 according to per-term average for the entire period were Stevens (31.3), Scalia (27.0), and Thomas (22.2), closely followed by Breyer (22.0).[10] Stevens wrote many more dissents per term than the other justices, and many more dissents than concurrences overall. Scalia's and Thomas's average totals speak for themselves—as the two justices often do, speak, themselves. But Breyer's relatively high opinion output calls attention to his regular production of concurrences and dissents. Indeed, he and Thomas vied for the third spot of the top three filers of concurring opinions on the natural Court from 1994 to 2005.

Numerically speaking, O'Connor was not the top concurring opinion

Table 2.2. Top Concurring Justices of the "Rehnquist Nine," 1994–2004

1994 Term	1999 Term
O'Connor (13)	Scalia (8)
Scalia (9)	Thomas (8)
Thomas (7)	Stevens (7)
1995 Term	Breyer (7)
Scalia (7)	2000 Term
Ginsburg (7)	Scalia (11)
Stevens (6)	Stevens (7)
Souter (6)	Thomas (7)
1996 Term	2001 Term
Scalia (9)	Scalia (9)
O'Connor (6)	Thomas (7)
Breyer (6)	Breyer (7)
1997 Term	2002 Term
Scalia (11)	Stevens (10)
Stevens (8)	Scalia (7)
Breyer (8)	Thomas (7)
1998 Term	2003 Term
Scalia (7)	Scalia (10)
Thomas (7)	Stevens (9)
Stevens (6)	Kennedy (7)
Kennedy (6)	2004 Term
	Breyer (12)
	Thomas (11)
	Stevens (9)
	Scalia (9)

Source: *Harvard Law Review* 109–119, annual statistical summary of the Supreme Court term.

writer; in only two terms in the last decade of the Rehnquist era was she among the top three concurring justices. Yet two factors argue in favor of her essential contribution to the individualist conception of judicial power the separate opinion writing on the Rehnquist Court reflected. First, her opinions in the 1980s, including those under Chief Justice Burger, established that concurrence could be constitutively important, as the journey of her "unduly burdens" test for abortion regulation and endorsement test for religious establishment demonstrated (Maveety 1996). Second, because she was among the regular concurring opinion writers on the Rehnquist bench, she helped to sustain the trend and, more than occasionally, accent its jurisprudential effectiveness. No *one* justice, after all, could be *single*-handedly critical to the Court's *choral* decision making, but single justices could repeatedly show their decisional singularity and, by doing so aggregatively, manifest chorality.

Despite the frequency of a given justice's concurring behavior, nearly all the Rehnquist justices followed a similar pattern for the relative frequency of concurrence type, according to one contemporary study. "Signaling" concurrence, or sending a specific message to a target audience as to the points of law the justice wished to revisit in a future case, was the least frequent concurring activity (Way and Turner 2006, 15). Moreover, this same study found that for the concurrences filed from 1991, with the seating of Justice Thomas, through the 2001 term, both "weakening" or limiting concurring opinions and "ground-laying" concurring opinions, which offer a substantially different legal approach or interpretation, correlated with the presence of joiners (Way and Turner 2006, 25). These more substantive separate opinions were also the more choral in terms of number of voices supporting them. Interestingly, one action on which the individualistic Rehnquist justices could agree collectively was individuated but plurally chimed commentary on the Court's doctrinal promulgation.

Different types of concurring opinion rhetoric can be extracted from the single best example of Rehnquist-era choral decision making. In 1997 the Court held that Washington's prohibition of physician-assisted suicide did not violate the liberty interest of Fourteenth Amendment due process. Although the judgment in *Washington v. Glucksburg* was unanimous in an opinion for the Court by the chief justice, there were five separate concurring opinions: one regular concurrence filed by O'Connor and joined in part by Ginsburg and Breyer and four special concurrences filed by Stevens, Souter, Ginsburg, and Breyer. The opinions ranged in length from Ginsburg's one-sentence concurring statement to Souter's lengthy dissertation on the origins and application of substantive due process. Language in these several concurring opinions exemplified signaling, weakening, and ground-laying arguments, and these concurrences also illustrated that a single opinion can invoke more than one type of argument. Both Stevens and Breyer, for instance, combined signaling and weakening rhetoric in their opinions concurring in the judgment. O'Connor also engaged in an interesting bit of signaling to state legislatures in her regular concurrence, urging "the laboratory of the States" to "strike the proper balance between the interests of terminally ill, mentally competent individuals who would seek to end their suffering and the State's interests in protecting those who might seek to end life mistakenly or under pressure." Table 2.3 classifies the type of arguments found in the *Glucksburg* concurrences.

Taken together, this section's findings on the frequency, authorship, and content of concurrence suggest that the members of the Rehnquist Court were collectively committed to what they individually saw as accurate interpretation of a particular legal issue. If they were mindful of the impact of this commitment on the institutional legitimacy of the Court, it was in the sense of adhering to the "institutional interest in the forthrightness of different justices' views." "Auxiliary way-paving" was the unofficial motto of this Court, with individual justices making sure that the decisional record reflected the exact parameters of the Court's opinion so that it would not or could not be misapplied to constrict or distort the next opinion in the doctrinal line. Tellingly, such accuracy-oriented auxiliary way-paving commentary on the doctrinal promulgation of the majority opinion was considered important enough to occasion the formation of a concurring coalition that competed with the majority opinion coalition.

PROMINENT EXAMPLES: MULTIVOCAL DECISIONS AND RULE-MAKING CONCURRENCES

Another indicator of the importance of concurring opinions on the Rehnquist Court was the degree to which they mattered to the Court's jurisprudential output; the previous section intimated that O'Connor's individual influence was felt in this area.

As judges, Supreme Court justices must express their policy preferences over case outcomes in the form of legal argument and doctrinal rules. As such expressions, concurring opinions have the potential to alter a majority opinion's jurisprudential message or propose distinctive ones of their own. The Rehnquist Court decisional record, then, potentially included two types of decisional phenomena: doctrinally multivocal rulings and legally salient concurring opinions. Did the Rehnquist Court's noteworthy or distinctive jurisprudential contributions to constitutional law come in these decisional formats?

Assessing a Court's contributions to constitutional legal policy is a notoriously subjective enterprise, but several areas of the law would seem to stand

Table 2.3. Types of Concurrence Found in a Single Rehnquist Court
Decision, *Washington v. Glucksburg*

Concurrence Type	Definition	Opinion	Example
Signaling	Indicates points of law to (re)visit in a future case	Stevens	"The differences the majority notes in causation and intent between terminating life support and assisting in suicide . . . may be inapplicable to particular terminally ill patients and their doctors. . . . How such cases may be decided will depend on their specific facts."
Weakening	Limits scope or reach of majority opinion	Breyer	"The Court describes . . . a 'right to commit suicide with another's assistance. [I would consider] a different formulation . . . [that] would use words roughly like a 'right to die with dignity.'"
Ground-laying	Offers different legal approach or interpretation than majority opinion	Souter	"I write separately to give my reasons for analyzing the substantive due process claims as I do."

out as issue areas in which the Rehnquist Court formulated new doctrinal
policy or established a new direction in its decisional outcomes. Commerce
Clause powers vis-à-vis the states, privacy-related concerns, and religious establishment questions were a few such areas of new doctrine and/or a new
direction of decision making; all were products of rulings marked by choral
decision making.

Although anecdotal evidence from the case record is at best merely illustrative, the multivocality in important policy rulings suggests the ingrained
nature of the Rehnquist Court's choral legal policy making. This is because
these "important" rulings are the ones in which legal clarity and thus judicial

unity should be of overweening concern. One could argue that civil liberties issue areas raise especially contentious questions of policy and are thus pre-destined to produce judicial conflict and multiple resolutions on any Supreme Court. Yet even in areas where the Republican-dominated Rehnquist Court was presumed to speak with one voice, such as states' rights limits on federal commerce power, it seldom did. Even a cursory survey of this Court bloc at its most unified around achieving a policy goal—in its defense of states' in-dependence of federal directives pursuant to the Tenth and Eleventh Amend-ments—concurring voices with respect to the promulgation of doctrine were nevertheless raised. In 1997, both *U.S. v. Lopez* and *Printz v. United States*—each a path-breaking five-to-four departure from settled jurisprudence on federal-state relations—garnered two concurrences apiece: two from Thomas and one each from O'Connor and Kennedy. Later rulings limiting the regulatory reach of federal commerce power, such as the five-to-four decision in *U.S. v. Morrison* (2000), continued the multivocal presentation of new doctrine with one concurrence filed. Two major rulings on Eleventh Amendment protec-tion of state immunity from suits pursuant to federal law, *Kimel v. Florida Board of Regents* (2000) and *Board of Trustees of the University of Alabama v. Garrett* (2001), were veritable festivals of chorality: Thomas and Kennedy each filed partial concurrences in *Kimel*, Stevens's partial concurrence in the same case gained three votes, and Kennedy and O'Connor each filed a solo concurrence in the five-to-four case of *Garrett*.

The importance of these various concurrences lay in their ability, by their very presence, to problematize the direction and application of the holding. That this happened in the area of federalism, one of priority and fundamen-tal agreement as to policy outcomes for a majority bloc, suggested justices' attachment to the concurring opinion as a vehicle for intellectual "clarifica-tion" of constitutional rules.

This pattern of multivocal, doctrinally qualified rulings and legally salient concurrences was even more striking in the major privacy and religious es-tablishment holdings of the Rehnquist Court. Doctrinally qualified rulings are decisions in which a chorus of majority coalition voices speaks in multiple separate opinions, including but not limited to a majority opinion. There was no more dramatic illustration of this phenomenon[11] than the multiauthored opinion for the Court on abortion rights in *Planned Parenthood v. Casey* (1992), which examined the precedent-setting *Roe v. Wade*. Much has been written about this case, but the recently opened judicial papers of Harry A. Blackmun

provide a window into the internal decisional processes and coalitional complications of the early Rehnquist Court. The archival material in the Blackmun
papers confirms much of the analysis already in print on *Casey* and sheds light
on the deeply ingrained nature of separate opinion writing on the contemporary Court. One example, though incidental, is instructive. In a memo of
June 16, 1992, Blackmun's principal clerk on his opinion for the case remarks
that "there is much to be admired in the formation of the troika and the substance of their opinion"; in a later June 26 memo she comments, "I think
your opinion expresses that admiration" (Blackmun Papers, Box 602, Folder
4). Rather than disturbing, the unorthodoxy of a "troika" opinion signed by
three justices, O'Connor, Kennedy, and Souter, was "admirable"—perhaps
for its affirmation of "the importance of a united front—why else write a joint
opinion?" (Karst 2003, 425). Technically united yet multivocal—such was the
character of much Rehnquist-era decision making.

Jointly voiced decisions on the Rehnquist Court at times included legally
salient concurring opinions or those that came to be rule-making concurrences. Such separate opinions, by demarcating a distinctive doctrinal approach or presenting a new judicial rule or test, came to shape the law—the
Court's legal outputs—in a given issue area. In such circumstances, a justice
who may not have been the most frequent concurror on the Rehnquist bench
nevertheless contributed a concurring opinion that was legally influential and
thus an important milestone of the Rehnquist choral Court record. There was
no better example of this phenomenon of legally salient separate writing than
the Rehnquist justices' various tests for First Amendment religious establishment cases. Many of these tests began as doctrinal alternatives offered in
solo-authored concurring opinions; discussion of the tests and weighing of
their relative merits became the centerpiece of a full-fledged judicial debate as
to the constitutionally appropriate stance of the state with respect to religious
activity. Not only did this interjudicial debate produce (or reproduce) multivocal decisions in Establishment Clause cases but also the jurisprudential
debate took place overtly within opinions of the Court themselves.

Especially illustrative of this approach to Supreme Court decision making
was *Lee v. Weisman* (1992), examination of which also benefits from access to
Harry Blackmun's record of memos and drafts in the case. After the vote at
conference, Chief Justice Rehnquist assigned Justice Kennedy to write the
original majority opinion upholding the graduation prayer in the case; Blackmun's clerks were planning an opinion that spoke for the dissent, which

included Stevens, O'Connor, and Souter.[12] But as Kennedy divulged in a March 30, 1992, memo to Blackmun, "After writing to reverse, . . . my draft looked quite wrong." He also acknowledged that after the "barbs" exchanged between the two of them in previous establishment cases (through the vehicle of separate opinions, one might add), "it [is] most important to write something that you and I and the others who voted this way can join" (Blackmun Papers, Box 586, Folder 6). Despite Kennedy's vote switch and attempts to reach across the great jurisprudential divide, Blackmun and Souter filed concurring opinions in order to reaffirm their broader positions on church-state separation. Souter filed a separate opinion "to show where I stand on some, though hardly on all, of the points on which such cases turn"—his words to Justice Kennedy to explain his concurrence, "since this is my first Establishment case."[13]

Stevens joined both Blackmun's and Souter's concurring opinions, as did O'Connor, although she had originally begun to write separately. But all four justices also joined Kennedy's majority opinion, resulting in a plethora of tests and readings of tests: coercion into religious exercises by the state, endorsement of religion by the state, endorsement without necessarily coercion, and, only minimally, explicit reiteration of the *Lemon* test that came from the 1972 majority opinion in *Lemon v. Kurtzman*. Indeed, the separate opinions made it quite clear that Kennedy's use of the coercion principle to resolve the case did not reflect a majority's commitment to that doctrinal approach. Yet rather than objecting to the majority coalition's multivocality, the coalition seemed to welcome it. Not only was Souter eager to get his own unique views on impermissible religious endorsement on the table, but Stevens wrote in a memo to Kennedy copied to the majority justices: "I think you have done a fine job both in explaining the central problem of the case and in doing so in a way that *we can have a Court opinion without unnecessary controversy about the proper way to formulate the standard.*"[14] Agreement and univocality as to the doctrinal rule of a holding by the Court no longer seemed essential to a good decision by the Court.

The Court's later establishment pronouncements continued if not embraced the choral practice, with the concurring voices in the cases resonating with significant doctrinal content. *Zelman v. Simmons-Harris* (2002), which addressed the school voucher question, produced six opinions in total, including one concurrence apiece from O'Connor and Thomas. Much of O'Connor's concurrence was devoted to refuting dissenting Justice Souter's notion that the neutrality-based ruling was a departure from extant Establishment Clause jurisprudence; Thomas devoted himself to noting that "it may well be that state action should be evaluated on different terms than similar action by the federal government [in the context of the Establishment Clause]." Even the unanimous holding in the 2004 Pledge of Allegiance case of *Elk Grove Unified School District v. Newdow* occasioned three separate concurring opinions to discuss the substantive questions not reached by the majority ruling, which disposed of the claim on a jurisdictional (standing) basis. Justices O'Connor and Thomas each wrote separately and also partly joined Chief Justice Rehnquist's concurring opinion. Of these concurring writings, O'Connor's envisioned the greatest future import for itself, with its four-part, fact-sensitive "ceremonial deism" test for permissible governmental use of religious symbolism or acknowledgment of religious heritage. Indeed, the test was invoked by the parties' briefs in the two Ten Commandments display cases of 2005, *Van Orden v. Perry* and *McCreary County v. ACLU*. Yet separate voices still proliferated, for one of O'Connor's principal allies on the endorsement-of-religion approach to First Amendment questions, Justice Souter, had already spoken in his *Lee* concurrence of ceremonial religious messages. An addition to the end of his third draft concurrence in the 1992 case stressed that even the "ceremonial" conveys an endorsement of religion when "armed with the state's authority" (Blackmun Papers, Box 586, Folder 7).

The Rehnquist Court continued to offer its jurisprudential approaches to establishment questions in concurrence in its last rulings, *Van Orden* and *McCreary*, in June 2005. Justice O'Connor again spoke separately, and separately from a putative ally, appending a concurring opinion to Souter's opinion for the Court in the *McCreary* case, which invalidated Kentucky's display of the Ten Commandments for lacking a legitimizing secular purpose. But most noteworthy was Justice Breyer's concurrence in the judgment in the *Van Orden* case, which upheld Texas' display of the Ten Commandments on government property. Breyer's vote, critical to the five-justice disposition in the case, turned on his admission that "none of the Court's various tests for evaluating Establishment Clause questions can substitute for an exercise of legal judgment" to resolve such fact-sensitive cases. Such exercises of legal judgment, although not personal (as Breyer took pains to proclaim explicitly), seemed inclined to take the form of personalized separate opinions.

CONCLUSION: WHITHER THE CONCURRENCE EXPLOSION?

Was the Rehnquist Court's durable resort to choral decision making a temporary detour into judicial individualism, a "chiefless" justice interlude in the decade's process of consolidating a conservative Republican majority on the Court, or did the Rehnquist era profoundly change the Supreme Court as an institution?

Although it is still early for prognostication about the post-Rehnquist future, there is reason to suspect that the decision-making behaviors practiced during the Rehnquist period leave a legacy for the next Court era. This is the case in two ways.

First, it is worth noting that the 1940s Supreme Court's "step[ping] up [of] its production rate of dissents until previously unheard of levels of disagreement were attained" (Friedman 2002, 181–182, citing attitudinal scholar C. Herman Pritchett) precipitated the midcentury exploration of the role of the Court and the rise of the "countermajoritarian difficulty" in legal theorizing about judicial review (Friedman 2002, 184).[15] Chapter 4 in direct comparison takes up the question of whether the Rehnquist Court decisional record, including its propensity for multivocal policy pronouncements, had a similar galvanizing force and ideational impact on judicial scholars' views of the institution.

Second, according to historical institutionalist scholars of the Supreme Court, its members' preferences and behavioral expressions are shaped by the institutional practices through which they find themselves and their role constituted. Justices who have "learned" a choral, discursive model of High Court leadership with respect to doctrinal policy making could be expected to continue that approach, and thus reconstitute it for new colleagues just joining the Court.

O'Connor's contribution to this feature of individuated judicial power was as a teacher of the convention, by being a confirmed practitioner. In this, she was not so different than her colleagues Stevens and Scalia, except that she was an associate justice whose centrist coalitional position during the Rehnquist period maximized the impact of her votes, separate opinions, and thus doctrinal views. She was, in this sense, the "poster justice" for the notion of concurring opinions serving a rule-making function that enhanced the doctrinal promulgation authority of individual justices. Her role-model influence is of course difficult to verify, as it is rare for judges to acknowledge their motivations candidly or even to understand them (Klein 2002, 137–138). Nevertheless, O'Connor's associates—whatever their motivation—exhibited concurring behaviors consonant with the above notion and with a role orientation toward judicial individualism. Some, like Stevens, Scalia, and O'Connor, attempted to justify separate opinion writing, in off-the-bench writings, but most others let their separate judicial voices do the talking.

Flash in the pan or deeply ingrained, Rehnquist-era multivocality became a touchstone for the new Roberts Court. Initial reports of its placidity and unanimity (Savage 2006) gave way to sightings of "dueling opinions" in the 2006 Fourth Amendment ruling that featured Chief Justice Roberts's first dissent, and the almost wistful notation of "a tone of banter between old adversaries, as if after some months of forced and unaccustomed unanimity, [the justices] were now free once again to acknowledge their differences" (Greenhouse 2006a). Chapter 5 takes up the question of whether other rulings of the 2005 Roberts term evidenced similar dissensus. Whether the Rehnquist Court was the first or the last choral Court is beyond the scope of this study, but the Rehnquist associates who remain on the bench may prove resistant to more modest visions of individual judicial power.

As a convention of decision making, as a customary practice, writing separately seems firmly and positively entrenched in the minds of at least one group of Supreme Court personnel—its clerks, if Justice Blackmun's clerks from the early 1990s are any indication. In their memos to Blackmun, they regularly presented the option of concurrence and seldom suggested its drawbacks. Indeed, in one memo from May 1990, regarding the Equal Access Act case of *Board of Education of Westside Community Schools v. Mergens*, the clerk who was advising the justice how to vote and what to write seemed to have no conception of the Court's "voice," seeing only individual writings and their respective positions and interpretations. Tellingly, the clerk noted that "all three opinions [in the case] are excellent" and "you could join any one of them without upsetting me in the least" (Blackmun Papers, Box 549, Folder 9). If clerks—their presence, their number, and their importance on the modern bench (Peppers 2006, 191–192)—are driving the increase in separate filings, as some scholars suspect (Best 2002; Ward and Weiden 2006, 148), it may be partly because they have internalized the value and validity of separate opinion writing. Still, not all clerks view themselves as the factor driving separate opinion writing. As a former clerk to Warren-era Justice Tom Clark posited, "Some judges happen to have strong views about an issue, which they happen to be on the losing side [of] all the time. But more it's that there are some judges like there are some board members in a board meeting that just can't resist being heard" (Ward and Weiden 2006, 234). The strong views of individual justices are pertinent in more ways than one, for contemporary judicial scholars have noted the relationship between selection of law clerks and polarization on the Supreme Court, arguing that the relationship between the justices' ideological positions and the positions of the lower court judges from whom they drew their clerks became stronger for the 1975–1998 terms of the Court.[16] This is relevant to separate opinion output because "polarization [within the clerk ranks] could make the Court's decisions *even more the sum of individual positions* and less the product of collective consideration that they were in the past" (Ditslear and Baum 2001, 869 [emphasis added]). Still, not all of the modern justices' clerks appear ready to seize upon multivocal decision making as a modern template. In another memo from another Blackmun clerk, on March 14, 1990, regarding the case of *Austin v. Chamber of Commerce*, she observes that both the force of the circulating dissents and the impetus for others' concurring writings were the weakness of the draft majority opinion. "Now," the clerk laments to Justice Blackmun, "we are stuck with a fragmented Court and no solid and unified majority position. I hardly know what to suggest. You might want to concur separately, but it's hard to see how more writing would help at this point" (Blackmun Papers, Box 549, Folder 6).

Whether "more writing helped" the Rehnquist Court's communication of its doctrinal policy directives must await the verdict of history. But it is clear that this Court found its voice in serial concordance, accentuating the potential importance of each individual justice—and each future appointment—to the U.S. Supreme Court.

3

The previous chapters argued that decision-making processes and doctrinal promulgation procedures on the Rehnquist Court accentuated the importance of individual justices at the expense of the chief justice and the Court institution as a whole. Decisions produced by the aggregation of individual voices and resulting from individualized policy leadership efforts were typical outcomes during the Rehnquist era. The outcomes of both separate opinion writing and diffused leadership activity were nurtured by the individualistic judicial behaviors of the Court's associate justices; by her example, Associate Justice Sandra Day O'Connor played an important role in sustaining and promoting such behaviors. The Court was "hers" in the sense that her approach to being an associate justice was critical to the decentralized and multivocal character of the institution. But that institutional character developed fully only because the "O'Connor approach" governed other associate justices' behavior as well. Individualistic decision-making conventions became the overall decision-making process.

Procedurally, O'Connor-style judicial individualism engendered a loosened standard of "collegial" behavior, whereby the collective product of the Court was more aggregative than coordinated and cooperation took on a decidedly atomistic cast. The combined effect of this novel standard of collegiality with the jurisprudential reasoning, constitutional interpretation, and substantive doctrinal promulgation of the Rehnquist era is the subject of this third chapter. Linking procedure and substance highlights the mechanisms by which and the degree to which individual associate justices shaped the Rehnquist Court's jurisprudence. By examining doctrinal rule making, this chapter directly confronts the question of whether "O'Connorism" in the justices' decision-making behavior carried over into "O'Connorist" jurisprudence, that is, jurisprudential outputs heavily influenced if not decisively shaped by O'Connor-style legal reasoning.

Much has been written about the jurisprudential contributions—or lack thereof—of the recently ended Rehnquist Court. Most extant accounts attempt to characterize that jurisprudence in terms of certain substantive principles, among them the Court's ideological conservatism, antiregulatory policy, and hostility to civil litigation (Siegel 2006). Some analysts find some accounts undertheorized, such as those identifying the Court's "conservative" judicial policy making, which therefore provide an inadequate understanding of the ideological content of judicial conservatism (but see Keck 2004); other analysts suggest the Court's own jurisprudence was undertheorized and fundamentally incoherent because of its perpetual divisiveness (Tushnet 2006). A strong theme of minimalism pervades many explications of the Rehnquist Court's work ever since the publication of Cass Sunstein's *One Case at a Time* (1999), which both identified and defended modest and incompletely theorized decision making on the contemporary Court. O'Connor's legal reasoning was singled out by Sunstein as best exemplifying minimalism (1999, 62; 2006).[1] The "O'Connor style" came to stand for a kind of principled restraintism, or neutral principles–informed judicial prudentialism and self-constraint (Molot 2004). Still, such characterizations said little about how such broad doctrinal trends turned into specific legal policies or why a Court might proffer such minimalist constitutional doctrine.

Shortly after the publication of Sunstein's book and his pronouncement that O'Connor's minimalism and judicial modesty constituted the legal persona of the Rehnquist Court, the Court seemed to morph into something else, judicially and politically. The "federalism five" stepped up their doctrinal defense of the sovereign dignity of states (Whittington 2004); broadly rights-protective rulings such as the Texas sodomy and juvenile death penalty decisions were rendered; and, of course, the Court's political judgment in *Bush v. Gore* was issued. Although Justice O'Connor supported all of the aforementioned judicial policies, it was neither her voice nor, arguably, "her" minimalist jurisprudence that prevailed. "One case at a time" seemed to have been succeeded by "one supreme ruling, for all time," but with the proverbial judicial finger held up to the prevailing political wind.

One of the difficulties scholars who wrote about the Rehnquist Court experienced was its elusiveness. Each underlying trend identified—ideological conservatism, minimalism, "juricentrism"[2]—seemed to melt away the following June. But perhaps the Court's slippery identity was the result of using the wrong categories to make sense of its jurisprudence, and can be attributed instead to its uniquely individualistic nature as a deliberative decision-making body.

Arguably, the Court's jurisprudence was never substantively coherent, but rather was the predictable product of a coherent set of intra-Court procedures. In positing this, I offer a new analytical focus for reframing the doctrinal legacy of the era. That analytical focus embraces the main claim of this book: that the Rehnquist Court's "supremely individualist" conception of judicial power was its primary contribution to the development of the Supreme Court and constitutional law in American politics, and that this institutional contribution was facilitated by an empowered associate justice and associate-empowering justice, Sandra Day O'Connor. Thus, the Rehnquist Court's doctrinal legacy must be reframed as *associates' justice*, that is, case-fact-sensitive jurisprudential pragmatism that occurred as individual associate justices vied for influence from the center and with one another. The aggregative and cumulative nature of both policy leadership and decisional rule promulgation on the Rehnquist Court, combined with the Court's lack of an overarching ideological unity, favored the jurisprudential result of contextual-factor, reasonableness-based balancing.

Legal pragmatism, like its philosophical namesake, embraces the "practical application of concepts" and, like the legal realist movement to which it belongs, challenges foundationalism and conceptualism in legal theory (Broughton 1999, 60–61) in favor of contextual reasoning "embodied in practices" (Grey 1989, 798). This jurisprudential approach views law in terms of "experience [as] tradition interpreted with one eye on coherence and another on policy" (Grey 1989, 814).[3] Elsewhere, such jurisprudence has been termed "split-the-difference reasoning," a methodology that deploys particular doctrinal tools for expressing legal policy solutions. Fact-dependent tests and the relaxation of constraints on judicial discretion in applying them are the critical tools (Wilkinson 2006, 1980–1981), and the jurisprudential doctrines that result "utilize a legal and rhetorical framework of express compromise" (Wilkinson 2006, 1977).

However described, this jurisprudential result occurred even in issue areas in which the Court possessed a relatively cohesive majority bloc where the justices were divided but a durable majority coalition existed—such as in federalism or commerce power. In such areas, as well as those in which the justices were fragmented, such as abortion or church-state relations, rule-of-thumb balancing approaches dominated. Moreover, various individual associate justices were doctrinal promulgators. That these attributes persisted across issue areas suggests that ideological cleavage and the polarization that resulted did not alone account for the style of Rehnquist Court jurisprudence. This pattern suggests that the justices did not simply default to rule-of-thumb approaches but opted for them out of procedural commitment. What procedural commitment? The Court consisted of a set of justices determined to record their diverse individual views, yet cooperative enough to accede reciprocity in doing so. Thus, alongside tacit acceptance of institutional decentralization and chorality was acquiescence to—albeit at times over objection—the inevitability of median-point, pragmatic doctrinal formulations.

In pursuing the claim that associate-empowering behavioral conventions affected substantive outcomes, I first delineate how the Rehnquist bench used rule-of-thumb balancing approaches for its constitutional policy making. The major rulings of the Rehnquist Court on constitutional structure and rights are the source material for demonstrating this. I then consider the "coincidence" of the judicial individuality of associates' justice and rule-of-thumb balancing in Rehnquist Court jurisprudence. Because the rule-of-thumb approach consists of individually conducted totality-of-factors or reasonableness balancing, idiosyncrasy in application is palpable—and is consistent with and even promotes the practice of judicial individualism. When used by an individualistic justice in an influential position, collegially speaking, such rule-of-thumb jurisprudence becomes the legal methodology of the Court's pronouncements. Jurisprudential consistency across the Court's constitutional policy making can come, then, from an individual's dominance in the decision-making dynamic—to the extent that a single individual's authorship of various doctrinal rules and tests guarantees their overall coherence. But although influential centrist O'Connor was the source of many of the Rehnquist Court's rule-of-thumb precedential rulings, other associate justices crafted doctrinal pronouncements for the Court that followed her jurisprudential style. The consequences of this, for the Court's overall jurisprudential output, were more "rule-of-thumb-ism" and "more thumbs."

Did a cognizable jurisprudence emerge, then, from associates' justice, rule-of-thumb balancing, from the serial and "explicit personalization of constitutional interpretation" (Wilkinson 2006, 1993)? A few aspects of the "rule of thumbs" must be investigated and, in a sense, "measured" to answer this question adequately. The first aspects are the structural similarity and common prudential orientation of the rule-of-thumb approaches, collectively articulated. The next aspect concerns the correspondence between output and process, or whether the associate practitioners of judicial individualism contributed equally[4] to the Court's median-point doctrinal formulations for various constitutional issue areas. The presence of structural similarity and common prudential orientation in the rules of thumb, combined with plural judicial contributions, suggests a recurring doctrinal approach grounded in practical policy and so a cognizable jurisprudence overall. Plural judicial contribution also presents an operationally reliable measure of individual judicial importance that indicates a widely shared and exercised understanding of the individual judicial function[5] on this collegial appellate Court. Finally, the recurring doctrinal approach by multiple justices provides a precise substantive meaning for the queen's Court.

In illustrating how the institutional convention of judicial individualism coordinated with an individually oriented jurisprudential method, I next raise the question of which Rehnquist-era judicial predilections are likely to leave an enduring mark on constitutional law. I explore this question more tentatively than conclusively in the final section of this chapter. Constitutional change is, of course, a product of the choices justices make, but because judicial choices are interdependent, they are not unaffected by personnel changes on the Supreme Court. Thus, the ideological alignment of the Court, a product of the judicial selection process, can predict which justices matter in terms of decisive votes cast. But ideological factors alone cannot predict whether the rule-of-thumb jurisprudential approach will be the decisive one on a multimember Court. In spite of the influence of the centrist conservatives on the Rehnquist Court, it is not obvious that a rule-of-thumb balancing doctrine would necessarily be the approach of the pivotal centrist justices on a divided bench[6]—or that its perpetuation depends on such justices.

In considering which juridical conditions produced and will affect the durability of the Rehnquist-era rule-of-thumb balancing tests as precedents, we must invoke the larger question of which forces shape constitutional development. Court scholars working in the American political development tradition concern themselves with how doctrinal settlements are reached and become entrenched, along with what makes legal doctrinal developments "sticky" (Kahn 2006; Kersch 2006). Broader institutional conditions affect which "constitutive stories" are likely to sustain a political or jurisprudential regime (Kersch 2006), but broader institutional conditions also interface with the internal dynamics on the Court. Intra-Court dynamics were obviously of great consequence during the Rehnquist era, enabling Justice O'Connor— predisposed to be moderately conservative—to perform as a strategic centrist blessed by the circumstance of a divided Court produced by a regime of divided government. Arguably, then, it was only her pivotal voting position that enshrined her individual style of doctrinal balancing into law, and the latter will not survive her stepping down from that pivotal voting position—unless institutional conditions ordain a similar type of jurist to succeed her in it.

This theory suggests that all eyes should be on Kennedy—or Breyer, or Roberts, or whoever might move into "O'Connor's role," coalitionally and jurisprudentially, on the Roberts bench—because such judicial behavior by one of the current Court's moderates is vital to the preservation of O'Connorist jurisprudence. But what would the fact of another pivotal centrist situated to perpetuate it *who then perpetuates it* indicate: simply the act of strategizing for judicial power or something more developmentally significant? Would such judicial behavior, preserving O'Connor-style jurisprudence, in fact also demonstrate that the individually oriented, rule-of-thumb standard is an entrenched jurisprudential regime—one that became entrenched because it resonated with the judicial individualism consolidated during the Rehnquist era? The latter continuity would imply that the O'Connorist doctrinal method has become a "sticky" jurisprudential settlement (although it would not tell us why). Still, *even* a pivotal centrist carrying on O'Connor-style jurisprudence would surely be *suggestive* of its deeper juridical appeal—and contribute to the "constitutive story" to sustain it. And that story might well be one of the pluralism of associates' justice, that is, of how a disunified bench of judicial individualists collectively produced a pragmatic, fact-sensitive, and incrementalist constitutional method, crafting decisions that prioritized workable, not categorical, rules in individualized, not autonomic, application.

The doctrinal formulations of the divided and divisive Rehnquist bench were elevated by certain court commentators to a kind of distinction: rule-of-thumb pragmatic balancing as nonideological legal compromise that averted constitutional stasis and political crisis. Indeed, it is difficult not to read this message into the many laudatory accounts of such decisions as the joint opinion for the Court in the 1992 decision of *Planned Parenthood v. Casey*. But whether rule-of-thumb jurisprudence is substantively good or bad is not the point of this chapter. The point is to show its utility for a particular, supremely individualist Court, and to suggest which existing and persisting institutional conditions may perpetuate the Rehnquist era's rule-of-thumb balancing, as both precedent and methodology.

RULE-OF-THUMB RULINGS: THE DECISIONS

In this section I have two objectives. First, I summarize the major rulings of the Rehnquist Court, explicating the doctrinal approach supported by the Court's decision and showing how it was a rule-of-thumb balancing approach. Second, I identify the individual justice making the rule-of-thumb judgment call in the case, or in the course of case-by-case adjudication of the issue. My objective is to ascertain whether the associate practitioners of judicial individualism were equal contributors to the Court's doctrinal formulations for various constitutional issue areas, or whether certain justices accounted for more of the Court's judge-made balancing tests. These two lines of inquiry will shed some light on the jurisprudential coherence of the practice of the rule of thumbs and offer another perspective from which to inquire whether a "queen's Court" existed during the Rehnquist years.

Encapsulating a Supreme Court era can be done in many different ways by summarizing different kinds of Court data. Decisional content is one kind of data, and such a summary of it involves identifying the major rulings of the Court. Any list of such case rulings is bound to be subjective, to some degree, although there are various methods employed by court scholars to limit personal discretion in selecting the most salient or important decisions of a term or an era. These include identifying those cases receiving above-the-fold coverage in "major" newspapers, headnoting by court reporters in such publications as *U.S. Law Week*, and inclusion in casebooks. The method also references expert opinion, such as articles in leading law reviews and attention from leading court scholars. Since so much retrospective writing on the Rehnquist period or portions of it has already occurred, there is some convergence of opinion around those decisions that are most memorable and evocative of a distinctive Court era and most portentous in their legal or political impact.

One moment of such convergence functions as my case-selection device for this chapter. In the fall of 2006 a not unexpected discussion thread occurred on a listserv of legal academics and political scientists who study law and courts: scholarly opinion as to a decisional synopsis of the Rehnquist Court period.[7] Reflecting his field's penchant for taking stock of judicial eras, a list member posed the question, "What were the Rehnquist Court's greatest or most important constitutional decisions?" With "most important" taken to mean politically or legally significant, a fair amount of consensus emerged in the responses, producing these thirteen cases listed alphabetically:

Bush v. Gore
City of Boerne v. Flores
Clinton v. Jones
Dickerson v. U.S.
Gratz/Grutter v. Bollinger
Hamdi v. Rumsfeld
Kelo v. City of New London
Lawrence v. Texas
Planned Parenthood v. Casey
Shaw v. Reno
Texas v. Johnson
U.S. v. Lopez
Zelman v. Simmons-Harris

Admittedly, this is an idiosyncratic and unscientifically derived list (as are most such lists), but it still reveals certain things. First, these cases taken together endorse neither political or constitutional conservatism nor political or constitutional liberalism. The decisions collectively chart a moderate course in terms of public and legal policy. The various majority opinions, where there were majority opinions, were the work of several different judicial hands. Only four were O'Connor opinions for the Court: *Grutter, Shaw v. Reno*, and *Hamdi* as a judgment of the Court; and *Casey* as a joint O'Connor opinion and an opinion for the Court in part. Still, O'Connor supported the majority outcome in all but three cases: the *Texas v. Johnson* flag-burning ruling, the *Kelo* Takings Clause decision, and the substantive assumption about free-exercise law behind the separation-of-powers holding in *Boerne v. Flores.*[8] Only two of the Rehnquist Court decisions could be described fairly as rule-bound, absolutist rulings (as uncompromised and uncompromising legal policy commandments): *Lawrence v. Texas*, in which the Court in pursuit of the value of personal dignity extended privacy protection to homosexual, intimate associational conduct, and *Texas v. Johnson*, in which the Court un-equivocally mandated First Amendment protection for the expressive conduct of flag-burning. The argument could be made that *Boerne v. Flores* and *Dickerson v. U.S.* were also absolutist commandments, but if we consider each in turn, we find problems with this interpretation. *Boerne* did assert judicial exclusivity in interpreting the parameters of constitutional rights protections, limiting the Section 5 enforcement powers of Congress under the Fourteenth Amendment to preventative and remedial actions that impinge upon neither the Court's own power nor the prerogatives of states. But rather than being the last or definitive judicial word on the subject, *Boerne* engendered a series of cases further articulating and fine-tuning the limits of that congressional power and its application to other areas of civil rights enforcement. *Dickerson* did unilaterally preserve the constitutional rule regarding protection against self-incrimination articulated in *Miranda v. Arizona* from any congressional superseding, and cited *Boerne* as its separation-of-powers precedent in doing so. But *Dickerson* also acknowledged that the Court had recognized (and, presumably, would continue to recognize) rule-of-thumb-based, balancing-of-circumstances exceptions to the *Miranda* warning requirement, and conceded that these could be taken to indicate the less-than-absolute validity of that practice. *Boerne*, *Dickerson*, and the two adamantly civil libertarian holdings aside for the moment, then, the vast majority of the above-listed rulings were judicious compromises notably using fact-based and even multifactor balancing. Finally, none of the decisions was unanimous with a single opinion for the Court: even nine-to-zero *Clinton v. Jones* was annotated by a concurring opinion, and most were close and multivocal decisions, five-to-four or six-to-three, with several shades of opinion to the majority coalition.

Are any noteworthy rulings missing from the above list? Whether *Roper v. Simmons* in the final 2004 term just misses being remarkable or was omitted in the haste of e-mail-based chat, this policy decision was not identified by a listserv member as "great" or "important." Many court scholars would probably take issue with this verdict on a decision that set aside state usage of capital punishment for juveniles by extending the application of "evolving standards of decency." Also not named were any of the Court's federalism rulings—decisions that collectively precipitated a "federalism revolution" by articulating the integrity of states and their immunity as "inviolable" sovereigns from certain federal regulation. These lacunae may show nothing more than the unsystematic nature and unreliable quality of "greatest hits" rankings. Or they may be connected to this vital fact about the Rehnquist Court: even its most significant decisions, in terms of their legal policy and political repercussions, were highly nuanced renderings of a rule of law—complex to summarize, mixed in their effect, sensitive if not quite fully satisfying compromises. Isolated Rehnquist Court cases—*Roper*, *New York v. U.S.*,[9] and its Tenth and Eleventh Amendment progeny—are forgivably forgettable not because they were unimportant but because each was an incomplete or unfinished mandate—each, like so many of the Court's "major" rulings, settled some big thing but left only a framework for settling many other, related things—a framework that entailed in its future use a perceptible amount of individual judgment-calling.

Flawed though the above case list might be, it has the virtue of the familiar and the fairly uncontroversial in content. With the agreement to include *Roper* as consequential for criminal justice policy,[10] and with the understanding to discuss the Rehnquist Court's definitional forays into states' rights, the list suffices as an acceptably abbreviated summation of the Court's jurisprudential contributions to constitutional law, and therefore as a defensible sample for exploring the Court's rule-of-thumb jurisprudential style.[11]

In considering the doctrinal approaches of the decisions and the qualifications of each as rule-of-thumb balancing, it is useful to begin with those rulings from the list that are clearly exceptions—though are still illustrative of the force of associates' justice during the Rehnquist era. Both *Texas v. Johnson* (1989) and *Lawrence v. Texas* (2003) are difficult to defend as examples of contextual-factor, reasonableness-based balancing that pragmatically fosters compromise. Neither shrank from an absolutist and potentially politically polarizing policy conclusion: that the First Amendment protects conduct expressing an unpopular viewpoint through a controversial medium—burning of the American flag as political speech in *Johnson*—and that the liberty interest of the Fourteenth Amendment includes protection of privacy in intimate association—the invalidation of state criminalization of homosexual sodomy in *Lawrence*. *Texas v. Johnson* was a five-to-four ruling, with the majority opinion authored by Justice William Brennan, and a brief concurrence written by Justice Kennedy "not to qualify the words Justice Brennan chooses so well . . . but with a keen sense that this case . . . exacts its personal toll" (491 U.S. 397, 420). The eloquent and powerful opinion of which Kennedy spoke is thus more accurately thought of as the last precedent of the "Brennan Court" than as an anomaly of either the Rehnquist period or the era of O'Connorism.

Its fundamental faith in the liberty of expression, broadly defined, combined with its staunch defense of the expression of unpopular ideas, marked the Brennan ruling as neither a doctrinal nor a political compromise. It was liberal jurisprudence and a libertarian holding in the face of difficult real-world circumstances, as Kennedy's separate opinion acknowledged. Similar things can be said of Kennedy's majority opinion in *Lawrence*, which also was rhetorically expansive in its defense of the importance of personal intimacy choices to the Fourteenth Amendment liberty interest and its connection to "the autonomy of self" and "the dignity of free persons" (539 U.S. 558). No fact-dependent tests were offered by Kennedy; his doctrinal rule was absolutist and bright-line with respect to state interference with private conduct in adult relationships. This aspect of the decision was fodder for Justice Scalia's equally absolutist dissent, which found no "right to 'liberty'" to justify the Court taking sides in the culture war. Experts on Kennedy's jurisprudence have labored to explain his position in the six-to-three *Lawrence* case,[12] connecting it to a libertarian streak, a commitment to nondiscrimination against gays espoused in his *Romer v. Evans* (1996) decision,[13] or a deeply felt obligation to engage in the judgment function (Barnett 2003; Brust 2003; Parshall 2004; Tushnet 2006, 177; Ward 2004). But whatever the explanation for it, the doctrinal approach in *Lawrence*, like that in *Johnson*, uses a categorical rule, not reasonableness balancing. These legal doctrines are thus unlikely to engender the idiosyncrasy in application that marks judicial individualism as a decisional methodology or practice. Nevertheless, these two significant precedents from the Rehnquist Court on constitutional rights illustrate how important its individual associate justices were to its creative product.

THE EARLY YEARS OF O'CONNOR'S AND O'CONNORIST JURISPRUDENCE

It is in the balance of the Rehnquist Court record of important decisions that we find rule-of-thumb jurisprudential solutions: individually oriented reasonableness standards as the doctrinal approach for an issue area, authored by different justices on the Rehnquist bench. These decisions are best reviewed chronologically, by decade and in light of personnel changes, with some grouping by subject matter. This format yields from the 1990s seven major or at least memorable contributions to constitutional law: *Planned Parenthood v. Casey* (1992), *Shaw v. Reno* (1993), *U.S. v. Lopez* (1995), *New York v. U.S.* (1992), *Printz v. U.S.* (1997), *Clinton v. Jones* (1997), and *City of Boerne v. Flores*

(1997). Three of these seven rulings were not the product of the "mature" Rehnquist Court or the Rehnquist era during its last natural Court period. That period commenced in 1994 with the seating of Justice Stephen Breyer to replace retiring Burger Court veteran Harry Blackmun. *Shaw*, *Casey*, and *New York v. U.S.* were the work of earlier iterations of the Rehnquist Court; *Casey* and *New York* were decided before the seating of either Breyer or Ruth Bader Ginsburg and in the first term of service of conservative appointee Clarence Thomas. By the time of *Lopez* in 1995, the nine who would serve together for more than ten years were already in place on the bench; indeed, the five-to-four lineup in that ruling would be a familiar coalitional ordering for the rest of the Rehnquist era: a conservative majority bloc consisting of the chief, Scalia, and Thomas plus Kennedy and O'Connor; and a liberal-centrist opposition bloc usually led by Stevens, including Souter, Ginsburg, and Breyer. But as in so many cases featuring this lineup, *Lopez* revealed the limits of coalitional fastness among the Rehnquist justices: Kennedy, joined by O'Connor, concurred to qualify and limit the majority's holding; Thomas, speaking from the Court's right, concurred to urge more radical action yet. The dissenters spoke separately and somewhat distinctly. Even though the reach of congressional commerce power was an issue on which the conservative justices were relatively united, the proper degree of rule-of-thumb balancing to espouse was a question for them, and a matter that fractured their univocality as to doctrinal promulgation.

Most of these rulings, including *Lopez* but especially the line of reasoning in *New York/Printz*, produced progeny of great importance in their own right as doctrinal formulations by the Court. But the initial significance of the rulings of *Casey*, *New York v. U.S.*, *Shaw*, *Lopez*, and *Clinton v. Jones* was the legal policy innovation of using a noncategorical rule and context-sensitive test *that would settle controversies in the particular and contentious issue area in terms of a balance between two or more factors, thus likely not settling individual instances of that issue controversy identically.* Whether this method was a jurisprudence of legal pragmatism or simply a recipe for pragmatic outcomes can be addressed by comparing the doctrines of each issue area for similarities in the execution process. Such similarities are putative evidence of some attachment to a jurisprudential approach as opposed to mere discrete instances of ends-oriented advancement. Of course, pragmatic balancing is more likely to produce pragmatic compromises, so similar procedural methods might be chosen *because* they produce reliably similar kinds of outcomes. Regardless of judicial motive, the jurisprudential approach of rule-of-thumb balancing as describing the doctrinal legacy of the Rehnquist Court still must be documented with illustrative case evidence.

One decision by the Rehnquist Court surely stands out as emblematic of the Court period, its finessing of doctrinal difficulties, and its pragmatic orientation to its role in policy debates. No case has consumed as much attention in the Rehnquist Court record as the 1992 decision in *Planned Parenthood v. Casey* (505 U.S. 833), chronologically the first case in our list of the most important decisions of the Court era. Analyzed in Chapters 1 and 2 for its manifestation of diffused leadership activity and choral doctrinal promulgation, the actual doctrinal rule spelled out in the joint opinion for the Court was the "undue burden" test, whose individually sensitive reasonableness standard for what constituted an "obstacle" to a woman seeking an abortion was explicitly defended by the Court's opinion and specifically attacked by both dissents.

An "undue burden" was determined by the factual context of the state abortion law, the conditions that law put upon a woman seeking to terminate a pregnancy, and the balance the state struck between the woman's individual privacy right and the state's legitimate interests in protecting maternal health and fetal life. On its face, the undue burden approach was rule-of-thumb balancing—a "rule" that was context-determined and oriented toward the individual judgment of the reviewing judge. Indeed, in spite of the acknowledged fact that "the concept of an undue burden [had] been utilized by the Court as well as individual Members . . . in ways that could be considered inconsistent," the *Casey* joint opinion by O'Connor, Kennedy, and Souter did not shrink from pursuing a "controlling standard" and "guiding principles" using the concept (505 U.S. at 876, 877). This portion of the opinion was supported only by a plurality, as the justices outlined that standard and those principles to include (1) recognition of the central right but rejection of the rigid trimester approach of *Roe v. Wade* and (2) use of the undue burden concept to test the validity of a law regulating abortion: if the law's purpose or effect is to place a "substantial obstacle" in the path of a woman seeking an abortion before the fetus attains viability, then it is unconstitutional (505 U.S. at 878–879). More interesting, though, than the justices' articulation of the rule-of-thumb approach to the privacy right and the abortion choice was their explicit if backhanded defense of rule-of-thumb jurisprudential solutions: "Even when jurists reason from shared premises, some disagreement is inevitable. That is to be expected in the application of any legal standard which must accommodate life's complexity. We do not expect it to be otherwise with respect to the undue burden standard" (505 U.S. at 878).

That standard's "inherent manipulab[ility]" attracted the ire of dissenting Justice Scalia (505 U.S. at 986)—although in a passage toward the end of his dissenting opinion he inadvertently detailed the operation of rule-of-thumb jurisprudential approaches as well as their practitioners had. After pillorying the test's "empty phrases," he observed that "one must turn to the 23 pages [of the joint opinion] applying the standard to the present facts for further guidance" as to its meaning and directives (505 U.S. at 990). The joint opinion itself emphasized that Section 5 of the Fourteenth Amendment, considering the separate sections of the statute at issue in the case, indeed further "refined" the undue burden standard (505 U.S. at 879).

Whether it was a standard "not built to last," in the words of Chief Justice Rehnquist's *Casey* dissent (505 U.S. at 965), two things are incontrovertible about the undue burden approach to abortion regulation: it mandates rule-of-thumb, plural-factor assessment and interest balancing, and it had its judicial origin in the separate opinions of Justice O'Connor in prior abortion cases (Maveety 1996). The rearticulation of the undue burden test and its "refinement" in an opinion coauthored by O'Connor is thus no surprise. Although it was arguably the "heresthetic" introduction of the dimension of choice regarding stare decisis and "institutional integrity" that moved the key vote of opinion coalition member Kennedy,[14] his and Souter's support for O'Connor's undue burden rendering of *Roe* allowed for both jurisprudential and policy compromise on abortion rights, abortion services, and abortion restrictions. None were defined by a bright line, facilitating the recurrence of conciliatory resolutions but necessitating constant judicial oversight to do so.[15]

An O'Connor-authored doctrinal standard that *was* "built" to last, and did, but partly because it was initially even less precise in its parameters than the undue burden test, was found in a second issue area adjudicated in the same term as *Casey*. O'Connor's opinion for the Court in the 1992 federalism ruling in *New York v. U.S.* (505 U.S. 144) has received substantially less fanfare than her abortion opinion efforts, but the decision in the *New York* case articulated a legal policy that commanded more than equivocal support from a Rehnquist Court majority. That legal policy was the protection of states' rights under the Tenth Amendment, limiting how far into that rights realm Congress could intrude with its commerce and regulatory powers. The two governmental interests did have to be balanced, but O'Connor placed the judicial thumb on the state side of the scale. The *New York* case addressed the rather technical question of federal policy making for radioactive waste disposal; the congressional enactment in question induced certain state actions of compliance with the federal policy by using both positive and negative incentives. O'Connor's opinion drew the line at the negative incentives and mandated state actions prescribed in the statute, saying this:

> No Member of the Court has ever suggested that a federal interest would enable Congress to command a state government to enact *state* regulation.
>
> No matter how powerful the federal interest involved, the Constitution simply does not give Congress the authority to require the States to regulate. . . . Where a federal interest is sufficiently strong to cause Congress to legislate, it must do so directly; it may not conscript state governments as its agents. (505 U.S. at 178)

Although the "outer limits" of the states' "residuary and inviolable sovereignty" were not well specified by O'Connor's opinion, she dismissed the idea that this "basic truth . . . easily overlooked, like the air around us," had led to a "formalistic" constitutional result in *New York* (505 U.S. at 187). Yet in a few short years, the Court's restatement of the *New York* ruling took on a decidedly more formal, formulaic cast.

O'Connor's admittedly strong personal commitment to federalism, expressed in her *New York* majority opinion but also present in her political background as a Republican from the West (Biskupic 2005; McFeatters 2005), became, in Justice Scalia's hands in the 1997 decision of *Printz v. U.S.* (521 U.S. 898), the "incontestable" constitutional establishment of "dual sovereignty." *Printz* addressed certain provisions of the Brady Handgun Violence Prevention Act, which compelled states neither to enact nor to administer a federal regulatory program but rather required state officials to conduct background checks as part of enforcing the new federal gun control law. "We held," Scalia scolded in his majority opinion, that Congress cannot "compel the States to execute federal law." As he continued:

> It is the very *principle* of separate state sovereignty that such a law offends, and no comparative assessment of the various interests can overcome that fundamental defect. We expressly rejected such an approach in *New York*, and . . . we adhere to that principle today, *and conclude categorically, as we*

concluded categorically in New York: "The Federal Government may not compel the States to enact or administer a federal regulatory program." (quoting from New York at 188; emphasis added)

Whether the Court "categorically" concluded anything in New York is doubtful, given that O'Connor expressly declined to delineate the outer limits of state sovereignty that insulates states from federal mandates. Tellingly, she herself concurred in Printz, with a short opinion interpreting the majority opinion as "appropriately refrain[ing] from deciding whether other purely ministerial reporting requirements imposed by Congress on state authorities are similarly invalid" (emphasis added). This phrase seemed to elucidate O'Connor's "outer limits"—though she had not provided this demarcation of permissible congressional requirements in her New York opinion, nor did Scalia's majority opinion in Printz give any real indication of any limit to the "principle of separate state sovereignty." Only its annotation by O'Connor's concurrence provided the sense of nuance or gradation in the application of the "New York approach."

The New York/Printz sequence suggests a couple of things. First, O'Connor's vision of federalism—the doctrine of a revitalized state sovereignty inherent in the constitutional structure—became firmly established in the case law. It is true that she was neither the singular spokesperson for nor the sole adherent to states' rights structuralism, so its adoption by the Court was as much a result of Rehnquist's dedication or Thomas's fervor[16] as O'Connor's statement in 1992.[17] But with the benefit of hindsight, we can see that her commonsense approach to federalism and governmental powers questions was the position around which the five most states rights–oriented justices could rally continuously. This consolidationist quality of O'Connorist states' rights federalism is even clearer in the Eleventh Amendment rulings later in the Rehnquist era, such as the relatively (for the Rehnquist Court) univocal decision in Alden v. Maine (1999). Second, O'Connor's context-sensitive jurisprudence was at times maddeningly and misleadingly vague. Even more than the roundly criticized test in Casey, the state sovereignty test in New York was a "truth" so "basic" that it needed no explicit utterance—and thus had little precise content. This led to the broadening of the test into a bright-line principle by a justice of a different jurisprudential persuasion than O'Connor. One of the dangers of rule-of-thumb doctrinal approaches is their susceptibility to personal variation in handling: because they are not formulaic, the results of their application are variable. *New York* represented the outer perimeter of this feature of rule-of-thumb juridical pronouncements: it was such an amorphous and unarticulated standard of state sovereign immunity that the ruling could be interpreted to support ends—policy or interpretive—that diverged from its contextual meaning. To a degree, this is a problem endemic to O'Connorist jurisprudence, but it is mitigated by the usable and meaningful verbal formulations of reasonableness-based balancing the jurist is able to supply. *New York* was especially unmitigated in this regard, but it was not an isolated case of judicial inarticulateness.

Another O'Connor majority opinion from the same period shared this distinction—although O'Connor herself helped fill in its definitional gaps in subsequent adjudication. An O'Connor-authored, individually oriented reasonableness standard was the doctrinal approach for a third issue area dealt with by the Rehnquist Court in the 1993 decision of *Shaw v. Reno* (509 U.S. 630), with race as the sole-factor threshold for identifying impermissible racial gerrymandering in electoral districting. Unlike *Casey*, which (temporarily, anyway) ended a legal policy debate, *Shaw* instigated one by holding that classifying citizens by race for the purpose of reapportionment plans constituted an equal protection claim and warranted a different equal protection analysis than districting that diluted the voting strength of a protected minority group of citizens. That different analysis involved the level of scrutiny applied to race-based classifications. Strict scrutiny—which had previously *not* been applied to cases of race-conscious districting to remedy existing racial vote dilution—made it much less likely that a state's use of a race-based classification would be upheld as constitutional. Policywise, the ruling essentially recognized that "reverse discrimination" against white voters could result from the race-conscious districting remedially required for fair and effective representation for minority voters under the Voting Rights Act of 1965—although both the white claimants and O'Connor in her opinion for the Court phrased their concern as "the constitutional right to participate in a color-blind electoral process" (509 U.S. at 641–642). However the harm was named,[18] the five-justice O'Connor-led majority concluded that when racial considerations were used in an "effort to segregate voters into separate voting districts" without sufficient justification, a constitutional violation was present. That "sufficient justification" included, of course, the equal voting rights commandments of the 1965 act and the Fifteenth Amendment; thus the *Shaw* ruling demanded balancing two different interests or rights claims in representation. But what really rendered *Shaw* a rule-of-thumb jurisprudential approach was its standard for recognizing the impermissible use of race: redistricting legislation "so extremely irregular on its face that it rationally can be viewed only as an effort to segregate" (509 U.S. at 642). How "extremely irregular"?

The "difficulty of proof" regarding racial gerrymandering was handled under the *Shaw* standard in classic rule-of-thumb form: as the O'Connor opinion put it, "reapportionment is one area in which appearances do matter" (509 U.S. at 647). The resemblance of this individually oriented judgment about unconstitutionality to Justice Potter Stewart's infamously subjective "I know it when I see it" approach to pornography and First Amendment protection was hard to disguise; in spite of the opinion invoking such traditional districting practices as compactness as touchstones, the determination of gerrymandering essentially turned on an individual judge's impression of district "bizarreness." Still, O'Connor's analysis attempted to provide the kind of guidance in using the *Shaw* standard that her joint opinion in *Casey* had provided for the undue burden test: let the facts of each case be the guide. She was rather explicit in this: "We express no view as to whether 'the intentional creation of minority-majority districts, without more' always gives rise to an equal protection claim. We hold only that, *on the facts of this case*, appellants have stated a claim sufficient to defeat the state appellees' motion to dismiss" (509 U.S. at 649 [emphasis added]).

Shaw "has been viewed by virtually all commentators as the most important voting rights case decided by the U.S. Supreme Court in the 1990s" (Grofman 2006, 3). O'Connor's context-sensitive approach to discerning the impermissible use of race in electoral districting—which "may balkanize us into competing racial factions" (509 U.S. at 657)—recognized the impermissible more in terms of its prospective threat than its actual harmful existence, but was nevertheless repeatedly invoked as a standard to guide redistricting efforts in subsequent decisions. In *Miller v. Johnson* (1995), for example, the 1995 Kennedy majority opinion relied on the "circumspect approach and narrow holding" of *Shaw* to craft a refinement in the test for unconstitutional racial gerrymandering: redistricting in which race has served as the "predominant" factor violates the Equal Protection Clause (515 U.S. 900). O'Connor's own concurrence to the five-judge majority opinion in *Miller* refined the refinement, stressing that "application of the Court's standard"—presumably on a case-by-case basis—"does not throw into doubt the vast majority of the Nation's 435 congressional districts . . . even though *race may well have been considered* in the redistricting process" (emphasis added). Excessive reliance on race is constitutionally invalid, but O'Connor was careful—in *Shaw* and in her *Miller* concurrence—not to condemn all race-conscious districting. One critic of O'Connor's line-drawing and splitting-the-difference doctrine observed that the result has been that the Court "review[s] challenged districts one by one and issue[s] opinions that *depend so idiosyncratically on the unique facts of each case* that they provide no real guidance" (Karlan 1996, 288 [emphasis added]). Practically speaking, O'Connor's *Shaw* standard required constant retooling in new case circumstances; rhetorically speaking, her warnings about the risks of a "racial apartheid system" for electoral politics struck an unusually hectoring tone for O'Connor opinion language but added impetus to her *Shaw* call for a careful, multifactor, reasonableness-balancing approach to the issue area. Either way, it is fair to say—as did the first edition of the leading law text on the subject—that the racial gerrymandering cases beginning with *Shaw* "confirmed O'Connor's pivotal role" (Issacharoff, Karlan, and Pildes 1998, 581).

U.S. v. Lopez (514 U.S. 547) in 1995 was not an O'Connor decision, and although she was critical to the five-justice majority in support of the Court's reordering of congressional power over interstate commerce, she was neither responsible for nor vocal on the decision's "substantially affects" test for the exercise of congressional commerce power. Still, that test qualifies as a rule-of-thumb jurisprudential approach because of its contextual method of ascertaining when the effect of an intrastate matter on interstate commerce is sufficiently substantial to trigger congressional regulatory authority. Rehnquist's opinion for the Court was short on verbal details about the test, never providing formulaic phrasing for it and suggesting its refinement through case-by-case inquiry. The *Lopez* case addressed the constitutionality of the Gun-Free School Zones Act, which authorized Congress to regulate firearm possession in school zones under the Commerce Clause. Rehnquist's opinion dismissed the idea that the presence of guns and the threat of gun-related violence in the educational setting had enough of an impact on interstate commerce to justify the reach of federal power, but he failed, as Thomas's concurring opinion pointed out, to fashion a coherent test to distinguish between what is national and what is local. Instead, Rehnquist said only that "a gun in a local school zone is in no sense an *economic activity* that might, *through repetition elsewhere*, substantially affect any sort of interstate commerce" (emphasis added). This formulation hinted at the factors that would determine the regulability of a local activity: whether it was economic or commercial in character, and whether it recurred in multiple settings and thereby magnified its effects on commerce. Nevertheless, Rehnquist left off from assessing such factors and conceded that identifying whether an intrastate activity is commercial or noncommercial "may result in legal uncertainty." He admitted, moreover, that defining the outer limits of congressional commerce power would not yield "precise formulations."

Kennedy's concurrence, which O'Connor joined, stressed the limited nature of the holding in *Lopez* and the need for "practical" Commerce Clause jurisprudence, recalling the imprecision of an earlier era's content-based boundaries "used without more" to define the commerce power. Clearly fearing that the majority opinion could be read as "resuscitat[ing] the abandoned abstract distinction between direct and indirect effects on interstate commerce," the Kennedy concurring opinion cited the *New York v. U.S.* decision as supplying the "more"—the needed clarity and fact-based specificity for reviewing exertions of national power—that should guide reviewing courts. Such exertions of the commerce power should not, he wrote, "foreclose the States from experimenting and exercising their own judgment in an area to which States lay claim by right of history and expertise." It is interesting that whereas Rehnquist seemed more concerned with federal power overreach, Kennedy and O'Connor were activated by the harm to state sovereignty; the respective "tests" of the majority and concurring opinions thus focused on different contextual factors.

Lopez was an important decision in the Rehnquist Court's revitalization of judicially enforced federalism. It has been an important precedent reshaping the balance between federal and state power and the separation-of-powers balance between Congress and the Court. Its "substantially affects" test was refined in subsequent adjudication, and not all congressional exertions of commerce power were invalidated by the *Lopez* majority.[19] Neither *Lopez* nor its progeny blocked the policies or defined the policy goals in question as illegitimate so much as they redirected political activity from the federal level toward the states (Whittington 2004). In this, the commerce power decisions show the influence of O'Connor's vision of federalism in *New York*. But the *Lopez* opinion coalition and its multiple opinions revealed the internal splits that fragmented the conservative judicial bloc even on issues on which it fundamentally agreed, and the specific nature of its fragmentation—over the framing of the contextual-factor test that would govern the issue area in

question—gives credence to the argument that the rule-of-thumb jurisprudential approach informed the doctrinal reasoning of more than one or two
justices.

By the 1997 decision in *Printz*, it was becoming clear that doctrinal approaches exhibiting multifact-based reasonableness balancing were most
likely to appeal to the Court's median point and thus to garner majority support. The 1997 decision of *Clinton v. Jones* (520 U.S. 681) demonstrated this
as well in its approach to the question of presidential immunity from civil
suit, along with the identification of those presidential actions performed
within the zone of immunity authorized by the Constitution. The case was
part of the long, sad saga of events—or politically vituperative saga of events,
depending on one's point of view—that led to Clinton's impeachment. The
ruling in the case has been called "the goof of the decade" and "the stupidest
decision in the Court's history" (Miller 1999)—not the typical attributes of a
decision from a Court's "greatest hits" list. *Clinton v. Jones* earned these moni-
kers because of its rejection of Clinton's argument for temporary immunity
for sitting presidents from lawsuits over nonofficial conduct or stemming
from actions taken before the president's term. The suit that precipitated
the Supreme Court case, Paula Jones's civil action over inappropriate sexual
advances made to her by then-governor Clinton, thus went forward, leading
to discovery proceedings that revealed an improper relationship with White
House intern Monica Lewinsky—but not before President Clinton denied the
relationship in his deposition and unleashed impeachment proceedings for
perjury and obstruction of justice. Whether the holding in *Jones*, combined
with the events that unfolded afterward, "undermine[s] the institution of the
presidency by exposing its occupants to harassing lawsuits in a political climate that encourages them" (Harriger 2004, 90) depends in part on whether
the decision is viewed as a broad and sweeping commandment or a narrowly
framed directive for case-by-case resolution of presidential immunity claims.

Clearly, Stevens's opinion for the unanimously supported holding in *Clinton v. Jones* saw itself as the latter, that is, as the rejection of a "categorical
rule" requiring federal courts to stay private actions during a president's term
(520 U.S. at 706). The question of the treatment for a specific assertion of
immunity, Stevens concluded, "is more appropriately the subject of the exercise of judicial discretion than an interpretation of the Constitution" (ibid.).
It would be difficult to find a balder statement than this promoting an individually sensitive standard of what pending litigation might "distract or

preoccup[y]" a public official and a relaxation of constraints upon judicial discretion in applying that standard. Its rule-of-thumb credentials are apparent, and the actual judgment call made in the *Clinton* case suggests the lack of guidance provided by the decision's rule-of-thumb approach of the Court. This was the point of the lengthy opinion concurring in the result filed by Justice Breyer, who observed that the majority opinion had not "delineated" the "contours" of the principle that a federal judge's scheduling of a civil trial may not interfere with the president's discharge of his public duties. He acknowledged that "we need [not] now decide whether lower courts are to apply [the principle] directly or categorically through the use of presumptions or rules of administration" (520 U.S. at 710–711), although he worried that the upshot of the ruling would be to grant a single judge significant power to second-guess a president's reasonable determination of his scheduling needs, and would require courts to develop administrative rules applicable to such cases in order to implement the basic constitutional directive (520 U.S. at 723). Breyer seemed to be cataloguing the areas in which the rule-of-thumb approach proffered by Stevens would need supplementing, and anticipating that such supplementing would unfortunately have to come in subsequent costly litigation. His statements support the characterization of the rule announced in *Clinton v. Jones* as pragmatic and nonformulaic but also inchoate as to the exact parameters of and justification for temporary executive immunity.

Attention to the 1997 ruling in *City of Boerne v. Flores* (521 U.S. 507) completes the review of the Rehnquist Court record of important decisions from the 1990s. A key step in the Court's exposition of its allegedly supremacist theory of judicial power,[20] *Boerne* nevertheless can be interpreted as the application of a noncategorical rule and fact-sensitive test for interbranch conflicts over identifying and remedying constitutional rights violations. *Boerne* did contain some rather unilateral statements about Congress encroaching on judicial power when it legislates premised on constitutional views at odds with the Court's precedent (Johnsen 2004, 119–120), and various journalistic and scholarly commentators interpreted the decision as a gauntlet thrown down before Congress. Other commentators, although recognizing the decision as espousing a "preeminent branch theory" of constitutional interpretation, still saw it as a "transitional case" asserting a new form of judicial control over congressional Section 5 powers under the Fourteenth Amendment (Post and Siegel 2003, 6).

The *Boerne* case had a history and a subtext. In 1990, in the decision of *Employment Division v. Smith*, a narrowly divided Rehnquist Court had held that under the Free Exercise of Religion Clause of the First Amendment, neutral laws of general applicability may be enforced against religious practices even when not supported by a compelling state interest. The burden of the law on religion, whether substantial or incidental, was not relevant to constitutional analysis as long as prohibiting religious exercise was not the object of the law, said Scalia's majority opinion for five justices.[21] O'Connor concurred in the judgment only and did not embrace the majority's alteration of the standard of review for laws that allegedly impair religious exercise; the three then-serving liberal justices dissented. It was to the *Smith* ruling that Congress had responded with the Religious Freedom Restoration Act (RFRA), as it "restored" the compelling state interest test and made it applicable against all federal and state laws, whether statutory or otherwise, and their implementation. The issue in *Boerne* was a local zoning decision that allegedly ran afoul of RFRA by denying a building permit for enlargement of a church because of the structure's coverage under a historic landmark ordinance. The case challenging this local decision as violating a federal statute protecting religious practice became the vehicle for the Supreme Court to invalidate congressional enforcement of religious freedom, and explain why.

Kennedy authored the majority opinion in *Boerne* and, as in his *Lopez* concurrence, rebuked Congress for its intrusion into traditional state prerogatives. In this key aspect of the decision, O'Connor was a supporter—despite the fact that she dissented from the Court majority because its position was premised on the erroneous view of the current constitutional law on free exercise of religion found in *Smith*, to which the congressional statute at issue was a corrective response. That the congressional correction in RFRA was an illegitimate one in terms of the separation of powers was a fundamental but not fundamentalist point for O'Connor. She agreed with Kennedy's "proportionality review" of the congressional corrective legislation: that the standard for congressional power encroachment was not bright-line but one of degree. Kennedy's majority opinion argued that the "sweeping coverage" of RFRA, its lack of adaptation to preventing or remedying "mischief and wrong," and its "lack of congruence between the means adopted and the legitimate end to be achieved" marked the act as improperly curtailing states' general regulatory power (521 U.S. at 532–534). Although in the last analysis "this Court's precedent" must control constitutional interpretation, Kennedy's jurisprudential method in *Boerne* used the factual context—the circumstances of constitutional rights determination and the actual regulatory parameters of the statute in the case—to determine congressional overreach under Section 5. O'Connor agreed with both the principle and the method; she parted company with the Kennedy majority over the correctness of the judicial constitutional construction stipulated as the "Court's position" pre-RFRA.

Boerne's status as a rule-of-thumb opinion depends on two characteristics. First was its qualified, conditional approach to identifying a separation-of-powers violation of the kind represented by the case. The Kennedy majority opinion stressed that "legislation which deters or remedies constitutional violations can fall within the sweep of Congress's enforcement power even if in the process it prohibits conduct which is not itself unconstitutional" (521 U.S. at 518). So although "Congress does not enforce a constitutional right by changing what the right is," Congress retains "the duty to make its own informed judgment on the meaning and force of the Constitution" as long as it acts within its own sphere of powers and responsibilities and does not intrude upon the federal-state balance (521 U.S. at 525, 535). The Court drew these lines between legitimate and illegitimate exercises of congressional constitutional interpretation based on (1) judicial judgment as to whether Congress had acted within its "sphere" and (2) extant judicial precedent on the constitutional right in question. Second, *Boerne* was a rule-of-thumb jurisprudential approach in contrast with and in light of the decisions that succeeded it, for their application of its rule regarding judicial supervision of Congress's Section 5 enforcement power produced less context-sensitive refinements and a more categorical approach to the entire question.[22] "Strong assertions of interpretive supremacy" for the judiciary is the way one scholar characterized post-*Boerne* rulings on the scope of Section 5 power (Johnsen 2004, 139), although another study observed that the Rehnquist Court "speaks loudly but strikes narrowly" (Post and Siegel 2003, 43), suggesting that the rhetoric did not match up with the practice in *Boerne* or elsewhere. Nevertheless, *Boerne*'s framework allowed for and ultimately required subsequent case-by-case adjudication, a quality associated with rule-of-thumb rulings.

In reviewing the 1990s decisions in chronological order and examining the doctrinal approach each articulated, we see rule-of-thumb balancing spreading beyond the majority opinions of the erstwhile lone accommodationist O'Connor and into opinions for the Court authored by other justices. Of the seven cases I discussed, O'Connor wrote three of the Court's decisions: *Shaw*,

New York v. U.S., and (jointly) Casey. Associate Justice Kennedy wrote two decisions: Boerne and also jointly Casey. The opinions for the Court in the remaining three cases were written by different justices: the chief in Lopez, Scalia in Printz, and Stevens in Clinton v. Jones. O'Connor's doctrinal approaches governed certain big issues the Court addressed during the decade, such as abortion regulation and race-based electoral districting. But "O'Connor jurisprudence" on the Rehnquist Court was, by the end of the decade, more accurately described as O'Connorist jurisprudence, that is, in use by various justices to consolidate conservative majorities, as in Lopez or Printz, or to coalesce ideologically mixed or cross-cutting coalitions of justices, as in Jones or Boerne.

THE LAST DECADE OF O'CONNOR'S AND O'CONNORIST JURISPRUDENCE

The opening of the third millennium includes many of the Rehnquist Court's marquee decisions, beginning with Bush v. Gore (2000). But this decade on the Supreme Court was also noteworthy for beginning the Eleventh Amendment sequence of Alden v. Maine (1999), Kimel v. Florida Board of Regents (2000), Alabama v. Garrett (2001), and Tennessee v. Lane (2004). This decisional sequence was itself an extension of the state sovereignty principle recognized first in New York v. U.S. and phrased more categorically by Scalia's opinion in Printz. Several other significant decisions were issued during this period: Dickerson v. U.S. (2000), Zelman v. Simmons-Harris (2002), Grutter v. Bollinger (2003), Hamdi v. Rumsfeld (2004), Roper v. Simmons (2005), and Kelo v. City of New London (2005). These rulings applied rule-of-thumb balancing frameworks across a range of constitutional topics, from individual rights principles to structural concerns and governmental powers.

By the time of these decisions by the Rehnquist justices, O'Connor was sharing the doctrinal promulgation spotlight with several of her associate colleagues and, on occasion, with the chief. All of them authored opinions for the Court that can be described as "O'Connor-esque" in purpose and in content. But as with the rulings reviewed in the previous section, the decisions of the last years of the Rehnquist era must be tested for the presence of a particular legal policy innovation: a noncategorical rule and context-sensitive test that would settle controversies in the particular contentious issue area in terms of a balance between two or more factors, thus likely not settling individual instances of that issue identically. The recurrence of this legal policy approach confirms the Court's continued use of rule-of-thumb jurisprudence and intimates what kind of jurisprudential coherence can be found in Rehnquist-era legal doctrine.

The turn of the millennium at the Supreme Court was marked by one of the most politically significant and legally controversial actions by the judicial institution in its 200-plus-year history. The Rehnquist Court's decision regarding the 2000 presidential election dispute in *Bush v. Gore* (2000) is a topic of which the contours extend far beyond the scope of this study. Whether what the Court did was right or wrong constitutionally speaking, partisan or nonpartisan in motivation, or harmful or not harmful to the legitimacy of the institution has been the subject of analyses addressing the case and the Supreme Court in American political life (Ackerman 2002; Banks, Cohen, and Green 2005; Dworkin 2002). Our concern here is narrower: did the characteristics of the decision corroborate general trends observed in the Rehnquist era? Certainly the Court's unusual two-justice per curiam opinion adorned by a concurrence with three named joiners and the chorus of four dissenting opinions suggest judicial individualism in decisional process and content (not to mention the expedited nature of the case disposition). But the per curiam opinion itself—a product of the combined work, by process of judicial elimination, of Justices O'Connor and Kennedy—displayed certain rule-of-thumb doctrinal qualities. It famously stated that its finding of an equal protection violation in Florida's standardless manual recounting of punch-card ballots was a "consideration . . . limited to the present circumstances" (531 U.S. 98 [2000]). In other words, the opinion for the Court offered no description of the minimum procedures necessary to protect the fundamental right of each voter in the special instance of a statewide ballot recount. It concluded only that the recount procedures then under way in the state of Florida did not satisfy that minimum and could not be conducted in compliance with equal protection of the law "without substantial additional work."

These veiled allusions to actual, exacting standards for evaluating and interpreting a valid vote, combined with the blunt statement as to the limited nature of the holding, are almost a parody of rule-of-thumb jurisprudence and its fact-dependent, case-by-case adjudicative method along with the incrementalist approach to the generation of doctrinal rules. *Bush v. Gore* provided no more than a resolution of the "present controversy" with its rights-claim acknowledgment pregnant with implications for the future but utterly undeveloped doctrinally in the opinion that announced it. It was a pragmatic decision in the sense that its orientation was toward settling a political dispute;

the "compromise" it articulated to do so was simply to end the contentious vote count battle because it could not be resolved with inarbitrary treatment of voters unless the time frame was extended and "additional work" was done. This the Court majority was unwilling to order, and so its recognition of an equal protection violation hung in the air, a right without a remedy.

Doctrinally spare though it was, the ruling had identifiable practical consequences. The finality of the ruling ended the legal phase of the election contest and made more probable presidential candidate Al Gore's eventual concession to the victorious George Bush. The decision's condemnation of Florida's recount efforts also precipitated congressionally mandated funding for nationwide modernization of vote tabulation mechanisms. Fear of legal challenges to election outcomes inspired a flurry of electoral reform activity at the state level as jurisdictions scrambled to standardize voting procedures and take advantage of the federal funding opportunity for replacing existing balloting methods with "touch-screen" voting machines. So although the O'Connor-Kennedy opinion in the case had limited its holding to the circumstances at hand, the implications of its ruling were broadly—if somewhat diffusely—felt in the political system. Concern about the articulation of a new cause of action under the Equal Protection Clause was expressed—gleefully, and with some irony, by the decision's opponents—but no cavalcade of litigation occurred. Hands were wrung over the impact of the decision on the legitimacy of the judicial institution (including the hands of one of the Court's dissenters, Justice Stevens), but public opinion studies revealed that *Bush v. Gore* has had only the most minimal effect on public attitudes toward the Court (Kritzer 2005).

For the reasons of both its high-stakes political context and the foreshortened doctrinal content of the per curiam opinion, *Bush v. Gore* was an unusual if not sui generis example of rule-of-thumb jurisprudence. It displayed rather prominently both the polarization and the fragmentation for which the Rehnquist justices were becoming known. Yet it did not particularly well exemplify rule-of-thumb reasoning that offered a position of consensual compromise for a majority coalition. Another decision at the beginning of the new century was this more representative type of decision in the Rehnquist Court record. *Dickerson v. U.S.* (530 U.S. 428) in 2000 was a more typical expression of the O'Connorist doctrinal approach, though it did not come from an O'Connor opinion for the Court. *Dickerson* was, somewhat like *Lopez*, an instance of a Rehnquist majority opinion written so as to garner support across the jurisprudential and policy spectrum: the heterogeneous majority alliance for the decision included the chief plus Stevens, O'Connor, Kennedy, Souter, Ginsburg, and Breyer. The case addressed whether Congress could alter by statute the *Miranda* warning rule for confessions used in federal court criminal proceedings; it asked, essentially, whether Congress could define differently than Court precedent what was a voluntary statement for the purposes of the Fifth Amendment protection against self-incrimination. The Court's determination in *Dickerson* turned, then, on the validity of the *Miranda v. Arizona* (1966) precedent and on whether the Supreme Court had announced a constitutional rule in *Miranda* or had "merely exercised its supervisory authority to regulate evidence in the absence of congressional direction" (530 U.S. at 437). To recognize the latter would limit the reach of *Miranda* and allow the Court to uphold the federal statute narrowing the application of its warnings.

It is worth noting that the U.S. solicitor general's office refrained from defending the statute in question in *Dickerson*, something that rarely happens when the constitutionality of a federal law is challenged in the Supreme Court. How important this signal of tepid support from the solicitor general—the so-called Tenth Justice—was to the chief is difficult to say, but his opinion for the Court's moderate conservatives and left-leaning moderates was an interesting and somewhat unexpected exercise in pragmatism, coming from him. Rehnquist's *Dickerson* decision recognized that the Court had throughout the 1980s and 1990s made context-specific exceptions to the *Miranda* rule—these with the support of Rehnquist himself—and conceded that language in some of these rulings suggested that the protections announced in *Miranda* were not constitutionally required under all conditions. Such acknowledgment of the Court's own qualification or uneven application of one of its precedents was reminiscent of the *Casey* Court's commentary on the vagaries of the undue burden standard. Yet revealingly, and also as with *Casey*, the *Dickerson* Court cautioned against reading too much into such action and upheld the "core ruling" of the precedent at issue in light of the persuasive force carried by stare decisis (530 U.S. at 443)—although in doing so the Rehnquist majority opinion, predictably, did not cite the *Casey* experience. *Dickerson* interpreted the Court's previous rule-of-thumb-like, circumstantial exceptions to the *Miranda* rule as fine-tuning but never countermanding the absolute validity of the judicially authored constitutional rule. The *Dickerson* ruling thus also contained elements resembling the majority's separation-of-powers argument in *Boerne*, a case the Rehnquist opinion did cite (530 U.S. at 437). But just as *Boerne's* defense of judicial preeminence in constitutional interpretation is nuanced if read closely, the *Dickerson* decision also contained this intriguing statement about the practical need for rule-of-thumb amendments to otherwise absolutist Court rulings: "No constitutional rule is immutable. No court laying down a general rule can possibly foresee the various circumstances in which counsel will seek to apply it, and the sort of modifications represented by [the *Miranda* exceptions] are as much a normal part of constitutional law as the original decision" (530 U.S. at 441).

That this statement came from the "O'Connorist" Rehnquist Court is not too terribly surprising. That it came from the "lone ranger" and (previously) uncompromisingly conservative justice Rehnquist is mildly so—although his assuming the job of chief did correlate with him modifying his previously expressed judicial positions (Rosen 2007a, 112; Whittington 2003), of which the decision of *Dickerson v. U.S.* is an example.

In addition to *Bush v. Gore* and *Dickerson*, the final years of the Rehnquist Court occasioned a series of rulings that qualifies as an important cumulative issue ruling, because the decisions illustrate the use of a particular rule-of-thumb doctrinal approach. The Eleventh Amendment case sequence that began with *Alden v. Maine* in 1999 and continued with *Kimel v. Florida Board of Regents* in 2000, *Alabama v. Garrett* in 2001, and *Tennessee v. Lane* in 2004 broadened—though not unilaterally—the extent of state sovereign immunity from suit in state and federal courts. The doctrine developed to justify this legal policy was revealing for its application and extension of the sovereign "dignity" principle recognized in the O'Connor opinion in the federalism case of *New York v. U.S.* (1992). The content origins and jurisprudential style of the doctrine point to O'Connor's importance to the Rehnquist Court's work even when she was not speaking or speaking for a Court majority.

An early sign that certain members of the Rehnquist bench wished to clarify the extent of state sovereign immunity came in the 1995 decision of *Seminole Tribe v. Florida* (517 U.S. 44). The case addressed a cause of action provided by the Indian Gaming Regulatory Act and a suit by the Seminole Indian Tribe against the state of Florida in federal court to compel certain good-faith negotiations over tribal gaming regulation. The "federalism five," led by Chief Justice Rehnquist, held that the federal commerce power did not support congressional abrogation of states' Eleventh Amendment immunity in the act. Concerned that sovereign entities be protected from the "indignity" of suits by parties against their consent (517 U.S. at 58), Rehnquist's opinion for the Court held that Congress must "unequivocally express" its intent to abrogate state immunity and act "pursuant to a valid exercise of power" (517 U.S. at 55). The statute at issue in *Seminole Tribe* failed the latter test. But it was not until the 1999 decision in *Alden v. Maine* (527 U.S. 706) that the *Seminole Tribe* holding received theoretical and jurisprudential elaboration. *Alden* provided this and more.

The same five *Seminole Tribe* justices, led by Kennedy, endorsed *Alden*'s ruling that the Fair Labor Standards Acts did not authorize private suits for monetary damages against states in their own courts without their consent. Kennedy's opinion for the Court featured a lengthy elaboration as to why not, invoking basic constitutional structure as the source for the sovereign immunity of the states. There was, without a doubt, an absolutist formalism to Kennedy's reasoning: he announced that state immunity—"sovereign dignity" and state "residuary and inviolable sovereignty" (527 U.S. at 715)—neither derived from nor was limited by the terms of the Eleventh Amendment but came from the structural principle of "the constitutional sovereignty of the states" (527 U.S. at 729–730, 732). A lengthy historical analysis followed, with "the essential principles of federalism" (527 U.S. at 748) "accord[ing] the States the respect owed them as members of the federation" (527 U.S. at 749). Such dignity and respect afforded to a state were what immunity—in state and federal courts—was designed to protect. Not only was state financial integrity at stake but decision-making ability and governmental accountability would be strained by a generalized Article I federal power to authorize private suits for money damages against states, subjecting state administrations and their public affairs to the mandates of judicial tribunals (527 U.S. at 750–751). Although Kennedy did acknowledge various limits to state sovereign immunity, including the federal government's "appropriate" enforcement of the Fourteenth Amendment (527 U.S. at 756), his *Alden* opinion intimated more of a bright-line rule than a rule of thumb for adjudging state dignity and integrity. "Form mirrors substance," Kennedy intoned dramatically but cryptically at the close of his majority opinion (527 U.S. at 758).

Was *Alden* an anomalous deviation from the doctrinal approach that characterized so many of the Rehnquist Court's rulings? Perhaps as an initial statement of principle it was, but the developmental trajectory of the Eleventh Amendment federalism cases was toward a more rule-of-thumb-like balancing approach to resolve states' rights claims. This is evident in the three sovereign immunity decisions that followed *Alden*. *Kimel v. Florida Board* of *Regents* (528 U.S. 62 [2000]), *Alabama v. Garrett* (531 U.S. 356 [2001]), and *Tennessee v. Lane* (541 U.S. 509 [2004]) explored the parameters and articulated the nuances of the "sovereign dignity test" as presented by *Seminole Tribe* and *Alden*. The test had three fact-based components to its application: first, had Congress unequivocally expressed its intent to abrogate state immunity from suit in its legislative exercise; second, was the legislation pursuant to a valid exercise of federal power; and third, where applicable, what "appropriate legislation" pursuant to Congress's Section 5 enforcement power under the Fourteenth Amendment qualified as such a valid exercise? *Seminole Tribe* had articulated the first two components of the test and applied them to the facts of that case but did not elaborate as to what theoretical vision of intergovernmental relations such a test furthered. *Alden* devoted itself to this latter matter and merely observed that the third component—what was "appropriate legislation" under Section 5—*might* limit the state sovereign immunity that supported its elaborated theory of intergovernmental relations. The two "valid exercise" components of the sovereign dignity test each seemed to require an individual judgment call as to what was reasonable or appropriate for the federal government to do, according to the particular judicial reading of the constitutional structure. Such individualized judgment of reasonableness was made manifest in the rulings in *Kimel*, *Garrett*, and *Tennessee v. Lane*.

Collectively, the post-*Alden* decisions expressed qualified support for state sovereign immunity, and demonstrated that the Court's Eleventh Amendment jurisprudence was using a rule-of-thumb doctrinal approach. *Kimel* in 2000 and *Garrett* in 2001 addressed provisions of the Age Discrimination in Employment Act and the Americans with Disabilities Act (ADA), respectively, and continued the trend begun in *Boerne v. Flores* of placing conditions of "congruence and proportionality" on congressional choice of means in implementing its Section 5 enforcement power (Post and Siegel 2000). The provisions in each statute authorizing private actions for money damages as mechanisms for enforcing nondiscrimination by state employers were found to lack both congruence and proportionality between means and ends; the breadth and scope of the means chosen and the lack of evidence of a widespread and pervasive harm justifying them rendered the provisions invalid Section 5 enforcement exercises. Without a valid exercise of federal power, the statutory authorizations of suits against unconsenting states were barred by the doctrine of sovereign immunity in the Eleventh Amendment.[23] Both O'Connor's opinion for the Court in *Kimel* and Rehnquist's in *Garrett* focused on the factual details of the case record, statutory history and purpose, and specific policy context in question; neither opinion spent much time addressing the theoretical principles about intergovernmental relations already laid out in *Alden*, though each implicitly depended on those principles. Still, O'Connor's and Rehnquist's focus was on applying a fact-based standard for determining the validity of the abrogation of state immunity.

Tennessee v. Lane in 2004 was a similar exercise in applying the fact-sensitive components of the sovereign dignity test, but the Court reached a different result in that case, finding Title II of the ADA, which implemented the right of access to courts, a valid exercise of congressional authority under Section 5. This time, O'Connor sided with the wing of the Court that had dissented in most of the previous Eleventh Amendment cases, joining Stevens's majority opinion, which faithfully applied the *Alden/Kimel* test but found a salient factual difference in the *Tennessee* situational context. Whereas *Kimel* and *Garrett* had involved statutes authorizing private parties' suits for money damages for employment discrimination by state actors, *Tennessee v. Lane* addressed enforcement of the basic constitutional guarantee of access to public services, including access to courtroom facilities and activities. Because physical and other sorts of barriers to access had "had the effect of denying disabled people the opportunity to . . . exercise fundamental rights guaranteed by the Due Process Clause," a right of action for money damages and equitable relief was a remedy congruent and proportional to the violation of rights because of evidence of a history and pattern of such violations (541 U.S. at 515, 521). Serious, "intractable," and "persistent" (541 U.S. at 531) was what made the harm of denial of access to public services warrant the measures specified in Title II—measures "*reasonably targeted* to a legitimate end" in the words of Stevens's opinion for the Court (541 U.S. at 533 [emphasis added]). The holding and the reasoning approach in the *Tennessee* case suggest that the Court's sovereign dignity test was indeed a rule-of-thumb jurisprudential standard, a noncategorical rule providing flexibility in application and compromise in result. This interpretation is further supported by the multiple separate opinions Stevens's decision occasioned, in which concurring and dissenting justices each offered their own take on how the test had been deployed with respect to the facts of the case and on the proper inferences to draw from what the Court had done.

The Eleventh Amendment decisions owed their theoretical foundation to O'Connor's majority opinion in *New York v. U.S.*, which Kennedy cited repeatedly in his *Alden* majority opinion. The foundational importance of O'Connor's doctrine was also evident in the 2002 establishment of religion case, *Zelman v. Simmons-Harris* (536 U.S. 639). Throughout the 1980s and 1990s, in a series of rulings on church-state relations, O'Connor had pushed for a doctrinal innovation she termed the "endorsement" of religion test (Maveety 2003). Designed to modify the separationist rigidity of the 1971 tripartite *Lemon* test (*Lemon v. Kurtzman*, 403 U.S. 602) and to avoid the accommodationist laxity of the conservatives' nonpreferentialist approach to religious establishment, O'Connor's approach asked whether a "reasonable observer" would "draw from the facts" of a particular government aid of religion "an inference that the State itself is endorsing a religious practice or belief" (*Zelman v. Simmons-Harris*, 536 U.S. at 843, O'Connor, J., concurring in part and in the judgment). The "message of endorsement" was the critical determinant of a First Amendment violation, and it was identified through a "reasonable" apprehension of the facts of the situation. Clearly, this doctrinal approach was an example of rule-of-thumb jurisprudence. O'Connor articulated it again in her concurrence in *Zelman*, but it also informed Rehnquist's majority opinion.

Zelman addressed the use of state tuition aid in the form of vouchers for students to attend public or private schools of the parents' choosing, including religiously affiliated private schools. The question in the case was whether such state aid was neutral with respect to religion or whether its sponsorship of religious institutions violated the Establishment Clause. Although the four dissenters viewed the program as the use of public funds to pay for the indoctrination of thousands of Ohio grammar school children into particular religious faiths (Steven, J., dissenting, 536 U.S. at 684), the majority opinion for the Court emphasized the secular purpose of the program in assisting children in a failing public school system and its activation through the private choices of parents. Doctrinally, the *Zelman* ruling was a kitchen-sink assemblage of various First Amendment precedents and tests; the issue area has been one of the Supreme Court's most jurisprudentially confused for more than three decades. But, tellingly, the *Zelman* holding rested on contextual facts and used O'Connor's rule-of-thumb endorsement instrument to read those facts. "Any objective observer familiar with *the full history and context* of the Ohio program," the chief justice argued, "would *reasonably* view it as one aspect of a broader undertaking to assist poor children in failed schools, not as an *endorsement* of religious schooling in general" (536 U.S. at 655 [emphasis added]). Indeed, the intra-Court dialogue, especially between the majority opinion, O'Connor in concurrence, and Souter in dissent, featured a battle of the facts: how many dollars were being diverted from secular public schools to private religious ones, how many nonreligious private schools were program beneficiaries, and how to define the "choice" that the program presented.

The *Zelman* ruling had significant public policy implications with respect to the financing and management of public school systems and for the Republican Party agenda of encouraging faith-based initiatives and accommodating religion in public life. Its importance as a decision thus ranges beyond its illustration of rule-of-thumb jurisprudence and the latter's adoption by increasing numbers of Rehnquist justices. But *Zelman* also exemplified how O'Connor's perseverance with respect to her individual doctrinal solutions paid dividends in terms of the Rehnquist Court's doctrinal solutions. She converted her colleagues both substantively and stylistically—the latter conversion became even more apparent in the Court's final religious establishment decisions of 2005 and the several judicial opinions occasioned by *Van Orden v. Perry* and *McCreary County v. ACLU of Kentucky*. Argued together before the Court, these cases addressed public display of an image of the Ten Commandments, and raised the question of whether use of such religious objects had a valid secular purpose. The Court split, narrowly upholding the "passive monument" on the Texas state capitol grounds in *Van Orden* but invalidating Kentucky's courthouse wallboards of the documents in *McCreary* because of the sectarian history of that display. O'Connor joined the liberal, pro-separation-of-church-and-state coalition of justices in both rulings. Although Souter's majority opinion in *McCreary* implicitly involved the reasonable-observer and fine-grained contextualism of O'Connor's endorsement test (slip opinion at 17–19), it was Breyer's concurrence in the judgment to Rehnquist's *Van Orden* plurality opinion that carried forth the banner of O'Connorist jurisprudence. "No exact formula," he argued, "can dictate a resolution to fact-intensive cases such as this" (545 U.S. 677 [2005]). Breyer proceeded to exercise "legal judgment," in his words, and found as the "determinative factor" the length of time the Ten Commandments monument had stood without legal challenge. He, too, obliquely invoked the endorsement approach, observing that the forty years without legal objection "suggest more strongly than can any set of formulaic tests that few individuals . . . are likely to have understood the monument as amounting, in any significant detrimental way, to a government effort to establish religion."[24] No majority of the Rehnquist Court formally adopted the endorsement test as its preeminent doctrinal rule, yet the reasonable-observer approach of that test as a commonsense indicator of constitutionally impermissible church-state commingling enshrined fact-based balancing as the Court's jurisprudential approach for the issue area, and ensured the kind of split-the-difference compromises reflected by the Court's resolution of the Ten Commandments display cases.

Further evidence of O'Connor's substantive and stylistic influence on the Rehnquist Court is found in the 2003 affirmative action decision of *Grutter v. Bollinger* (539 U.S. 306). Recent scholarship on the *Grutter* litigation and that of its companion case, *Gratz v. Bollinger*, mentions the importance of conservative legal action groups such as the Center for Individual Rights in orchestrating a promising challenge to affirmative action using the two race-conscious admission plans of the University of Michigan and its law school (Teles 2008; Tushnet 2006, 231–232). Carefully selected test cases though they might have been, the upshot of the Michigan rulings was nevertheless that the Supreme Court took itself out of the affirmative action fight, at least for a while (Tushnet 2006, 239).

Advocates of multicultural diversity had battled with the proponents of a color-blind society since the Supreme Court weighed in on the constitutionality of affirmative action in *Regents of the University of California v. Bakke* in 1978, upholding "goals not quotas" but protecting universities' prerogatives to use racial considerations in admissions to achieve the educational benefits of a diverse student body. Throughout O'Connor's career on the high bench, she was a swing vote on the preferential use of racial criteria in hiring, promotion, and termination of employment decisions, sometimes approving but more often invalidating affirmative action plans for their failure to incorporate a narrowly tailored use of racial classifications (Maveety 1996, 2003). The divisions among the Rehnquist Court justices meant that most affirmative action decisions were split, although the general policy direction was to limit the use of race as a selection factor except to eliminate the effects of identifiable past discriminatory action by government or private industry. By the 1990s, addressing general societal discrimination and providing minority role models clearly were not compelling enough justifications for race-conscious policies, raising the question of whether the *Bakke* diversity principle was still good law. Late in its final years, the Rehnquist Court considered the two cases from the University of Michigan and its law school; these became the vehicle for the majority's decisive and final statement on the policy practice of affirmative action.

The two affirmative action admissions programs differed in their particulars regarding the kind of diversity criteria eligible for "substantial weight" in an application and the threshold for enrolling a "critical mass" of underrepresented minority students, and the Court invalidated the undergraduate admission program in *Gratz* but upheld the law school admission program in *Grutter*. O'Connor's opinion for the Court majority in the latter case was the more important of the two because of both the policy message and the legal standard it communicated. First, student body diversity was a compelling state interest justifying the use of race in admissions. "Context matters when reviewing race-based governmental action under the Equal Protection Clause," O'Connor pointedly reminded the readers of the *Grutter* opinion (539 U.S. at 327). Second, even though racial and ethnic diversity was a legitimate goal, the use of race to achieve it must be narrowly tailored. The Michigan Law School admissions procedure met this test because it was "flexible enough to ensure that each applicant is evaluated as an individual and not in a way that makes race or ethnicity the defining feature of the application" (539 U.S. at 337). "Flexible *enough*" was the key, for O'Connor's opinion both approved the "holistic" review of law school applicants' files and rejected the idea that the university must first exhaust other race-neutral means of achieving diversity. Finally, and more as a comment than a hard-and-fast rule, race-conscious admissions policies should be limited in duration; O'Connor identified a sunset provision of twenty-five years, expecting by then that "the use of racial preferences will no longer be necessary to further the interest approved today" (539 U.S. at 343).

Together, the holdings in *Grutter* and *Gratz* proffered a compromise, and the *Grutter* ruling was styled as a consensus-building position on the contentious question of race-conscious selection policies under equal protection of the law. The question is whether it did this without providing a clear doctrinal framework giving clear guidelines for other decision makers on the status of other affirmative action programs. Indeed, one of the most serious questions about the *Grutter* ruling is whether any judge other than O'Connor could apply her *Grutter* doctrinal elements—particularly, distinguishing between seeking a "critical mass" of minority admittees and out-and-out racial balancing or identifying individualized but holistic consideration of applicants and their diversity credentials.[25] But it has also been argued that the mechanics of application were beside the point, for *Grutter* was meant as a signal, not a doctrine. This reading of O'Connor's jurisprudential statement in the decision placed special emphasis on her admittedly curious sunset provision at the end of the opinion and attributed to it this meaning:

> O'Connor was telling everyone, including those who might be appointed to the Court over the next few years, that it was done with affirmative action for the foreseeable future. Technically, new justices could reopen the issue, but O'Connor's opinion meant that they would have to confront not only the issue of affirmative action itself but the preliminary issue of stare decisis. (Tushnet 2006, 247–248)

Although the evidence for this interpretation of O'Connor's intention or motivation is far from conclusive, Tushnet's is a plausible synopsis of the consequence of the Rehnquist Court's final affirmative action decision. O'Connor-esque though its rule-of-thumb doctrinal approach was, the real importance of her *Grutter* opinion for the Court was its status as a definitive ruling. This result suggests the significance of even imprecise and highly personalized doctrinal standards: to be set aside, they must officially be repudiated or at least officially reconsidered. O'Connor's jurisprudential legacy may have whatever legs it does for the reason of general judicial reluctance to seem activist more than any innate durability of her flexible and adaptable doctrinal standards. Such "legacy by default," although now somewhat doubtful with respect to *Grutter*,[26] still applies to *Casey*, *Shaw*, and, to a lesser degree, *Zelman* because of the latter decision's acknowledgment but not adoption of O'Connor's endorsement test for Establishment Clause violations.

An opinion with less closure than *Grutter* but no less magnitude was authored by O'Connor in one of the most politically sensitive cases of the entire Rehnquist era: the 2004 case of *Hamdi v. Rumsfeld* (542 U.S. 507) regarding the constitutional legitimacy of President Bush's detention of U.S. citizens as "enemy combatants." Indeed, *Hamdi* may have earned the distinction of being the most importantly indeterminate of the Court's rule-of-thumb doctrinal promulgations, in that its holding on executive power in the "war on terror" precipitated an ongoing saga of presidential and congressional responses to its prompts, along with continuing judicial reactions to these measures.

Only a plurality of justices supported O'Connor's opinion in the *Hamdi* case, which was a classic example of reasoning "for purposes of the case at hand" (542 U.S. at 516). As a result, the rule the decision generated was context-bound, an effort to balance and accommodate multiple conflicting and rather case-specific concerns. The first question the Court considered was whether the Authorization for Use of Military Force (AUMF) resolution, passed one week after the September 11, 2001, terrorist attacks, authorized the executive to designate and detain those persons defined as part of or supporting forces hostile to the United States or allied armed forces in the subsequent military operations in Afghanistan. In permitting the president to use "necessary and appropriate force," the O'Connor opinion concluded that Congress had clearly authorized detention, but "in the narrow circumstances considered here" (542 U.S. at 519). O'Connor was cautioning that indefinite detention for the purpose of interrogation was not authorized, that authority to detain was for the duration of the relevant conflict, and that this understanding was based on "long-standing law-of-war principles" (542 U.S. at 521). Next the Court considered what due process was constitutionally owed a citizen who disputed his enemy combatant status; absent congressional suspension, that process is to appeal the writ of habeas corpus in an Article III court, a right that remains available to every individual detained in the United States. Stipulating that no suspension had occurred under the AUMF, O'Connor's opinion also rejected the government's argument that a court's factual review of Hamdi's case was limited to investigating whether legal authorization existed for the broader detention scheme. Rather, a "judicious balancing" of the private interest affected by the official action against the government's asserted interest and burdens faced in providing due process must occur (542 U.S. at 529), and in "striking the proper constitutional balance" between the rights and privileges of American citizenship and the needs of the nation during ongoing combat, O'Connor held that a detainee had to be provided "a fair opportunity" to rebut the government's factual assertions about his classification before "a neutral decision maker" (542 U.S. at 533).

Although the plurality opinion in *Hamdi* did not describe in detail "to challenge meaningfully" or define definitively "an impartial adjudicator" (542 U.S. at 535), it did make clear that "an appropriately authorized and properly constituted military tribunal" might satisfy the concerns for due process but, absent that, a court that received a habeas corpus petition from an alleged enemy combatant must itself ensure that due process was being achieved (542 U.S. at 538). This affirmed the opinion's earlier and now famous statement that "a state of war is not a blank check for the president"—that the judicial branch serves as an important check on the executive's discretion in the realm of detentions (542 U.S. at 536). It was this part of the Court's judgment with which Justices Souter and Ginsburg concurred, in order "to give *practical effect* to a majority's rejection of the Federal Government's position" (Souter, J., concurring in part, dissenting in part, and concurring in the judgment, at 540). Given the content of their opinion, which disagreed with the plurality reading of the wartime authority provided by the AUMF, that announced stratagem was pragmatically results-oriented in the extreme.

The important ways in which the ruling was indeterminate are several. First, it conceded something to both sides: presidential authority to designate detentions under the congressional resolution, and a curb on executive power during wartime by protecting citizens' personal procedural liberty. Yet neither concession was absolutist, and this was the second way in which the ruling was indeterminate. Executive detention decisions were restricted by norms of international law, the particulars of which were not spelled out, and civil libertarian limits on executive action were themselves limited in scope and scale, but these limits were expressed more hypothetically than conclusively. *Hamdi* thus left room for future courts to fill in some of these gaps by making future adjudication of the issues almost a certainty, as the executive tested the limits of the restrictions on wartime powers in the special logistical circumstances of the war, and enemy combatant detainees further explored the rights of citizens and challenged the treatment of noncitizens in accordance with the principles of due process and judicial review defended by the *Hamdi* Court.

The fallout from the rule-of-thumb standards announced in *Hamdi* was seen almost immediately in the first Roberts Court term. With Chief Justice Roberts recused because of his participation on the case in the D.C. Circuit Court, the Supreme Court considered in *Hamdan v. Rumsfeld* (126 S. Ct. 2749 [2006]) the constitutional operation of the military commission option for combatant status review it had mentioned in *Hamdi*. *Hamdan*, however, was not about a citizen but an alien detainee at the American prison in Guantánamo Bay, Cuba. In a more sweeping opinion and condemnation of presidential overreach than *Hamdi*, the Stevens majority ruled in *Hamdan* that the military commission trial had not been expressly authorized by any congressional act and furthermore violated the Uniform Code of Military Justice (UCMJ). The Court also dismissed out of hand the government's argument that the Detainee Treatment Act of 2005 had repealed Supreme Court jurisdiction to review the decision by the lower court on which then-judge Roberts had sat and with which he had voted in support of the tribunal's review of Hamdan's detention. "Rais[ing] separation-of-powers concerns of the highest order," in the words of Kennedy's concurrence in part (126 S.Ct. at

2800), the *Hamdan* ruling relied on *Hamdi*, but chiefly the interpretation in that decision of the president's AUMF-authorized war powers including military commissions in *appropriate circumstances*. Finding none, the *Hamdan* holding precipitated the subsequent legislative override of its recommendations in the Military Commissions Act (MCA) of 2006, which offered a more expansive vision of executive power and the categorical rule limiting review of executive and executive-authorized commission detention decisions. At this writing, the constitutionality of the MCA is a matter of dispute because of questions as to its application to U.S. citizens, disallowance of the invocation of the Geneva Conventions, and removal of federal court jurisdiction to hear petitions relating to any aspect of the detention of unlawful enemy combatants. Although the presidential power questions spawned by the act are grounded in the "no blank check" position the Rehnquist Court took in *Hamdi*, the MCA also depends on that decision, which acknowledged that executively constructed tribunals could satisfy due process concerns, for its authority.

Hamdi's splitting of the difference, constitutionally and in terms of policy, has already had visible and palpable consequences, suggesting that the open nature of O'Connorist jurisprudence facilitates less compromise than continuing struggle over the meaning of its legal standards. The rule-of-thumb doctrinal approach appears to be impermanent by design. However, *Hamdi*'s imprecise stance on executive power is a function of the limited circumstances in which it held impermissible an exertion of executive power, meaning that its context-bound rule of thumb does not prevent the decision from being read as a broadly applicable but general statement about constitutional limits on executive authority. Available to serve a variety of positions on executive power and produce recurrent fine-tuning, *Hamdi*'s O'Connorist—and, in this instance, O'Connor-authored—doctrinal formulation rather ensures its versatility and, arguably, its longevity as a precedent.

The last two decisions in our sample from the Rehnquist-era final years were cases in which O'Connor dissented from the opinion of the Court. Both *Roper v. Simmons* (543 U.S. 551 [2005]), addressing the application of the Eighth Amendment to capital punishment for juvenile offenders, and *Kelo v. City of New London* (545 U.S. 469 [2005]), regarding the definition of "public use" within the meaning of the Takings Clause of the Fifth Amendment, were curious examples of O'Connor dissenting from rule-of-thumb doctrinal statements. Her dissents can be explained by her not seeing the decisions as such rules, but whether they actually were is a matter for debate. In *Roper*, the

Kennedy majority opinion applied the "evolving standards of decency" approach from prior capital punishment rulings to determine that a consensus had emerged that to impose the death penalty for crimes committed when an offender was under eighteen was cruel and unusual punishment. O'Connor's dissent essentially argued that the Court had misapplied the elements of moral proportionality and objective evidence of contemporary social values in ascertaining "evolving standards of decency," and had thereby derived a categorical rule about capital punishment for seventeen-year-old offenders that was unjustified under the rule-of-thumb doctrinal standard it applied. In *Kelo* it was O'Connor's turn to reason categorically against a Stevens majority opinion that rejected the bright-line rule that economic development is never an appropriation of private property for public use. O'Connor's dissent retorted that all private property was now vulnerable to being taken and transferred to another private owner if, in the opinion of the legislature, it might be "upgraded." "The specter of condemnation hangs over all property," she warned, uncharacteristically skeptical of the Court's "rightful admission" that "the judiciary cannot get bogged down in predictive judgments" about the public benefits of a property transfer (125 S.Ct. at 2676). In both *Roper* and *Kelo*, O'Connor joined the three most conservative justices, Rehnquist, Scalia, and Thomas; in both *Roper* and *Kelo*, her fellow moderate conservative, Justice Kennedy, was the standard-bearer of fact-based balancing-of-interests jurisprudence.

Just three years prior to *Roper*, the Court had held in *Atkins v. Virginia* (536 U.S. 304 [2002]) that standards of decency in punishment had evolved such that execution of people with mental disabilities was considered excessive and thus cruel and unusual punishment under the Eighth Amendment. The Court referenced the same indicia of a national consensus in that case as it did in *Roper*: passage of state laws prohibiting the practice in a majority of states, infrequency of the use of the practice even where it remained in the law, and consistency in the trend toward abolition of the practice. Kennedy and O'Connor had joined Stevens's opinion for the Court in *Atkins*; their differences with each other in *Roper* appeared to turn on the definitiveness of the factual evidence of an emergent national consensus. O'Connor was thus reluctant to prohibit death sentences categorically for criminal defendants who were seventeen at the time of their crime, preferring to leave the determination of maturity and responsibility to capital sentencing juries. "I would demand a clearer showing that our society truly has set its face against this practice before reading the Eighth Amendment categorically to forbid it," she concluded, indicating that it was not the rule-of-thumb doctrinal approach with which she disagreed but the flawed result of its improper application in the specific Roper situation (543 U.S. at 588). "Let me [make] clear," she emphasized, "that I agree with much of the Court's description of the general principles that guide our Eighth Amendment jurisprudence" (ibid.).

If Roper was a case of disagreement over the outcome dictated by an agreed-upon rule-of-thumb doctrinal standard, it was also a case that illustrated the variation in result produced by the diversity of the thumbs in action. The indicia of a national consensus of evolving standards of decency were subject to interpretive variation, or individual differences in interpretation of the dispositiveness and directionality of the multifactorial evidence of consensus. Kelo demonstrated a different sort of dispute between O'Connor and the majority, and between O'Connor and Kennedy. Kennedy, it should be noted, concurred in the takings case, arguing that the Court needed a more fact-sensitive and stringent framework for adjudging when a legitimate public-use taking of private property had occurred. His three-part test identified the factors that, if present, would signal unconstitutional taking of private property; these factors—including possessing only pretextual public benefits and showing impermissible favoritism to private parties—were intended to supply greater analytic precision than Stevens's formulation, which was generally deferential to the legislative branch, and to provide guidance for judicial oversight of the Fifth Amendment Takings Clause. O'Connor was dismissive of the possibility of sorting through incidental versus true public benefits, or "divin[ing] illicit purpose by a careful review of the record," as Kennedy's test promised (125 S.Ct. at 2675–2676), although she vehemently agreed with the need for an external judicial check if the public-use constraint on government action was to have any meaning (125 S.Ct. at 2673–2674). But Kennedy's Kelo concurrence had not specified "what courts should look for in a case with different facts, how they will know if they have found it, and what to do if they do not" (125 S.Ct. at 2675). The Court's opinion, too, came in for criticism from O'Connor for "put[ting] special emphasis on facts peculiar to this case" when "none has legal significance to blunt the force of today's holding" (125 S.Ct. at 2676). In an uncharacteristic and somewhat hypocritical swipe at fact-based or context-generated jurisprudential compromises, O'Connor's Kelo dissent charged that "there is nothing in the Court's rule or in Justice Kennedy's gloss on that rule to prohibit property transfers generated with less care, that are less comprehensive, that happen to result from less elaborate process" than that ordered by New London, Connecticut (ibid.).

Although the Court's holding and reasoning in *Roper* appear to have been accepted by the public, in spite of O'Connor's objection to the ruling, the policy position of her *Kelo* dissent clearly resonated with the general public and state legislatures. Public reaction was intense and overwhelmingly negative, judging by the U.S. House of Representatives' denouncement of the decision and the forty or more states that have passed or considered post-*Kelo* legislation restricting eminent domain powers (Somin forthcoming). O'Connor was thus markedly unprescient at the end of her dissenting opinion, where she proclaimed that it was "an abdication of our responsibility" for the Court to suggest that property owners turn to their state legislatures to impose appropriate limits on economic development takings. "States play many important functions in our system of dual sovereignty, but compensating for our refusal to enforce properly the Federal Constitution," she scolded, "is not among them" (125 S.Ct. at 2677). Rather, in vivid support of O'Connor's vision of state sovereignty, so enshrined elsewhere in Rehnquist Court jurisprudence, such a function obviously belongs to states.

Overall, the last years of Rehnquist Court decision making did embody O'Connorist jurisprudence, in that all the rulings considered from this period—even those from which O'Connor herself dissented—effectuated the legal policy innovation of a noncategorical rule and context-sensitive test for the particular issue area with which they were concerned. These rules and tests ensured that controversies in that issue area would be settled in terms of a balance of two or more factors identified by the presence of certain factual conditions. The flexibility (or variability) of the doctrinal approach also ensured that individual instances of the particular issue would not be settled identically—that the outcome of application of the doctrine instead would be a compromise of "win some, lose some." Except for the previously discussed *Lawrence* case on privacy and homosexual relationships, there were few categorical rules about anything in the decisions that closed the Rehnquist era. Even its most formulaic pronouncements, about federalism and Eleventh Amendment immunity, were less than black or white in application, as the sequence from *Kimel* to *Garrett* to *Tennessee v. Lane* arguably showed.

In terms of O'Connor's versus O'Connorist jurisprudence, four rule-of-thumb doctrinal promulgations for the Court were O'Connor's: *Kimel*, *Grutter*, *Hamdi*, and the per curiam opinion in *Bush v. Gore* in part, with Kennedy. The other decisions—*Alden*, *Garrett*, *Tennessee v. Lane*, *Dickerson*, *Zelman*, *Roper*, and *Kelo*—were authored by Rehnquist (three), Stevens (two), and Kennedy (two). The penultimate Rehnquist Court was no more likely to evidence the rule-of-thumb doctrinal approach in its most "important" rulings than it did in the 1990s, although Chief Justice Rehnquist was somewhat more frequently the author of the Court opinion that did so. One could interpret this latter trend as the price the chief paid, doctrinally, for holding on to control of the majority opinion, which he clearly desired to do as titular Court leader in high-salience, high-stakes cases such as *Dickerson* and *Zelman*. In spite of these wishes, it is clear that certain associate justices, because of their seniority or centrality or predisposition, were the privileged creative actors of the Court's rule-of-thumb doctrinal approach.

Was the doctrinal legacy of the period, then, a "queen's Court" of O'Connor-style legal reasoning across the board? Based on the rulings reviewed in this chapter, the answer would have to be yes. The decisions authored by other justices either depended overtly on O'Connor's own jurisprudential formulations—such as *Alden*'s reliance on her federalism theory in *New York v. U.S.* or *Zelman*'s evocation of her "endorsement test" for religious establishment—or they embraced her context-based and multifactor doctrinal style and garnered her support in doing so—such as *Tennessee v. Lane* and *Roper*. *Kelo* was an outlier of sorts, in that O'Connor seemed the voice of objection to fact-based jurisprudence. But careful examination reveals that the intra-Court debate was really about whether the Stevens majority or the Kennedy concurrence had spelled out a workable rule of thumb for controversies in the issue area—not about whether rule-of-thumb-ism was valuable or desirable as a jurisprudential approach.

Balancing of interests is not the type of jurisprudential theory embraced openly with the fervor of the true believer or the enthusiasm of the intellectual purist. It is neither a straightforward nor an elegant and parsimonious jurisprudential approach. Yet quietly, incrementally, and for the most part unacknowledged, it became the predominant judicial methodology of a majority of the Rehnquist associates. This begs the question of whether there was any legal coherence to associates' justice "rules of thumb." At the outset of the chapter, I proposed to gauge this by testing for two conditions: first, predominant use of rule-of-thumb doctrinal solutions in the Court's important rulings and, second, structural similarity and common prudential orientation in the rule-of-thumb approaches overall. Both conditions were satisfied, indicating that whatever coherence rule-of-thumb, balancing-of-factors legal pragmatism has, the Rehnquist Court's version possessed it.

This was the case in spite of plural judicial contributions to the Court's body of rulings. The repeated rule-of-thumb balancing contributions of

O'Connor, Kennedy, Stevens, and Breyer—and, even, from time to time, of Rehnquist—provide evidence of a commonly shared and widely exercised understanding of the judicial function on the collegial appellate Court. Although not the same as substantive coherence, such common behavioral orientation contributes to it because opting for rule-of-thumb approaches suggests a judicial procedural commitment to the idea of the Court as a set of justices determined to record their various individual views, yet cooperative enough to accede reciprocity in doing so. Thus, the Rehnquist justices settled into nonformulaic doctrinal formulations that accommodated both policy compromise and a plurality of "reasonable observers." Indeed, constitutional doctrine accommodating a plural number of reasonable judicial observers was the O'Connor Court made manifest, jurisprudentially speaking.

As with the reasonable observer approach of O'Connor's rule-of-thumb endorsement test, the flexible nature of rule-of-thumb jurisprudence has its imprecise, less than coherent, less than consistent side. Tests that mandate balancing of multiple factors are susceptible to variation in handling, in part because the presence of those factors first must be determined—calling forth Breyer's infamously phrased and essentially idiosyncratic "exercise of legal judgment." So not only are the results of the application of rules of thumb variable, but the open nature of O'Connor-style jurisprudence facilitates a continuing struggle over the operational meaning of its legal standards. Continual struggle means continual negotiation through recurring judicial fine-tuning or adjustment, and it also means that the balancing approaches are always potentially available to serve a variety of positions on the policy issue in question.

Yet, perversely, that open-texturedness and susceptibility to continual negotiation help ensure the longevity and, possibly, the utility of the doctrinal formulation. This leads to one final question that remains to be answered about the decisional record of the Rehnquist Court: was its O'Connorist jurisprudence a "sticky" doctrinal settlement? The final section of the chapter addresses this issue and offers a prognosis regarding rule-of-thumb balancing and the future direction of judicial policy making on the post-Rehnquist Court.

RULE-OF-THUMB RULINGS: THE PROGNOSIS

The inquiry as to what conditions will perpetuate the Rehnquist-era rule-of-thumb balancing precedents really consists of two questions: What are the persisting judicial behavior predilections, and what are the existing jurisprudential constructs that could contribute to a continuation of the rule-of-thumb methodology used by the Rehnquist-era associate justices? Let us consider each of these dynamics separately.

Is there, first of all, a predictive rule or model of precedential survival? According to Hansford and Spriggs's 2005 study *The Politics of Precedent* there is, but certain commonly presumed relevant factors do not seem to be related to the predictive model. With respect to multivocal judicial decisions—the kind typically produced by the choral Rehnquist Court and the kind thought to lack legal clarity and thus precedential power—Hansford and Spriggs found that "the number of special concurring opinions accompanying the precedent increases the probability of negative interpretation but does not decrease the likelihood of the precedent being treated positively. . . . Precedents set by relatively small majorities appear more likely to be interpreted either positively or negatively" (Hansford and Spriggs 2005, 72). In other words, "justices are simply more likely to interpret a precedent, either positively or negatively, when the precedent case's majority coalition was smaller. . . . [Moreover,] there is *not* much support for the contention that concurring opinions weaken the precedent and make it more vulnerable to being overruled by a subsequent Court" (Hansford and Spriggs 2005, 90 [emphasis added]).[27]

This finding speaks more to case characteristics than to judicial personnel tendencies. But the Hansford and Spriggs study also investigates the impact of judicial ideology on the preservation of a precedent. According to them, precedent vitality—which they measure as the cumulative function of prior interpretations—acts to condition the effect of ideological distance between the Court and the policy established by a precedent. Nonetheless, even case characteristics connected to precedent vitality, such as the multivocality of the decision, are unrelated to precedent survival. In other words, the Rehnquist-era rule-of-thumb balancing tests announced in narrowly decided judicial judgment calls or through case-by-case adjudication are no less likely to endure as precedential rulings than unambiguous, bright-line rules promulgated unanimously.[28] Ideological agreement or disagreement with a precedent, standing alone, is simply not determinative of the perpetuation of the latter.

Such findings suggest that judicial personnel changes of the kind represented by the John Roberts and Samuel Alito appointments do not necessarily herald the replacement of Rehnquist-era rule-of-thumb balancing precedents. The survival of these precedents is arguably less related to the continuing tenure of a rule-of-thumb pivotal centrist justice than to their own vitality as frequently referenced doctrinal rules. Since the doctrinal rules of most of those precedents were the product of rule-of-thumb jurisprudential methodology, their referencing by subsequent judicial majorities helps to keep the precedents alive—if only as touchstones.

With respect to the impact of jurisprudential constructs or "jurisprudential regime" conditions on the preservation of precedents such as *Casey, Shaw, Grutter*, or *Hamdi*, we must remember that this kind of cognitive structure is specific to a given decisional issue area. Decision structures for a particular legal area "reflect core understandings of the bases on which cases should be decided, the interests or goals to which deference should be shown in situations of conflict, and the relevant roles of government institutions . . . and function as intervening variables influencing justices' decisions" (Richards and Kritzer 2002, 307, 308). As with Hansford and Spriggs's model of precedential survival, the thrust of the theory of jurisprudential regimes is that ideas matter as they become embedded in institutional frameworks. Judicial ideology and judicial personnel change can affect these institutional frameworks at the margins but certainly do not do so unilaterally.

Jurisprudential regime establishment is, then, enshrinement of a way of thinking—a frame for how judges think about legal policy issues, how they evaluate others' actions, and how they try to persuade others to adopt their own perspective. Although empirical evidence confirms the operation of jurisprudential regimes in discrete areas of the law, such as reproductive freedom of choice or representation rights in electoral districting, whether a macrolevel regime such as the rule-of-thumb jurisprudential approach can be said to influence judges in their reliance on precedents awaits conclusive demonstration.[29] Did the Rehnquist justices bequeath such a global jurisprudential regime or merely a series of issue-area regimes? How we may begin to know will depend on whether the entire rule-of-thumb jurisprudential approach survives or only selected rule-of-thumb legal doctrines are retained, such as the endorsement test for religious establishment or the state "sovereign dignity" test for states' rights and immunities.

The theory of jurisprudential regimes posits that ideas have impact, that ideational structures have manifest consequences. These manifest consequences include decisional behavior, and regular patterns of decisional behavior can become the constitutive stories that help make certain doctrinal developments stick. Unfortunately, political development scholars still know little about the actual mechanics of this process, and it is often more conclusively identified retrospectively than while in progress. This pattern suggests that it is difficult to tell whether the rule-of-thumb balancing approach that characterized so many of the Rehnquist-era doctrinal contributions is an entrenched jurisprudential regime that will continue in the Roberts era. All that can be said at this point is this: it will take purposive judicial actions of upheaval—direct repudiation of precedents—to dislodge the content of that jurisprudential regime. Given what we have observed about associates' justice in the Rehnquist period and what we can postulate theoretically, there is less reason to expect than not to expect this occurrence.

An "O'Connorist" Court thus may well be the doctrinal as well as behavioral legacy of the Rehnquist years. But it is important to note what this label means, and what a legacy does and does not include. "Associates' justice" relied upon the tacit acceptance of institutionally decentralized policy leadership and choral Court pronouncements, along with an acceptance of the median-point pragmatic doctrinal formulations that ensued. Because of the appeal O'Connorism had for O'Connor and her colleagues as a method, those median-point formulations took shape as rules of thumb articulated by a Court that embodied the "reasonable observers" their doctrinal approaches lauded. This was the O'Connor Court, and how ingrained its decision-making conventions are is still difficult to say.

Still, there is one other dimension of the Rehnquist Court's legacy that can be discussed, which has relevance for the continuation of both O'Connor-style collegial decision making and jurisprudential reasoning. That dimension is the conception of the institutional role of the Supreme Court in the American constitutional system that the Rehnquist Court displayed in its decisional behavior. The conceptualization of the judicial role furthered through the Court's actions was not a legacy entirely of its own making; it depended, in large measure, on the community of court commentators who framed the Court's work. To this aspect of the legacy of judicial power in the Rehnquist era I turn in the next chapter as well as to the synergistic nexus between the Court and its critics. The ideational legacy that resulted may prove more lasting than the Rehnquist Court's specific doctrinal one—but it may also, and somewhat counterintuitively, aid in preserving the O'Connorist jurisprudence of the Rehnquist years. In Chapter 4, I explain why.

4

Both heralded and feared as the onset of a new era of conservative jurisprudence, the Rehnquist Court, as I observed in the
previous chapter, has left that prognosis to its successor. Although early assessments emphasized the emerging conservative decisional trends on a bench dominated by Republican
appointees, like many early assessments, these missed the
mark—in part because of unexpected behaviors by the Reagan
and Bush judges, along with a working majority's coalescence
around Justice Sandra Day O'Connor's conservative but rule-
of-thumb balancing approach. With the close of the Rehnquist
era, the true implications of its performance can be assessed
more accurately. After twenty years of decision making and the
analyses such decisions inspired, it is evident that the Rehnquist Court era left a significant legacy that reached beyond its
jurisprudence to its ideational impact on scholarship about the
Supreme Court and its role in a constitutional democracy.

The Rehnquist Court powerfully shaped legal theorizing
about the Court, the judicial role, and judicial review, as did
the Warren Court. "The Warren Court," in the words of one
analyst, "taught the justices that the Supreme Court could
help shape public policy" (Tushnet 1993, 34). Neither was
this lesson lost on court scholars, for by the era of the Burger
Court—supposedly refashioned by Nixon's appointment of
strict constructionists—"the Court is activist and so are the
commentators" (Shapiro 1983, 236). The Rehnquist Court's
record changed those sanguine views of judicial involvement

in the political process and inaugurated instead a profound reconsideration of the influence and role of the Supreme Court in public policy making and in American life. Judicial activism was not defended but increasingly castigated. More significantly, a revivified version of judicial restraint, incorporating minimalist decision making and institutional limitations, supplanted a faith in broad and principled judicial review as the standard for the modern Court. If the restraintist verbiage of the new Chief Justice John Roberts—in both confirmation hearings and off-the-bench remarks—is to be believed, it *is* the new standard for the current Court.

To make this argument about the Rehnquist Court's legacy, I have divided this chapter into two segments. The first delineates the standard of "legal liberalism" that became central to the construction of the Supreme Court's role since the Warren era, then explains how the Burger Court's identity as "the counterrevolution that wasn't" facilitated the perpetuation and maturation of the defense of a progressively activist Supreme Court. This notion of the Court and its role became the contemporary standard of normalcy, and when applied to the new Rehnquist Court, occasioned apprehension from liberal commentators. The second segment of the chapter tells the story of the Rehnquist Court's alteration of court commentators' views of the judicial role and its obligations and aspirations—which it did, ironically, without becoming the conservative counterrevolution so long feared or anticipated. Indeed, this "Rehnquist era" ended with the effective resignation of the moderate conservative, Justice Sandra Day O'Connor. I conclude the chapter by asserting that the commentary informed by the Rehnquist period lives on, already shaping coming assessments of that Court's successor.

As with previous chapters, I also evaluate the specific contributions made by Associate Justice Sandra Day O'Connor to what I call in this chapter the ideational impact of the Rehnquist era. The nomenclature of a "queen's Court" conjures an unchecked judicial power and unrestrained judicial role so feared by critics of judicial activism. Specifically, an associate justice seizing the institution's leadership for individual satisfaction or purposes seems to demonstrate a Court out of control, both internally and externally. Yet the reality is that by the time of O'Connor's announced retirement and ultimate departure from the Supreme Court, she was praised as an enviable judicial minimalist who narrowed the grounds of decisions and allowed consensus around them (Sunstein 1999) and as a "model" justice "widely recognized as a jurist with practical values."[1] Judicial scholars mused that her brand of judicial pragmatism was of a type the institution cannot do without, and that her era on the high bench only reestablished and solidified this notion. So whereas the Rehnquist Court on which she served became the measure of all things to be corrected, judicially, Rehnquist Justice O'Connor—who contributed more to the Court's identity than its chief justice did—escaped largely untainted and was, indeed, extolled as a model to emulate.

In considering whether this discrepancy is logically possible or simply ironic, we must ask whether the reaction to the Rehnquist era was conceptually informed or, in actuality, ideologically motivated.

THE PRESENT-DRIVEN ENDEAVOR OF CONSTITUTIONAL THEORY

Until recently, the Warren Court, which ended in 1969, was the "window to the present" ideal of a Supreme Court in the American constitutional system (Powe 2000, xiv), and the Warren legacy, at least for its liberal enthusiasts, was that of the heroic activist Court. Even for its critics—and there have been plenty—the Warren Court was an ideal type of the countermajoritarian Court run amok. Alexander Bickel (1962), originator of the term "the countermajoritarian difficulty," took the Court to task for *not* deciding, when a decision would be improvident for the nation, highlighting the undemocratic nature of judicial review. Enthusiasts and critics were united by agreement over what the Warren Court established: the constitutional regime of "legal liberalism."

Laura Kalman, who coined this phrase in her 1996 book, defined legal liberalism as "trust in the potential of the Supreme Court to bring about . . . policy change with nationwide impact" (2). With *Brown v. Board of Education* as the "paradigmatic event" of this era of Court-produced transformative social reform, the law professoriate remained under "the spell of the Warren Court" and "kept the faith in 'the cult of the Court,' . . . [a] confidence in the ability of courts to change society for what judges believe is the better" (Kalman 1996, 4). Besieged by process theory in the 1950s and 1960s and interpretivism in the 1970s, obfuscated by the turn to legal hermeneutics and challenged by the originalist turn to history in the 1980s, legal liberalism eventually found a renewed classical republican refuge justifying judicial value choices in defense of positive freedoms and civic inclusion (Kalman 1996, 160). The revivified vision of the progressively activist Court helped ensure, in the words of one contemporary analyst, the perpetuation of "the standard, celebratory history of the Supreme Court" (McConnell 2004, 142).

Even denigration by the left[2] of a mythology termed *liberal legalism* could not interfere with the "cheery account of the Supreme Court's role as protector and defender of the Constitution" and civil rights (McConnell 2004, 144). The Warren Court's championing of an "idealized set of public values" (Powe 2000, 496) was emblematic of such a view of the Court. The judicial activism it married to those values by overturning precedent, voiding statutes, and expansively interpreting the constitutional text was embraced as "the sovereign prerogative" (Rostow 1962). The persuasiveness, and pervasiveness, of this account continued to find intellectual expression in theorizing about judicial constitutional interpretation in the mid-1990s. An example was Kahn's (1994) "constitutive approach" to understanding Supreme Court decision making as "seek[ing] coherence in polity and rights principles" (29). Kahn applied this legal values–oriented approach to analyze the decisions of both the Warren and the Burger Courts, arguing that instrumentalist assessments misunderstand the Supreme Court role. The subtle differences between the Courts that Kahn described—the Warren Court's view of polity made it radical, whereas the Burger Court was more liberal with respect to structural inequality than its predecessor (261)—were less important than his unshakeable belief in the Supreme Court as a principled decision maker.[3] Such a belief in the constructive force of judicial policy making is the appeal of legal liberalism.

Revisionist treatments of the Warren Court admit that a tension between liberal idealism and liberal realism affected its decision making (see Tushnet 1993), and that "history's Warren Court" (Powe 2000, 500) applied to only one period within the Warren era. Still, its cultural image as expositor of aspiratory values was so firmly enshrined that it became the touchstone against which all successor Supreme Courts would be measured.

The intellectual framing power of this cultural image would soon be realized. Legal liberalism was both descriptive and proscriptive in identifying the content and the method of the Supreme Court's decisional outputs. Evaluation of the Burger Court from 1969 to 1986 applied this framework but yielded unexpected results: "the Burger Court consolidated and occasionally extended the Warren Court 'revolution' . . . explain[ing] why the scholarly criticism of the 'Imperial Judiciary' emerged not during the heyday of the Warren Court era but rather during the Burger years, often taking aim directly at the Burger Court" (Lamb and Halpern 1991, 434).

As this view intimates, the Burger Court continued the civil rights–civil liberties orientation that was the hallmark of McCloskey's modern Supreme

Courts (2000), so much so that it reaped much of the praise and the criticism perhaps more appropriately directed at the Warren Court. Court commentators of the late 1970s and early 1980s such as Owen Fiss (1979), Jesse Choper (1980), and Michael Perry (1982) generally looked favorably on the Burger Court's record of continuing the judicial role of espousing individual rights versus government powers. Although other commentators such as John Hart Ely (1980) were critical of the reach of the Supreme Court during the 1970s, the Court's necessary engagement in support of democratic values was not disputed. To some observers, such commentary expressed the outlook of judicial scholarship "decidedly influenced"—or "distorted"—by the Supreme Court's prevailing civil libertarian focus (Lamb and Halpern 1991, 445).

Empirically (on the Court) as well as normatively (from court scholars), the standard of legal liberalism reigned supreme. Important continuities with the modern era of individual rights–based activism outweighed any decisional drift to the right under the Burger chief justiceship. This was evident in recent revisionist scholarship on the Burger Court, pronouncing it "pragmatic not dogmatic" (O'Hara 1998, 6), a Court without a common or shared "sense of mission" (Schwartz 1998, 261), yet a demonstration "that activism of one sort or another is here to stay" (Henry 1998, 43).

The Burger Court was not, and continued not to be through its final October 1985 term, a counterrevolution to the Warren era. Its majorities tinkered at the margins of civil rights and civil liberties jurisprudence, but its justices accepted the role and generally the precedential record of its predecessor Supreme Court.[4] Viewing ostensibly reactionary Courts as having less impact than expected (or feared) has an established pedigree in recent court scholarship, and no Court era provided more of an anticlimax than the Burger years. In 1983, Vincent Blasi edited an aptly titled book about the Burger Court, *The Counter-Revolution That Wasn't*. The contributors commented on the Burger Court's doctrinal contributions in various areas of constitutional law, opining that the Warren Court's legacy of liberal activism had generally withstood the Nixon appointees' retrograde efforts, but lecturing that the Burger Court's own activism was "rootless" (Blasi 1983, 211; see also Schwartz 1998, 268). With the onset of the Rehnquist era, the Burger years came to be seen as nothing more than an interregnum. Indeed, writing in 1987, legal scholar Herman Schwartz speculated darkly that "the Burger Court was only a transition from the liberal activism of the Warren Court to the reactionary activism of the Rehnquist Court" (xxv).

The Warren-Burger Court period of scholarship illustrates the reality that constitutional theory is a reaction by scholars to the events of constitutional law and politics occurring around them, as mediated by those scholars' ideological commitments. It is in this sense present-driven (Friedman 2004, 151). If it is also true, as Martin Shapiro (1983) has suggested, that each generation of court commentators is "happier with the Court that shaped its intellectual adolescence than the one it confronts when it reaches maturity" (236), then contemporary analysts' readings of the Rehnquist Court were particularly overwrought. If the Burger Court inspired a collective sigh of relief, albeit resigned, from its Warren-era examiners, the Rehnquist Court prompted gasps of astonishment of various kinds. As the years passed and the decisions accumulated, few could reasonably describe the Rehnquist era as "rootless" in its fundamentals, as the Burger Court's activism was pilloried. Even those right-wing detractors who lamented the insipid direction of some of its policy making by the moderate and contextually oriented conservatives on the bench did not see the Rehnquist Court as standing in the shadow of a more celebrated precursor, whose constitutional policies and role it fitfully (or vapidly) continued. The Rehnquist Court came to be seen as the true jurisprudential counter or opposite to the New Deal Court—most particularly in its reelevation of the interests of states in the constitutional mix of national power and federalism rights (Schwartz 2002, 19).

This shift in ideological valence of the Supreme Court would seem to have predicted a shift in constitutional theorizing about judicial review, according to law professor Barry Friedman in his observation of the politically contingent cycling of normative arguments about the Court and constitutional review (2004, 164). A shift in constitutional theory certainly did occur; whether it was precipitated simply by an ideological shift during the Rehnquist Court era is debatable.

A PRESENT-DRIVEN ENDEAVOR REDUX

Some have alleged that the Warren Court was the historical aberration, with the Rehnquist Court "regressing to the mean" with respect to judicial progressivism in decision making.[5] In terms of the content of Supreme Court decision making, then, the Rehnquist Court's policy conservatism arguably reflected the more usual ethos of the institution (since the Civil War) of representing forces and ideas of the right rather than the left (Friedman 2002, 151). There were surely elements of the ideological conservatives' legal agenda that a Rehnquist majority successfully pushed—most especially, states' rights federalism, the restoration of the protections of the Tenth and Eleventh Amendments, and the limitation of the reach of congressional commerce power. Whereas defenders linked such structural adjustment in the constitutional system to a restoration of originalist jurisprudence (Bork 1989), critics decried the judicial activation of this agenda as ideologically motivated activism.

Such "regression" notwithstanding, somewhat different majorities on the Rehnquist Court pursued progressive policy decisions—most particularly, the expansion of privacy rights to protect homosexual intimate association in *Lawrence v. Texas* and the application of "evolving standards of decency" to forbid the execution of juvenile defendants and those with mental disabilities. Even more confusingly, the Rehnquist Court worked cautiously within its own modern, inherited agenda: for example, preserving the essential holding of *Roe v. Wade* on abortion and maintaining elements of the *Lemon* test for church-state separation questions—although particular decisions in specific factual circumstances allowed legislative inroads of state regulation or religious sponsorship. As I detailed in Chapter 3, the rule-of-thumb balancing approach, although highly individualist in implementation, was essentially modest as to legal change, particularly as to precedent.

The hopes of conservatives—so long frustrated in the judicial realm—thus were not vindicated by the Republican appointee–dominated Rehnquist Court. One contemporary analysis offered this less than encouraging synopsis to policy advocates of the right: "Rehnquist Court jurisprudence can only be understood as the product of the interaction of the views of nine separate individuals, each of whom has an idiosyncratic view of the proper interpretation of the Constitution and appropriate role of the Court in the American political system" (Maltz 2003, 6–7). Hardly the stuff of a conservative legal juggernaut, this.

The March 2004 release to the public of the late Justice Harry Blackmun's papers confirmed the worst fears of legal conservatives by providing evidence of the pivotal vote switches by Reagan appointee Justice Anthony Kennedy, and of both his and Bush appointee Justice David Souter's "seduction" at the hands of ideological turncoat Justice Blackmun (Greenhouse 2005a). Indeed, Justices Kennedy and Blackmun—both third-choice, compromise nominees of Republican presidents with an agenda for the Court—played a role in muting the Rehnquist Court's ideological direction by siding with liberal or moderate justices in closely decided, highly polarized issue areas. Such individual judicial actions prevented the Rehnquist Court legacy from being that of a right-wing repudiation of the role or policies of its predecessors.

Given this mixed record, how and why did the Rehnquist Court alter court commentators' views of the judicial role, its obligations, and its aspirations? The Court did so by being, to borrow a phrase from Tom Keck, "the most activist Supreme Court in history" (2004) and thereby inspiring the recrudescence of a philosophy of judicial restraint and a limited vision of the judicial role in American political society. In a way, then, the Rehnquist Court was the direct, but mutated, descendent of the Warren Court, seizing the latter's activist role and magnifying the Court's power, institutional place, and constitutional presence (Powe 2003).

Early scholars of the Rehnquist Court saw no signs of this, predicting instead a fairly conventional, conservative counterrevolution (Friedelbaum 1994; Savage 1993). They expected its contribution to be right-wing policy activism and retrograde jurisprudence, and some contemporaneous commentators continued to characterize the later Rehnquist Court in such partisan terms (Gottlieb 2001; Schwartz 2002). Although simple ideological objection to the Rehnquist Court's decisional outcomes was not the whole story, it no doubt colored contemporary court scholarship defending the abandonment of judicial activism. But more important and central to the Court's causal ideational force[6] was its "distinctive post-Warren Court jurisprudence of an utter lack of deference to Congress" (Keck 2004, 283). "Post-Warren" in content but not necessarily in form, the Rehnquist Supreme Court forced a blunt discussion of the judicial function in creating constitutional law.

According to Keck, the Rehnquist Court engaged in two strands of judicial activism: conservative policy–oriented and rightist jurisprudential decision making, and moderately liberal policy outcomes united to judge-centered balancing tests. The reason for this, he argues, was simple: Justice Sandra Day O'Connor, who endorsed both. Critical to the Rehnquist Court's "modern conservative activism" was that none of its justices, including its judicial conservatives, attempted a consistent commitment to judicial restraint by exercising legislative deference. Also crucial was that its centrist conservatives, O'Connor and Kennedy, defended both conservative positions on limited government and individual rights–based constraints on government action (Keck 2004, 199, 203). A strong conception of judicial supremacy was the result (203, 208), as "no areas of law and policy [are] off-limits to judicial action" (253).

It was the seemingly unprincipled and unabashedly hubristic nature of such judicial action that made the Rehnquist Court the new "touchstone" of what is right and wrong, judicially speaking,[7] and gave it the conceptual power to shape an emergent intellectual consensus about the institution. That intellectual consensus came in two parts: disapproval of the Court's new-style judicial preeminence and defense of varying degrees of judicial limitation.

Scholarly disapproval of the Rehnquist Court's view that "the Court's legal expertise endowed it with exclusive authority to interpret the Constitution" condemned the idea of the "juricentric Constitution" (Post and Siegel 2003, 6, 17). According to this idea of judicial institutional preeminence, the constitutional views of nonjudicial actors, particularly Congress, are to be suppressed, and constitutional deliberation by nonjudicial actors is to be surpassed (Whittington 2004). Indeed, Congress, "by reason of its institutional differences from the Court, lacks the integrity needed to speak for a Constitution that must endure as fundamental and enduring law" (Post and Siegel 2003, 18). Certain decisions were considered emblematic of the resultant vision of the separation of powers: City of Boerne v. Flores (1997), Bush v. Gore (2000), and Board of Trustees of the University of Alabama v. Garrett (2001).[8] Other decisions, such as Dickerson v. U.S. (2000), rebuffed congressional efforts to substitute legislative standards for judicially crafted rights protections (Post and Siegel 2003, 21), or pointedly resisted succumbing to external political pressures, as some observers characterized the Planned Parenthood v. Casey (1992) joint opinion (Bradley 2004; Nagel 2004). In focusing American public attention and American policy makers' reliance on the judicial institution as in no other period of the polity's history (Kramer 2004a), the Rehnquist Court was therefore more than a simple ideological counterrevolution in relation to its predecessor. It inaugurated, institutionally, a very different Supreme Court.

Explanations for the Rehnquist Court's juricentrism varied. One critic of the Court argued that in building on trends begun in the Burger era, the Rehnquist Court continued the "employment of standard modern balancing techniques and [paid] insufficient attention to the requirements of legislative deference where judicially manageable standards [were] not available" (Wolfe 2004, 219). The result was a notion of judicial power that defied limitation, because ad hoc rule-of-thumb balances could always be struck. It is worth noting that the juricentrism lambasted here is essentially indistinguishable from O'Connorist jurisprudence, except perhaps in terms of tone.

Another, less muted, critic of the Rehnquist Court's untoward judicial supremacy asserted that political attacks prompt the Supreme Court to protect
its perceived turf from unwanted invasion (as the Marshall Court did in *Mar-
bury v. Madison* [1803] and the Warren Court did in *Cooper v. Aaron* [1958]),
and that the Rehnquist Court's distinctive assertiveness suggested that its
perception of a threat to its independence was delusional and overblown
(Powe 2003, 697, 732). Still, neither commentator disagreed that the Rehnquist Court carried the theory of judicial interpretive primacy developed by
its predecessors along a discomforting logical trajectory to a self-important,
unrestrained judicial preeminence.

Although it seems unlikely that the Rehnquist Court "will be remembered"
for *intentionally* "championing a measurably smaller role for the Supreme
Court" in American life (Garrow 2002, 281), that smaller role in the constitutional dialogue is what Rehnquist Court commentators recommended and
even forecast. The Rehnquist Court was the target of a number of studies urging a reconsideration of the power and prerogatives of the judicial branch.
Taken together, they collectively called for a minimalist judicial practice from
the Supreme Court. Such minimalist practice has both an interpretive dimension, which supports only narrow, modest interpretive claims and cautious
incrementalism, and an institutional limits dimension, which endorses Thay-
erian judicial restraint (see Perry 1994, 86–88; Vermeule 2006) in electing to
decide matters of fundamental moral and political concern.

The interpretive dimension of minimalist judicial practice rests on an understanding of the indisputable minimal content of the Constitution as narrow in its substantive commitments and not deeply theorized or embedded in
a distinctive set of underlying precepts (Sunstein 1999, 62–63). Modest claims
about the meaning of the constitutional text and cautious resolution of little
more than the single case at issue are the appropriate judicial response. Such
diminished judicial power to enforce national norms is a logical consequence
of the rejection of moral foundationalism in the civic republican writings by
scholars such as Perry, Tushnet, and Levinson during the late 1980s; this rejection understood constitutional principles as indeterminate prior to judges'
decisions (Kahn 1994, 213). Thus, when aspirations in the Constitution are
not clear and are contested in their policy manifestations, the Court must rule
so as to defer their resolution to a deliberative political forum. Some scholars identified this "substantive deference" school of constitutional theory as
necessary judicial adaptation to the contemporary political regime, where

much is contested (Peters and Devins 2005, 55) and much finds its way to the Court's agenda. In such a regime, substantive deference entails ruling narrowly, cautiously, and incrementally, and striving to harmonize established precedent and popularly endorsed legislation.

Minimalist judicial interpretation, then, is supposed to be nondisruptive. Sunstein, writing in 1999, found evidence that the Rehnquist Court was making minimalist decisions that did not preempt community deliberation of value questions. However, rulings during the final years of that Court suggested that his words were more proscriptive than descriptive.

There was also an institutional power dimension to the Court commentary that used the Rehnquist era as its foil. Drawing on a body of work establishing that constitutional interpretation goes on outside the courts (Tushnet 1999, x), the call for minimalist judicial practice accepted the Dahlian thesis about the political nature of the Supreme Court and circumscribed the countermajoritarian responsibilities of the institution.[9] The result was a call for diminished practice based on decreased expectations, with the Rehnquist Court as the Supreme Court in the analytical viewfinder. A diminished faith in judicial settlement of divisive policy questions sprang from that Court's inability to articulate the substantive values or vision that supported its defense of constitutional norms. Elaborating on the Rehnquist Court's "effort to avoid the grand style of Warrenism," one commentator characterized the inability in this way: "What has been lost is the basic ingredient of principled decision making, which is a commitment to judicial reason-giving. . . . [W]e have the spectacle of a Court exercising great power without offering publicly accountable reasons" (Rosen 1999, 50). Another scholar noted this about the Rehnquist Court's less-than-fulsome reasoning: "The Court derives its authority from its ability to 'explain and expound.' . . . This lack of clarity is a problem that runs through the jurisprudence of the Rehnquist Court and illustrates, I would argue, its profound misunderstanding of its fundamental responsibility. . . . It is the multiple concurring opinions and murky language that damage the confidence that the people should have in this Court's decisions" (Sracic 2000, B2). Again, none of this condemnatory language is inconsistent with the doctrinal style of O'Connor, whose substantive prescriptions were vague and certainly not grounded in grandiose normative assertions.

Whether the flaw lay in the atheoretical character of the Rehnquist Court's practice of judicial supremacism (combined with "supreme" judicial individualism) or in the problematic nature of judge-led constitutional construction more generally, the resultant proscription was the same. Without the capacity to perform the settlement function, the Court must decline to resolve "big" questions and thereby preserve space for contested issues to be decided democratically. One analysis defended the diminished judicial role as a "descri[ption of] the practices of courts in a constitutional regime whose aspirations have diminished" (Tushnet 2003, 141). Certain other commentators took the institutional limits dimension of a minimalist judicial practice so far as to advocate populist constitutionalism or coordinate constitutional construction (Devins and Fisher 2004; Kramer 2004; Tushnet 1999).[10] Whether the role of constitutional law in American politics or the role of the Court was the chastened one was of less significance than the general sentiment that with the Rehnquist Court, a turning point had been reached, systemically.

What distinguished this turn-of-the-twenty-first-century group of court studies from previous clarion calls to prevent judges from legislating from the bench (e.g., Bork 1989; Meese 1985) was that its scholars were not the typical right-of-center Warrenism bashers who previously could be counted on to attack judicial activism. Advocates of judicial modesty are of course nothing new, for New Deal–era court commentators (Jackson 1941; Shapiro 1983, 219–220), "passive virtues" advocates of legislative deference (Bickel 1961, 1962; Keck 2004, 61–63; Lasser 1988, 271–272; McCloskey 2000 [1960]), and a variety of political conservatives (e.g., Berger 1977; Franck 1996; Hand 1958; Kilgore 1977) have defended judicial restraint as the Supreme Court's proper stance in constitutional democracy. What was new, as a result of reflection on the Rehnquist Court's record, was the widespread scholarly skepticism of a jurisprudence of values and principled activism by the Supreme Court, including from (former) believers in legal liberalism.

In the law-and-courts field of political science, such skepticism is partly the result of the intellectual dominance of instrumentalist accounts of judicial decision making such as attitudinalism and the strategic model of judicial behavior (Geyh 2006, 14–15). But even academic lawyers, less affected by the orthodoxies of their social science colleagues, seemed to be discarding grand constitutional theorizing as the job of the Court.[11] It was as if the Rehnquist period engendered disillusionment with the entire project. Such disenchantment, moreover, applied to Court decisions across the ideological spectrum. The Rehnquist Court's Commerce Clause revolution, for instance, in rulings such as *Lopez v. U.S.* (1995) and *U.S. v. Morrison* (2000), was criticized for vindicating the constitutional principle of federalism without supplying an explanatory framework in the form of judicially manageable or even identifiable standards for intrastate activity with a substantial effect on interstate commerce (Wolfe 2004, 217–218). And when the Rehnquist Court's activist involvement in policy making included such "legal liberal" goals as preserving affirmative action, protecting expansive rights to expression (including hate speech and flag-burning), and broadening constitutional foundations for gay rights, the jurisprudential underpinning of these judicial commitments was disjointed, unrelated to an overarching philosophy of civil libertarianism. Instead, these rights-protective actions were indicative of something else: the ad hoc and *ipse dixit* nature of the Rehnquist Court's contributions overall.[12]

Thus the revisioning of the Supreme Court's role in the constitutional order: scholarship addressed a Court that, by virtue of its internal incoherence, replaced principle with result-oriented pragmatism. Although one sympathizer with the judicial minimalism talk noted that "to a neutral observer, it is suspicious that all of us liberals are making these claims about limited judicial power at a time when we don't control the power" (Tushnet 2003, 219–220, n. 165, quoting Michael Klarman), this recent intellectual dialogue about the judicial role was neither disingenuous nor disgruntled. Neither was it a straightforward illustration of Barry Friedman's ideological cycling of normative arguments by court commentators, for not all criticism directed at the Rehnquist bench was politically convenient. Ideologically conservative legal scholar (and federal appellate judge) Richard Posner joined the chorus lambasting the Rehnquist Court's "aggressive" political judgment of constitutional interpretation, and urged the "modest judge" approach where the justice is a "timid politician" (2004, 54–55). Not only did the minimal judicial practice commentators echo a strain of constitutional conservatism that had consistently critiqued judicial power (Keck 2004, 324, n. 7; Yoo 2006), theirs was an academic version of then current cautionary thinking about the Court in the public realm. Such cautionary thinking coming from across the political spectrum had already inspired, by the end of George W. Bush's first term, congressional campaigns to strip the federal courts of jurisdiction to hear cases on certain subjects, heated discussion of the Senate's role in examining the president's judicial nominees, and agitation about federal justices' life tenure. Additionally, suggestions for minimal as well as more maximal popular elements in the federal judicial system—from the appointment of judges with tempering political experience (Posner 2004) to the censure moves from the House Working Group on Judicial Accountability (Geyh

2006, 4)—indicated a dissatisfaction with contemporary appointees' inflated sense of their own judicial capacity. One study of congressional oversight of the judicial branch commented that these latest campaigns to curb the courts might be different from their predecessors, for "Americans have been steeping in a culture of legal realism for long enough that it may well have begun to color the way they and their representatives in Congress think the judiciary should be governed" (Geyh 2006, 21). If this is so, then the Rehnquist Court's seemingly unprincipled activist behavior cannot have helped matters— not if the strong sales of the conservative screed inspired by the Court's justices, *Men in Black: How the Supreme Court Is Destroying America* (Levin 2005), were any indication. That one particular Court had largely been the catalyst for such a range of court skepticism does not diminish the reality of the ideational trend.

Without being uniformly, demonstrably, or satisfactorily "ideological" in its activism, then, the Rehnquist Court altered court commentators' views of the judicial role and the obligations and aspirations of the judicial institution. That Court's activism, and its "imperialism in displacing and disparaging other constitutional interpreters" (Powe 2003, 731), triggered reflection on the constitutional role of the institution. Paradoxically, its centrist-moderate conservative justices' contextual, case-by-case, and balancing-of-facts approach to legal rule promulgation—what in Chapter 3 I labeled rule-of-thumb jurisprudence—guaranteed that issues *would* return to the Supreme Court for disposition (Keck 2004, 292–293; Tushnet 2003, 140). That continual judicial disposition, more than the doctrinal or policy directions of the Court's particular inclinations, inflamed those pronouncing on the judicial era.

Yet oddly enough, this was also the approach that marked it as the "queen's Court." The idiosyncratic nature of O'Connor's fact-sensitive resolutions ensured that "her" Court would be the central organ of "significant legal debate [at] the forefront of the intellectual development of the law" (Scalia 1994). And, as my findings in previous chapters suggest, O'Connor's vision of her associate's role also seems to have been embraced by her colleagues. It is plausible, then, to view the Court of "associates' justice" not only as supremely individualist but also as juricentrist.

The associate justices who were critical to the activism of the Rehnquist Court shared a decisional trait that arguably displayed their understanding of their individual roles as members of the Court. Examining them sheds some light on the kind of activist judging against which recent court commentators have railed. As one study reminds us, to explain the decision making of O'Connor, Kennedy, and other situationally pivotal justices, "and hence that of the Rehnquist Court itself," we should examine "their visions of the judicial role" (Keck 2004, 274).

In their behavioral expression of the roles of Supreme Court justices, O'Connor as well as Kennedy were especially emblematic but not necessarily unique on the Rehnquist bench. In its pronouncements, the O'Connor-driven Rehnquist Court united a devotion to judicial seriousness with a multivocal approach to decision making. Each of these traits requires explication, because neither received as much attention from court commentators as did the Rehnquist Court's assumption of a preeminent institutional role. But both aforementioned traits nevertheless played a part in altering scholarly views of the judicial job, its occupants, and their obligations and aspirations.

The devotion to judicial seriousness was stylistic as well as content-oriented, and reflected the justices' desire "to show that they are technically competent lawyers who do small things very well" and to "secure assent by demonstrating their seriousness as lawyers" (Tushnet 2003, 125–126). Speaking in another context, one analyst labeled it a "lawyer's aversion to making fundamental value choices" where decisions "reflect less an overriding calculus of fundamental values than lawyerlike attempts to resolve the given controversy as a practical compromise between both sides of the issues involved" (Schwartz 1998, 269). Although Justices Kennedy and Souter were accused explicitly of exemplifying "self-presentation as thorough-goingly serious" (Tushnet 2003, 126, 212, n. 61), O'Connor too epitomized this persona in her juridical identity as the Court's Solomon, as well as with her oft-repeated, desired epitaph of "here lies a good judge."

O'Connor was frequently lauded as the Rehnquist Court's chief pragmatist, but this epithet was also applied to—and embraced by—another Rehnquist justice, Stephen Breyer (Rosen 2005a). Moreover, Justice Breyer's bench writing from his Rehnquist-era tenure supplied another, more specific example of judicial "seriousness." In his separate concurring opinion in the final term's Ten Commandments display case, *Van Orden v. Perry* (2005), he agreed that the state's display of the religious symbol was constitutionally permissible, propounding, "I see no test-related substitute for the exercise of *legal judgment*" (emphasis added). He then engaged in a serious, lawyerly weighing of the decisive factors as he saw them. His off-the-bench writing elaborated further on this practical method as he saw it: "ordinary, professional judicial

approaches" to "gauging whether and to what extent [judges] have succeeded in facilitating workable outcomes" are the product of judges' "professional training and experience" or the "professional framework" (Breyer
2005, 110–111, 115).

Such was the Rehnquist Court's voice in highly salient constitutional pronouncements: a voice of confident, serious-minded competence.[13] Scholars
such as Keck stressed that that voice was frequently O'Connor's or Kennedy's; whether they unilaterally spoke for the Court, what was indisputable
was that Scalia's dramaturgical rhetoric or Thomas's juridical radicalism did
not. It was also clear, as detailed in Chapter 2, that the Court's voice was not
always, or only, found in its majority opinions. This was the second of the
two aforementioned behavioral traits of the Court during the Rehnquist era:
it was given to a multivocal approach to decision making consisting of separate opinions and separate writings—particularly concurrences—to present
choral doctrinal resolutions of constitutional questions by embellishing on,
clarifying, or limiting the doctrinal rule or reasoning of an opinion for the
Court. O'Connor and Kennedy were among the top three filers of concurring
opinions during the last natural Court period (1994–2004), but concurring
behavior was fairly widespread among the Rehnquist justices, with the chief
being the notable exception on his own Court (Maveety 2005). As Chapter 2
discussed, an upshot of the trend toward separate writing was a steady increase in the number of concurring voices per case over time and a marked
increase from that of the Burger Court (Maveety, Turner, and Way 2004).
That the Rehnquist justices took their own notes of judiciousness seriously is
strongly suggested by their penchant for choral communication.

Speaking seriously and speaking separately had the combined effect of
highlighting the (self-?) importance of the individual jurist to constitutional
law.[14] The long tenure of service without a personnel change of the last group
of Rehnquist justices only magnified this fixation on individual justices, as
court commentators emphasized the importance of the justices as medians,
crafters, accommodators, and creators. Tushnet (2005), for instance, demonstrated the popular appeal of this individualistic characterization of the
Court with chapter treatments by individual justices in a recent work intended
for a nonspecialist audience. Although studies and biographies of individual
justices are not new, the Rehnquist Court was persistently viewed as not the
creature of its chief justice, despite acknowledgment of his capable leadership. Instead, various individual associate justices contended—in the eyes of

court watchers—for creative control of the High Court's output (Edelman and Chen 2001; Irons 1994; Merrill 2003; Rosen 2001). And the Rehnquist Court's collective output was viewed as the product of separate and discrete theorizing by the Rehnquist Court's jurisprudential individualists (Maltz 2003)—so much so that a 2002 study began an analysis of whether there was a pattern to the Court's constitutional decision making by examining whether the individual justices on the Court had their *own* philosophies of law that might *accumulate* into a Court view (Chemerinsky 2002, 196).

Separate opinion writing was a facet of the contemporary judicial individualism embodied by the Rehnquist Court. So was the serious lawyerly "weighing in" certain Rehnquist justices had no qualms about expressing in individuated Court decision making. As a group, the Rehnquist justices were keen to inform the public and the bar precisely "about the state of the Court's collective mind" (Scalia 1994). The implication is that individualized earnest judgment was the currency of modern judicial integrity—for them and for us.

Whether the Rehnquist Court's enactment of the judicial role will extend beyond its tenure remains to be seen,[15] but it fit with the justices' *collective institutional faith in their own judicial voices.* Attention to such role orientation is fodder for any restraintist reformulation of judicial review, as "the justices' perception of their role is the true restraining influence" (Griffin 1996, 139) on their behavior as judicial actors.[16] Although some commentary on the Rehnquist era was histrionic at times, it was based on a plausible construction of the high-toned actions of the Court's justices. The Rehnquist justices styled themselves as pragmatic individualists and reasonable observers; how they came across was another matter. The fact that their Court became an advertisement for a restrained and modest institutional role lay less in the objective quality of their own work than in the nature of scholars' reactions to it.

Interestingly, if this ideational legacy results in a revivification of judicial restraint on the high bench, one perhaps unintended consequence of that revitalization may be the preservation of the Rehnquist Court's other, doctrinal legacy. Respecting rule-of-thumb precedents—that is, respecting the "'personalized jurisprudence' that allowed judges to impose their will without explaining their rationale" (France 1999)—could, ironically, demarcate the new judicial modesty. To return to a matter I explored in the previous chapter, the ideational legacy of the Rehnquist Court—the embrace of judicial restraint—may make existing, O'Connorist doctrine sticky by default. That default would be the embrace—induced or heartfelt—of nondisruptive behavior by the next Court's justices. Of course, a "disruptive" new Supreme Court—bent on revisionism—would also hammer home the Rehnquist-era restraintist lesson, albeit through defiance rather than unobtrusiveness.

THE END—AND A BEGINNING

The "Rehnquist" era effectively ended with the de facto January 2006 resignation of Justice Sandra Day O'Connor, whose moderate judicial conservatism and accommodationist voting behavior (Maveety 2003) were central to the activist, juricentrist, minimalist, and multivocal tendencies that defined the Rehnquist Court as a political institution and as a jurisprudential entity. The Rehnquist Supreme Court continued nominally until the 2005 death of the chief justice, but its ideational legacy had been established firmly long before his Court's demise. That ideational legacy acted as a catalyst for profound reconsideration of the influence and role of the Court in American life and public policy making. The summary comment by one judicial scholar on the judicial confirmation process as applied to future (and, as of this writing, recently confirmed) Supreme Court nominees is telling: "Experienced, competent, noncontroversial jurists *with a restrained understanding of the role of the federal judiciary in the political system* may be the best the modern system can offer" (Silverstein 1994, 171 [emphasis added]). Whether this is an accurate assessment of the first post-Rehnquist Court appointments, the statement proves that as a result of the Rehnquist period, the romance with the Warren era is dead indeed.

"We are surrounded by the rubble of Warren and Bickel, and the age of judicial heroics is mercifully past," wrote journalist Jeffrey Rosen, thanking the Rehnquist Court for curing the nation of the naive notion of salvation by the Supreme Court (1996, 43). That it did so in spite of itself is irrelevant now, for a reconstructed limited vision of the judicial institution is in place and influences the debate over the appointment of new Supreme Court justices. Indeed, a judicial restraint motif dominated the John Roberts and Samuel Alito nomination announcements and confirmation hearings from summer 2005 through winter 2006. As a new appointee, Chief Justice Roberts continued to emphasize that "if it is not necessary to decide more to a case, then in my view it is necessary not to decide more to a case" (Yen 2006). As a nominee, Judge Alito labored under the additional burden of being measured against the "model" Supreme Court justice he was putatively replacing.

What made Sandra Day O'Connor such a model was the role identity read into the reality of her centrist position and aptitude for jurisprudential balancing. According to Senator Patrick Leahy, in his opening statement at the Alito confirmation hearings on January 9, 2006: "Justice Sandra Day O'Connor serves as a model Supreme Court justice, widely recognized as a jurist with practical values, a sense of the consequences of the legal decisions being made by the Supreme Court." As Justice Breyer's writings urge and one Rehnquist Court analyst posited (Posner 2004, 91), such pragmatic adjudication of the Constitution can converge with judicial modesty or restraint. But it need not, and in O'Connor's case, arguably did not.

By winter 2006, when O'Connor finally left "her" Court, the Rehnquist Supreme Court and its most emblematic associate justice had already repaired to the realm of history, each having been replaced by a more vivid "simulacra" (Norton 1993). In other words, the Rehnquist Court commentators, through their vigorous defense of minimalist judicial practice in reaction to the Rehnquist Court, successfully created both a new judicial ideal—the "anti-Supreme Court"—and a newly idealized judicial entity—"O'Connorism." These identities stood in some contrast to their real-world inspirations, but they became the templates against which a new Court and its new justices were evaluated. How the Rehnquist Court could be both the juricentric villain to target and the location of a romanticized judicial past is the stuff not of misplaced legend but of constructed legacy. That legacy arose not so much from the Court itself as from its audience of commentators, who created a judicial mythology more compelling and memorable than its real, live version.

That creation was the hyperreal, didactic instrument of "history's Rehnquist Court." Its significance lay in the magnitude of the lesson drawn from its various performances. The primary lesson, a circuitous defense of judicial restraint, seems downright baffling, for paradoxically, of course, "history's Rehnquist Court" was already associated with the "model" Supreme Court Justice O'Connor. Yet this connection—in the face of the prorestraintist lesson—is not as nonsensical as it at first seems. This perspective suggests that the age of judicial heroes/heroines in fact persists, but that heroics lie more in temperance[17] than in transcendence. Whether the living justice was as temperate as the model justice does not diminish the ideational force of her memory.

To return to the question with which I began this chapter, is the discrepancy between the interpretations of the Rehnquist Court and Justice O'Connor's records logically resolvable or simply ironic? The Court on which O'Connor served became the measure of all things to be corrected judicially, and the justice who contributed more to that Court's identity than its chief justice became the contemporary gold standard for a judge: the practical jurist. This discrepancy is logically resolvable when we realize that although the reaction to the Rehnquist era was not ideologically motivated, the reaction to O'Connor's specific deeds of jurisprudential pragmatism probably was. Her status as a paragon of temperance was inseparable from her moderate actions of accommodating polarized policy positions through context-sensitive balancing approaches—which, hardly coincidentally, privileged her judgment. Such active judicial supervision of legal policy making was not tarred with the same brush as the Rehnquist Court's "juricentrism" because of the ideologically centrist and satisfying outcomes produced by her doctrinal compromises. Whether hers was a method of judicial restraint is of course debatable, but the approval of her judicial methodology in some quarters simply furthered the call for a modest judicial role—or, more accurately perhaps, for modest consequences from the next Supreme Court. This was less an irony or a logical contradiction than the deliberate obstinacy of refusing to see the Rehnquist Court's O'Connorism as political savvy dressed as minimalist jurisprudential methodology. Having "practical values" at times means being restraintist, but not always, and they are surely not the same thing in a judge.

Nevertheless, the *commentators'* Court and the *commentators'* O'Connor together constituted the Rehnquist-era discordant but progenitive ideational legacy. O'Connor's specific ideational importance, moreover, took full shape in the post-Rehnquist period. Chapter 5 takes up the topic of the end of the "O'Connor" era and looks at her influence during the transition period from fall 2005 to winter 2006. That influence continued to be both juridical and ideational, as it had been during the Rehnquist period. But by examining the end that is also a beginning, one can see clearly the several legacies of O'Connor's Rehnquist Court: its mixture of behavioral and jurisprudential individualism and the peculiar vision of judicial self-possession and self-control this mixture inspired.

5

In the previous chapter, I established that the Rehnquist Court had an ideational legacy grounded largely in court commentators' reaction to it—particularly to its assertion of a large measure of judicial oversight through the active application of its rule-of-thumb doctrinal solutions. I had argued in Chapter 3 that rule-of-thumb pragmatism depended heavily on Justice O'Connor's but also on her colleagues' exhibition of "O'Connorist" jurisprudence. The reasonable individual jurist standard and fact-based balancing approach of the Rehnquist Court were central reasons for critics' castigation of its supremacist judicial role; yet, ironically, they also were the centerpiece of the "Justice O'Connorism" that came to be associated with her iconographic role as a judicial model. To repeat, this perception was illustrated during the confirmation hearings for O'Connor's successor, Judge Samuel Alito, when Senator Patrick Leahy praised her in the following way in his opening statement: "Justice Sandra Day O'Connor serves as a model Supreme Court justice, widely recognized as a jurist with practical values, a sense of the consequences of the legal decisions being made by the Supreme Court." Those "practical values" and that sense of decisional "consequences" framed O'Connor's contributions to the behavioral, jurisprudential, and institutional legacies of the Rehnquist Court. Yet they also described the modes of juridical action that spurred a reactive revival of judicial restraintism. The "supremely individualist" Court was, paradoxically, both the motivation for the call to return to restraint and, largely, the doing of a "model" but mischaracterized judicial individual.

Because the legacy of judicial power during the Rehnquist era is, in so many ways, that of Associate Justice Sandra Day O'Connor, her departure was a critical juncture for the Court. After the death of Chief Justice Rehnquist in summer 2005 and his replacement following the successful confirmation of Judge John Roberts, O'Connor continued in her service on the Supreme Court from October through early January of the 2005–2006 term. Her offer to stay on after her announced retirement, so as not to leave the Court shorthanded, created a transition period—a regency, of sorts—and an opportunity to reflect on the difference O'Connor's retirement from the Court would make to its decision making. By the time Samuel Alito was seated, O'Connor had participated in and decided some twenty-six cases. This case record allows an examination of which Rehnquist-era legacies detailed in Chapters 1–4 persisted in the early months of the Roberts Court transition period. Did the "queen's Court" continue, but only as long as her tenure? Or did the early Roberts era suggest the institutionalization of the traits of its predecessor?

One early prognosis affirmed the latter hypothesis and offered this prediction about the new Court era: "The Roberts Court's modern Republicans . . . are going to have to decide how strongly they are committed to the criticisms of judicial activism they deployed quite effectively against their adversaries. . . . With nine individuals all pursuing distinctive variations on a single theme, the Roberts Court is likely to seem themeless overall" (Tushnet 2006, 358). The judicial individualism to which Tushnet alludes would seem to include both multivocal decision making and rule-of-thumb doctrinal approaches implemented by reasonable observers. And the reference to a wavering commitment to "criticisms of activism" intimates that the Roberts justices will find it hard to embrace a restraintist role.

Tushnet's comments suggest the endurance by default if not the active continuation of Rehnquist-era judicial traits. Although it is not possible to replicate perfectly my studies in the previous chapters of leadership patterns, opinion-writing behaviors, jurisprudential approaches, and institutional role orientation by way of court commentators' reactions, data on the Roberts Court "regency" period exist in journalistic coverage, decisional outputs, and the justices' own off-the-bench remarks. My observations in this chapter are directed in particular at evidence of O'Connor's continuing influence on the Court, of contributions she may have made to the legacy of the Rehnquist period she helped shape so much. Equally important, I also examine decision making in that portion of the first Roberts Court term following O'Connor's departure. Would "associates' justice" be perpetuated and bedevil the new chief?

THE FINAL DECISIONS OF THE QUEEN'S COURT

Two features of the last decisions in which Justice O'Connor participated shed light on their continuity with the Court practices and Court outcomes that immediately preceded them. The first is the degree of unanimity of the decisions. As I detailed in Chapter 2, one of the most visible markers of the Rehnquist era was its trend toward choral decision making, the tendency of the members of the Court to raise their separate voices in legal policy making and thereby to fracture or, at the very least, add complexity to, opinion majorities. Using a descriptive classification, we can measure the multivocality of the first decisions of the new Roberts Court, and assess how similar they were to decisions of the previous Court era.

The second feature is the presence, or clear absence, of O'Connorist jurisprudence in those rulings with significant substantive content or some setting of precedent. As I discussed in Chapter 3, the rule-of-thumb doctrinal approach engaged in fact-based balancing or the substitution of a reasonable (judicial) observer for a bright-line rule of law. Although presented as narrow in application to the specific circumstances of the case at hand, the balancing test/reasonable observer's judgment necessitated judicial fine-tuning and follow-up decision making, and almost guaranteed judicial disagreements as to the reach and use of any particular rule of thumb. Using evaluative assessment, we can appraise the early Roberts Court rulings on this content-based dimension.

These measures are all the more interesting as indicators of a "queen regent's Court" in light of Chief Justice Roberts's repeated statements about the importance of crafting narrowly grounded opinions on which a large majority, if not a unanimous Court, can agree.[1] As irreverent political commentator Dalia Lithwick (2007) summed it up: "John Roberts has been trying to sell judicial minimalism as a model of his jurisprudential mission." But the judicial minimalism referenced seems different from the jurisprudential approach for which O'Connor was once praised—perhaps inaptly—by law professor Cass Sunstein (1999). In the new chief's own words, "our job is to decide cases, not promulgate comprehensive rules" (Barnes 2007b). O'Connorist doctrine may have privileged "standards" over "rules," but comprehensive it surely was, for in its rule-of-thumb generality and contextual flexibility, O'Connor-style jurisprudence had a broad if somewhat Delphically imprecise applicability to new cases and controversies. Roberts's stated objective of jurisprudential sparsity with decisional unanimity would seem to counter directly the legacy he inherited. Thus, it is especially pertinent to examine how quickly, or how successfully, he has been able to counter it—with or without O'Connor on the bench.

Having said this, the final decisions of O'Connor's tenure are something of a mixed bag, but there is clear evidence of "Robertsian" judicial agreement. Eight of the twenty-six decisions of 2005–2006 in which she participated were per curiam, and eleven were signed unanimous opinions of the Court, although three of those garnered regular concurrences and one featured a concurrence in the judgment. But less than half of the Court's output during O'Connor's final months on the bench was standard-issue Rehnquist Court dividedness. There were only two five-to-four rulings in this period: one, a federal bankruptcy case that raised state sovereign immunity issues (*Central Virginia Community College v. Katz*), and the other a death penalty case involving state sentencing procedures (*Brown v. Sanders*). Even the two highest-profile cases decided during the early months of the 2005 term, on the Oregon Death with Dignity Law and the New Hampshire statute requiring parental notification for minors seeking abortions, were less divisive and fragmentary than they might have been. In *Gonzales v. Oregon*, the Kennedy majority of six justices found that the Controlled Substances Act did not allow the attorney general to prohibit doctors from prescribing regulated drugs for use in physician-assisted suicide under state law permitting the procedure; the "public interest" mandate granted the attorney general by the act did not empower him to make an independent assessment of the meaning of federal law. *Gonzales* potentially qualifies as the kind of narrowly grounded, thus widely supported, Supreme Court case disposition to which Chief Justice Roberts aspires for his Court. In the early Roberts Court's other closely watched, potentially high-stakes case, *Ayotte v. Planned Parenthood of Northern New England*, O'Connor wrote the opinion for a unanimous Court, which returned the parental notification law to the state legislature for repair on a procedural technicality; there was no substantive ruling in the decision on the health exception question and the undue burdening of minors' abortion rights. In sidestepping this larger and more contentious matter, the Court again seemingly did what Roberts proposes: decide on cases instead of promulgating comprehensively where it is not necessary to do so.

Some commentary on the early decisions of the new Supreme Court suggested that they "be understood as lowering the stakes in a time of transition," with the Court "simply avoiding highly controversial matters during Justice O'Connor's 'lame duck' term."[2] Some journalists saw the new leader as turning "the famously quarrelsome justices, at least for now, into a surprisingly agreeable group," although acknowledging that the Court normally hands down more unanimous decisions early in the annual term and holds the sharply divisive cases until the end (Savage 2006). As if on cue, a story later commented on a decision with "dueling opinions" that "drew back the curtain to reveal the strains behind the surface placidity and collegiality of the young Roberts Court" (Greenhouse 2006a). Indeed, in observing the exchange of majority, concurring, and dissenting opinions in the Fourth Amendment case *Georgia v. Randolph*, the reporter noted her impression that "there was a tone more of banter than anger to the exchange between old adversaries [Stevens and Scalia], as if after some months of *forced and unaccustomed unanimity*, they were now free once again to acknowledge their differences" (ibid. [emphasis added]).

There is another possible perspective on the 2005–2006 term—that its unanimity was really no more marked than other recent terms. One scholar commented that the "interplay between ideological and procedural values" in Supreme Court decision making means that unanimous decisions account for about one-third to one-half of the docket in most years (Eisgruber 2007). So even though 44 percent of the Roberts Court's decisions were unanimous in the 2005–2006 term compared with 30 percent of the Rehnquist Court's decisions in the 2004–2005 term, this range of variation is not considered remarkable by all judicial scholars. Thus, little can be inferred about the Roberts Court's decisional practices from the unanimity of its first term. Indeed, as the *Wall Street Journal* "Law Blog" recorded on April 18, 2007, "supreme disharmony" had replaced the judicial agreement with which the 2006–2007 term had started—which was much as the first term of the Roberts Court had started. Noting Roberts's summer 2007 statement to a meeting of Ninth Circuit judges that "it promotes the rule of law to have the Court speaking, to the extent possible, with one voice," the blog posting concluded—on the day of the announcement of the five-to-four ruling in the so-called partial-birth abortion case *Gonzales v. Carhart*—"so much for unanimity."[3]

Fits and starts in consensus aside, it is still difficult to claim that the Court of O'Connor's "regency" bore much of a mark of the Rehnquist years. Like its metaphorical namesake, it was a period of waiting until the coming, fully institutionalized personnel change. Oddly enough, it was the second half of the October 2005 term, with Alito replacing O'Connor, that bore a greater resemblance to the decision-making behaviors and decisional outputs of the queen's Court era. Whether this represented a legacy, the reality of harder cases later in the term, or—as the above quote about "forced and unaccustomed unanimity" intimates—a reactive adjustment or even resistance to a new order is difficult to say. Nevertheless, analysis of the O'Connor effect on the Rehnquist Court legacy is incomplete without some attention to that second half of the Roberts transition period.

POST-O'CONNOR: POST-REHNQUIST-ERA LEGACIES?

In her summary of the 2005–2006 term, *New York Times* Supreme Court reporter Linda Greenhouse ventured that the Roberts Court was "in name" but not "in fact." She continued:

> In the Court's most significant nonunanimous cases, Chief Justice Roberts was in dissent almost as often as he was in the majority. His goal of inspiring the Court to speak softly and unanimously seemed a distant aspiration as important cases failed to produce majority opinions and members of the Court, including occasionally the chief justice himself, gave voice to their frustration and pique with colleagues who did not see things their way. (Greenhouse 2006b)

Washington Post Supreme Court reporter Charles Lane was more biting and more succinct: "Kennedy Reigns Supreme on Court," read the regally themed headline to his story on the historic new term in which so little had changed (Lane 2006).

Both journalists emphasized that even within a term distinguished by a high number of unanimous rulings, old patterns died hard. Several major cases—on executive power, electoral redistricting, campaign financing, and environmental protection under the Clean Water Act—were decided by fractured sets of opinions. Roberts would later comment in an interview on his "frustration" by the degree to which the media focused on "a handful of divisive cases" rather than on the greater number of unanimous ones from his first term as chief, and also by the degree to which some of his colleagues "were acting more like law professors than members of a collegial Court" (Rosen 2007a, 105). The many separate opinions in *Rapanos v. U.S., Randall v. Sorrell, League of United Latin American Citizens (LULAC) v. Perry,* and *Hamdan v. Rumsfeld* seemed to display that "law professor model," or "personalization of judicial politics" (Rosen 2006, 224). This approach to adjudicating—which even the new chief admitted is deeply ingrained among some justices—foregrounds "being concerned with the consistency and coherency of an individual judicial record" rather than with working toward jurisprudence of the Court acting as a Court (Rosen 2007a, 106). True to form, the Roberts Court rendered a confusing and polarized resolution with Kennedy in the middle on wetlands regulation in *Rapanos;* split into three choruses of voices with no majority opinion in *Randall,* the campaign finance case; issued six different permutations of partial concurrence and partial dissent on racial and partisan gerrymandering in *LULAC;* and rendered Stevens's multipart judgment with important supplementary statements from Kennedy and Breyer in the military commissions case of *Hamdan.*

Consensus remains an elusive thing on the contemporary Supreme Court, and it does seem that the Rehnquist-era understanding of judicial power, both interjustice and interbranch, is responsible. To reiterate, the Rehnquist Court actualized its understanding of interjustice power relations as diffusion, parity, and plurality with respect to policy leadership, judicial voice, and doctrinal contribution. The Rehnquist justices' construal of interbranch judicial power was also judicially focused, but on the preeminence of the judicial institution rather than that of the judicial individual. The upshot was Court pronouncements that were unilateral and uncompromising with respect to the "judicial role" in constitutional interpretation, even when particular constitutional doctrines—whether by content or because of choral, plural presentation—gave the impression of compromise and balancing of interests. The legacy of the "queen's Court," behaviorally speaking at least, would seem to be surviving its namesake. Was the jurisprudential approach of this latter-day O'Connor-style Court also a continuation of a previously exhibited doctrinal style? It is hard to read the aforementioned case records as anything but highly fact-sensitive, conflicting individual reasonability standard renderings of constitutional problems, and they are attributable to O'Connorist jurisprudence per se in the sense that they perpetuate an associates' justice model of doctrinal promulgation.

Brief consideration of the jurisprudential approach taken in the majority opinion and the doctrinal modifications offered by the concurring chorus in each of the four decisions discussed here illustrates this conclusion.

Although this small group of decisions from the second part of the 2005 term is hardly indicative of an overall and continuing trend, the fact that each was a major policy ruling in its respective issue area, receiving extensive coverage in the *New York Times* and the *Washington Post*, makes the use of O'Connorist jurisprudence in any of these Roberts Court rulings potentially noteworthy. Moreover, one could cautiously generalize from the patterns exhibited in these rulings, as they were hardly the only fractured decisions rendered in the 2005–2006 term. As the detailing of "Split Decisions" by the *Wall Street Journal* indicates, several other decisions during the term featured justices peeling off from majority opinions in separate and, at times, hair-splitting concurring doctrinal statements.[4]

Rule-of-thumb juricentrism was on display in the content and stance of the early Roberts Court's resolutions in *Rapanos, Randall, LULAC,* and *Hamdan.* The fragmentation of the majority coalitions in the cases makes summarizing the doctrinal rules challenging. For instance, in *Rapanos,* interpreting the scope of the Clean Water Act protection of "navigable waters," Kennedy's concurrence in the judgment in a five-to-four holding rendered his reasoning the doctrinal guideline of the decision. He opted for the application of a "significant nexus" test between waterways that are navigable, and thus covered by the act, and the wetlands at issue in the regulatory controversy presented by the case. Though Kennedy did not originate this test in his separate opinion, he noted that neither the *Rapanos* plurality nor the dissenting opinion by Stevens had used it, and argued that the best course of action was to remand the case to the court of appeals for "proper consideration of the nexus requirement." He then went on to spend many pages reviewing the same facts, detailed statutory language, and relevant regulations as the other opinions in the case. Definitional differences were important to observe, as when Kennedy remarked with some flourish, "contrary to the plurality's description, wetlands are not simply moist patches of earth." "Nexus was lacking with respect to isolated ponds" but "intermittent or ephemeral streams" might have a sufficient connection to navigable and thus covered waterways, Kennedy stated later in his concurrence, revealing the fact-specific nature of his legal analysis and understanding of the application of the judge-made balancing test from the relevant precedent. "Reasonableness" was Kennedy's message in his *Rapanos* opinion, with the strong suggestion that a reasonable (judicial) observer's rendering of the commandments of the statute regarding water quality protection needed to be conducted.

Randall, decided toward the end of the term, reversed the lower court, invalidating Vermont's restrictive limits on both campaign expenditures and contributions as violating the First Amendment. The decision featured the unusual majority coalition of Breyer, Roberts, and Alito in the plurality, with Kennedy plus Thomas and Scalia joining with special concurrences. Breyer's opinion did little to advance or change the constitutional jurisprudence on political speech, relying heavily as it did on the framework of *Buckley v. Valeo*, itself a fact-sensitive and multipart balancing approach dating from the Burger era. Interestingly, although Alito joined most of Breyer's opinion and analysis of the constitutional problems with the Vermont statute, he parted company from Breyer and the chief in their defense of the *Buckley* precedent out of the concern for stare decisis and adherence to principles that have "become settled through iteration and reiteration over a long period" (slip opinion, 8–10). Though hardly full-blown juricentrism, Breyer's passage on the Court precedent did contain the requisite rhetoric of judicial self-confidence, such as "the rule of law demands that adhering to our prior case law be the norm." Arguably, this was just rhetoric, and not terribly strong or shocking at that; moreover, its purpose was more specific to the case at hand than especially revealing as to its author's vision of the Court's role.

Kennedy's brief concurring opinion also recorded his dissatisfaction with *Buckley*, but less obliquely than Alito's silent nonassent. "Viewed within the legal universe we have ratified and helped create, the result the plurality reaches is correct," Kennedy concurred. Yet, "given my own skepticism regarding that system and its operation," he noted that it seemed "appropriate" to concur only in the judgment. Thomas and Scalia's separate concurrence was even more direct. "The illegitimacy of *Buckley* is further underscored by the continuing inability of the Court (and the plurality here) to apply *Buckley* in a coherent and principled fashion," Thomas wrote. The nature of his objection as well as Kennedy's and Alito's expressions of discomfort with the precedent can be taken as indirect evidence of the early Roberts Court's perpetuation in *Randall* of a rule-of-thumb doctrinal approach as governing the issue of protection for political speech. Of course, this evidence also points to a nascent coalition supportive of replacing that rule-of-thumb doctrinal approach with something else, and something not necessarily rule-of-thumb in conceptualization or operation.

LULAC showed the continuation but also the continuing problems with the rule-of-thumb jurisprudence devised by Justice O'Connor, this time for questions of gerrymandered electoral districts. Kennedy's partial opinion, partial judgment of the Court was a careful but tortuous application of the fact-specific, reasonable-observer standard the Rehnquist Court had put in place for racial vote dilution and equal protection challenges to racial and political gerrymandering in rulings such as *Vieth v. Jubelirer*, *Georgia v. Ashcroft*, and *Thornburg v. Gingles*. As testimony to the future utility of O'Connorist jurisprudence, Kennedy's *LULAC* opinion is sobering. It gave life support to the context-specific analysis of the representation rights issue, but also exemplified the unhelpfulness of that analysis in guiding future districting plans. *Gingles'* three-part test and the "totality of circumstances" approach to adjudging impairments of minority groups' voting strength, along with the fact-rich discussion and assessment entailed by application of each, coexisted with Kennedy's detection—though not articulation—of "a successful test for identifying unconstitutional partisan gerrymandering." Spare and elegant Kennedy's opinion in *LULAC* was not, and his written stance on the problem of partisan bias in electoral districting added new vagaries based on old, O'Connorist opacities. According to Kennedy's description in his opinion, any new test for partisan bias in districting "must show a burden, as measured by *a reliable standard*, on the complainants' representational rights" (emphasis added). But aside from rejecting the petitioners' standard for identifying unconstitutional partisan gerrymandering, Kennedy offered no definition of a "reliable" one—only the cryptic clue that one might be devised, incrementally, in the course of future litigation.

Because the case concerned not only the partisan gerrymandering question but district-specific charges of racial gerrymandering, five separate and distinct partial concurrences/concurrences in the judgment/partial dissents followed Kennedy's plurality opinion. Some agreed with his use but not his actual application of a particular balancing test; others disagreed more sweepingly with his rule-of-thumb-style analysis. Scalia, joined by Thomas, not surprisingly was condemnatory of the rule-of-thumb doctrinal elements Kennedy employed, and completely opposed to political gerrymandering claims as justiciable; once again, this separate opinion was, by nature, indirect confirmation of the new Roberts Court's retention—by a slim majority, anyway—of O'Connorist legal reasoning and policy judgments dependent on judge-made balancing tests.

Finally, *Hamdan* contributed the least rule-of-thumb doctrinal approach but most juricentric policy statement of the four choral rulings of the earliest post-O'Connor Roberts period. It was also a classic exemplar of associates' justice—both in format and in that Chief Justice Roberts did not participate—having been part of the decision in the lower court.

I discussed *Hamdan*'s reliance on the guiding spirit if not the specific guidelines of the Rehnquist Court ruling in *Hamdi v. Rumsfeld* briefly in Chapter 3. Yet Stevens's opinion for the Court in part in *Hamdan* was a much less conciliatory judgment than was O'Connor's plurality opinion in *Hamdi*. Both cases addressed the 2001 joint resolution authorizing the president's use of military force against those involved in the al-Qaeda terrorist attacks, and whether it provided a mandate of executive authority regarding the treatment and prosecution of those detained as a result of the military invasion of Taliban-governed Afghanistan. One of these detainees was Yemeni national Hamdan, who had been held since his battlefield capture and subsequent transfer to the Guantánamo Bay, Cuba, prison facility in 2002 for unspecified crimes; he ultimately filed the federal habeas corpus petition that occasioned Supreme Court review.

"The rules specified for Hamdan's commission trial are illegal," said Stevens in the majority-supported portion of his opinion, not mincing words for the Bush administration. Finding that the president's military commissions to try the detainee enemy combatants at Guantánamo prison were not *expressly* authorized by any congressional statute, Stevens went on to dismiss the administration's argument based on the World War II precedent of *Ex parte Quirin*. Even this case, Stevens scolded, did not view the authorization of military commissions to try offenders of wartime law as a "sweeping mandate for the President to invoke [it] whenever he deems them necessary." Moreover, the structure and procedure of the military commissions outlined violated, by Stevens's assessment, both the Uniform Code of Military Justice (UCMJ) general requirements for courts-martial and the international law of the Geneva Convention on combat detention. Although this latter portion of his argument gained only a plurality, at every legal stage, Stevens's opinion confronted the executive branch. Its doing so from a juricentric constitutional position was clear from the outset of the opinion in the tone of its first segment on jurisdiction. He rejected the administration's urging that the Detainee Treatment Act (DTA) of 2005 gave the D.C. Circuit Court of Appeals "exclusive" jurisdiction to review the final decisions of combat status review tribunals for aliens detained at Guantánamo, rebutting the repeal of the Supreme Court's power to hear the habeas claim with "ordinary principles of statutory construction." In language, Stevens's ruling was much less limited to the "circumstances at hand" than was *Hamdi*, reacting as it did to executive one-upmanship in the DTA[5] and to suspected strategies to elide international laws and treaties. As such, it exhibited less balancing and compromise than emphatic judicial correction to perceived executive overreach,[6] to the effort to use a comprehensive military order to alter the procedural rights guaranteed by the Constitution. Stevens's opinion did acknowledge the relevance of *Ex parte Milligan*'s "controlling necessity" standard governing the president's power to convene military commissions without congressional approval, but declined to develop and apply this context-sensitive approach to *Hamdan*'s separation-of-powers conflict. "The duty which rests on the courts, in time of war as well as in time of peace," Stevens stated, quoting *Quirin*, is "to preserve unimpaired the constitutional safeguards of civil liberty."

Breyer's brief concurrence and Kennedy's concurrence in part were the more modest jurisprudential expressions in the Court's five-to-three ruling, and provided important substantive elements of the decision taken as a whole. Breyer, for instance, highlighted comity and consensus, disarming the majority opinion's uncompromising stance as merely supplying "judicial insistence" upon executive "consultation with Congress" in responding to national danger. Making the same point was Kennedy in concurrence, although with a somewhat more "justice knows best" tutorial quality: "It seems appropriate," he intoned, "to recite these rather fundamental points [about] the authority of Congress and the interpretation of its enactments." Kennedy also provided more doctrinal details than Breyer, reading the situation of Congress setting forth the governing principles for military courts in the UCMJ in terms of Justice Jackson's three-part scheme for adjudging executive action in *Youngstown Sheet and Tube Co. v. Sawyer*. Kennedy, too, had the most nominally rule-of-thumb approach of the majority opinion coalition, noting that "in assessing the validity of *Hamdan*'s military commission the precise circumstances of this case bear emphasis." "At this time," he concluded, "we must apply the standards Congress has provided" in the UCMJ for the prescribed limits on presidential authority. But with a tantalizingly juricentric final twist, Kennedy noted that "Congress can change them, requiring a new analysis consistent with the Constitution." And conducted by the Supreme Court, he need not add.

The four aforementioned Roberts Court rulings enacted the Rehnquist-era understandings of judicial power, both interjustice "associates' justice" modes of doctrinal promulgation and interbranch judicial preeminence attitudes, to various degrees and in various ways. The decisions showed a perpetuation of rule-of-thumb jurisprudence by applying rule-of-thumb-based precedents. From the O'Connorless half of the Roberts transition period, they suggest that the Rehnquist Court legacy is independent of a specific "O'Connor effect." O'Connor's presence on the Court, in other words, did not seem essential to the preservation of O'Connorism on the Court—at least during that first Roberts Court term. Still, the new median justice and the new putative five-to-four polarization of the bench harbored the possibility of rightward drift in the rule of thumbs.

THE PROGNOSIS FOR RULE-OF-THUMB DECISIONS AND OTHER LEGACIES

With Kennedy as that new median justice, the continuation of rule-of-thumb associates' justice coincided with a significant shift in the ideological direction of judicial policy making. "Exhibit A" is, of course, the April 2007 ruling of the Roberts Court in *Gonzales v. Carhart*. With Kennedy at the Court's center and as the voice of the majority coalition, the Roberts Court upheld the Partial-Birth Abortion Ban Act of 2003—with the lack of a health exception[7]— but also upheld the precedent and undue burden standard of *Planned Parenthood v. Casey*. Yet *Gonzales* was clearly a limitation of the *Casey* precedent, for the Kennedy majority permitted the ban on the "intact dilation and extraction" abortion procedure in previability pregnancy situations. The ban was not a "substantial obstacle," as Kennedy's opinion viewed it, to a woman seeking an abortion before the fetus attains viability, because other medical options for different and "less brutal" abortion procedures existed (slip opinion, 26). Moreover, that ban was justified as furthering important state objectives not only protected by the "balance" in *Casey* (slip opinion, 16) but "evident [in] a premise *central to its conclusion*[:] that the government has a legitimate and substantial interest in preserving and promoting fetal life" (slip opinion, 14 [emphasis added]). Recasting the "core holding" in *Casey* also allowed the *Gonzales* Court to recognize "additional ethical and moral concerns" about the so-called partial-birth abortion procedure "that justify a special prohibition" (slip opinion, 28). These included the "reality" that "respect for human life finds an ultimate expression in the bond of love the mother has for her child" (slip opinion, 28), cognizance of a "painful moral decision . . . so fraught with emotional consequence . . . [that] some women come to regret their choice . . . [and suffer] severe depression and loss of esteem" (slip opinion, 29), and promotion of a "dialogue that better informs the political and legal systems, the medical profession, expectant mothers, and society as a whole of the consequences that follow from a decision to elect a late-term abortion" (slip opinion, 30). Education, protection, and improvement of morals are thus coincident to the state's legitimate interest in respect for life and defensible under the constitutional framework of *Casey*, according to the Supreme Court that fashioned and currently interprets and applies that precedent. The rule-of-thumb quality of the undue burden approach to abortion access facilitated *Gonzales's* readjudication of the balance of interests affecting abortion rights as a policy matter. *Gonzales* proceeded to retain the idea but reconceptualize the actuality of an undue burden by continuing to use a rule-of-thumb doctrinal approach. Yet clearly, both the "thumb" and the operative content of the doctrine have changed.

"There is no better guide to where the Court is headed than a careful inventory of where Justice O'Connor has been," wrote one journalist in answer to the question of what to expect in the first post-O'Connor, 2006–2007 term (Liptak 2007). Where O'Connor left rule-of-thumb doctrinal guidelines, the opportunity to refashion their application to a particular factual circumstance exists. Kennedy's "refashioning" in *Gonzales* showed the perils of that opportunity and the flaws in the guidelines themselves. Refashioning their application includes the opportunity to reassess contextual facts and produce a more rightward, less centrist policy statement in a particular controversy. Rule-of-thumb jurisprudence continues in terms of style, with compromise shading toward a more conservative outcome in terms of substantive prescription. This is what O'Connorist jurisprudence makes possible. Is *Gonzales*, then, a continuation of or a departure from the rule-of-thumb undue burden doctrinal test? Or by being both, is it neither, and thus a demonstration of the vacuousness of O'Connorism, with or without O'Connor?

If the holding in *Gonzales* is any indication, it may not matter whether the Roberts Court nominally preserves Rehnquist-era precedents if it incrementally and in all but name overrules them. Still, it is interesting to note that O'Connor's jurisprudential solutions—and their moderate policy accommodations—were revamped by an "O'Connorist" process. If the current Court's decision in *Gonzales* is the beginning of a trend toward recasting existing rule-of-thumb doctrinal approaches, and if that trend manifests itself in specific decisional instances in the same "preserve yet incrementally weaken" way, then the Roberts Court could be seen as influenced by the legacies of its predecessor despite its departures from that predecessor. Supremely individualist, the Roberts justices would find no unanimity of purpose despite their chief's oft-stated commitment to one Court voice. Diffused policy leadership and choral communication of decisions and their doctrinal rules would leave the Roberts Court at the mercy of its median, and still plural-rule, promulgator. Rule-of-thumb balancing and case-by-case adjudication of issues would characterize the Roberts Court's conservative march and retain Court-centrism and Court-dependency for its constitutional project.

Speculation is just that, and speculation about the post-Rehnquist Court should not unduly color the analysis of that Court's legacies. It is more useful to ask what the political, judicial, or other conditions are that would cause the rule-of-thumb balancing approach to constitutional policy making to persist—and then to ask, as a separate, empirical matter, whether those conditions are present for the post-Rehnquist Court. These political, judicial, or other conditions are presumably the same conditions that caused the Rehnquist Court's own behavioral, decisional, and doctrinal judicial individualism.

If we review the possibilities, we come to no simple conclusions about the shelf life of O'Connorism beyond the Roberts transition. In terms of political conditions as a prospective cause, we might posit that an ideologically divided Court yields judicial individualism because a Court divided among conservatives, moderates, and liberals will cohere around no single jurisprudential approach. Each bloc will push for its own approach, with conservatives employing constitutional "rule from the grave" originalism or "lost constitution" textualism, liberals employing "living Constitution" legal liberalism, and moderates wavering issue by issue. This political condition described the Rehnquist justices according to many court watchers of the era, and continued in the early Roberts period. Does the use of rule-of-thumb jurisprudential pragmatism then depend on judicial moderates—even increasingly conservative ones—being in the balance of power on the Court? Possibly, as Thomas's and Scalia's separate concurring statement in *Gonzales*—that the Court's abortion jurisprudence, though correctly applied in the instant case, has no basis in the constitution—suggested, a winning coalition of "nonmoderate" justices would undo at least some of the current rule-of-thumb doctrines. Both new appointees, Roberts and Alito, joined Kennedy's tour de force on the balance of *Casey* in full, paying lip service to stare decisis and retention of the rule-of-thumb undue burden test.

In the end, however, political conditions—and the justices' ideological lineup—better predict polarization and accounting for unstable majority coalitions than explain the doctrinal *content* those conditions perpetuate. The interpretive complexity of rule-of-thumb jurisprudence "works" in political conditions of ideological divergence, but it is unclear how or why judicial divisiveness generates it. There still must be a mechanism—individual, institutional—that produces centrism-by-default doctrine. Nor does ideology alone really account for other decisional process aspects of judicial individualism such as choral decision making.

Judicial conditions are another possible cause of rule-of-thumb jurisprudence, and relate to institutionalized decision-making conventions or the breakdown of judicial institutional norms of consensus and univocality. The use, then, of rule-of-thumb doctrinal approaches depends on associate justice empowerment in a web of judicial individualist decisional conventions, because rule-of-thumb-ism privileges the creativity and sagacity of the individual jurist. But as an accounting of which of the O'Connorist-era balancing tests are likely to endure as precedent, the norms that govern internal decision making are necessary but perhaps not sufficient causal conditions. After all, not all judicial individualists are or would be jurisprudential pragmatists. Some, such as Scalia, are clearly not. Still, there may be other judicial dynamics that cause and thus would perpetuate behavioral aspects of judicial individualism, such as separate opinion writing, the elevation of speaking over winning, and the articulation of the "right position" (one's own) regardless of the ultimate outcome. These dynamics have been characterized as the "audience-based perspective on judicial behavior," and predict that winning personal esteem from a valued reference group audience is a judicial end in itself that fosters personal expression (Baum 2006, 23). Judges' personal expression as judges takes the form of individual opinions and other articulations of judicial philosophy, and serves to cultivate a positive public and media image (136–139) or win admiration from a policy group (123). Seeking such approval mandates personalistic actions, which could include legal doctrine with an unmistakably personalized stamp.

Stubborn adherence to principle and vocal reiteration of it were not new to the Rehnquist Court, but seemed to be more widely shared among its justices than those on previous Courts. Of course, to be fair, without a baseline of institutional unity, it is difficult to judge whether the Rehnquist era was typical or formative for judicial individualism. We lack that accurate baseline—for the simple reason that few thought to analyze the breakdown of unity and contemplate its cause(s) until the rampant individualism of the Rehnquist era.[8] The phenomenon of the Rehnquist period suggests but cannot confirm that the aforementioned judicial institutional conditions did cause and will preserve the behavioral and decisional aspects of judicial individualism. And although these judicial conditions predict less well its doctrinal content, the Court's greater pluralism in decision making and plurality of decisional outputs theoretically jibe with the personally tailored flavor of the O'Connorist-era doctrinal approach.

There is a final possibility in accounting for the judicial individualism that dominated the Rehnquist Court and explaining the persistence of the rule-of-thumb balancing approach to constitutional policy making. It is neither political nor judicial, strictly speaking. It is that the array of issues facing the modern Supreme Court has become so wide that voting coherence and doctrinal clarity are hard if not impossible to maintain. One currently sitting justice has herself posited that the increasing complexity of Supreme Court cases invariably produces no single opinion to express a clear majority.[9] The justices are left to parse matters for themselves, and their precedential rules—such as they are—are left to the lower courts to decipher. In such an issue climate, judicial individualism and rule-of-thumb jurisprudence are the only ways to manage. Multivocal decisions are inevitable and exemplify the balancing of interests that a choral body ultimately pronounces. O'Connorism copes without clarifying and might even make matters worse—though one could only charge this if one could claim that any other, better response to the Court's multifaceted contemporary agenda was available.

Is there one? Before addressing this question, we must admit that the Supreme Court's agenda has been diversifying for quite some time, and has always included issues of great policy significance, *pace* de Tocqueville. Its potential legal policy prescriptions, then, are arguably no more diverse and potentially fragmentizing now than they ever were—unless we wish to say that jurisprudential options have so proliferated as a result that juridical agreement is unlikely, if not impossible. If so, the only agreement likely is non- or adoctrinal: pure rule-of-thumb, case-by-case adjudication by aggregation of judicial votes. Since someone must write the opinion that frames or aggregates the decision, that someone will be he or she who articulates the inarticulate: a pragmatic "rule." The Rehnquist Court guided by O'Connor grasped this principle and embraced it, performing it again and again. O'Connorism was a response facilitated by O'Connor and her Court. O'Connor-era rule-of-thumb precedents were situational resolutions only; by definition, they have minimal intrinsic or extendable validity because they frame without giving guidance. The "model" Supreme Court justice simply understood her circumstances and adapted her Court to them.

If such an agenda-based account of judicial individualism is persuasive, then O'Connor's jurisprudence is a predictive though not necessarily inspiring model for the Roberts Court and the contemporary institution in general. The account and the model square with the record of the "queen regent's Court" in the Roberts Court transition period. But is the doctrinally pragmatist O'Connorist Court—likely in light of the aforementioned causal forces—the best one can expect in the modern constitutional and judicial age? Or is the commitment to an interpretively complex and coyly consequentialist doctrinal approach a commitment to promote the most ambitious, challenging, and ultimately dissatisfactory form of judicial decision making?[10] The concluding chapter considers this sobering question of the potentially problematic legacy of judicial power in the Rehnquist era.

Judges relish the power of their institution, according to political science and popular culture.[1] And unequivocal opinions, scholars of political development have assumed, enhance judicial power.[2] But the "victory" represented by a unitary opinion of the Court is far from guaranteed these days. "Today's appellate judges," observes legal scholar John Orth, "are less willing to unite in a single statement. . . . Multiple opinions [have] proliferated" (2006, 41).

Orth's point seems well illustrated by the decision summary for a recent Second Circuit Court of Appeals case addressing an application of the Voting Rights Act, which read as follows:

> The Court of Appeals (Jose A. Cabranes, Circuit Judge) concludes that the Voting Rights Act must be construed to not encompass prisoner disenfranchisement provisions such as that of New York. . . . Accordingly the Court dismisses plaintiffs' Voting Rights Act claims challenging New York Election Law sec. 5-106 and remands for further proceedings consistent with this opinion.
>
> Chief Judge Walker concurs in the judgment and in the opinion of the Court and files a separate concurring opinion, joined by Judge Jacobs.
>
> Judge Jacobs concurs in the judgment and in the opinion of the Court and files a separate concurring opinion.
>
> Judge Straub concurs in the judgment of the Court and in parts I, II, and IV of the opinion of the Court, and files a separate concurring opinion, joined by Judge Sack.

Judge Sack concurs in the judgment of the Court and in parts I, II, and IV of the opinion of the Court, and files a separate concurring opinion, part I of which is joined by Judge Straub.

Judge Raggi concurs in the judgment and in the opinion of the Court and files a separate concurring opinion, joined by Judge Jacobs.

Judge Parker dissents, in an opinion in which Judges Calabresi, Pooler, and Sotomayor concur.

Judge Calabresi dissents in a separate opinion.

Judge Sotomayor dissents in a separate opinion.

Judge Katzmann dissents in a separate opinion.[3]

Compare this with the decision summary for the Roberts Court's June 2006 ruling in the Texas redistricting case from its inaugural term:

Kennedy, J., announced the judgment of the Court and delivered the opinion of the Court with respect to Parts II-A and III, in which Stevens, Souter, Ginsburg, and Breyer, JJ., joined, an opinion with respect to Parts I and IV, in which Roberts, C. J., and Alito, J., joined, an opinion with respect to Parts II-B and II-C, and an opinion with respect to Part II-D, in which Souter and Ginsburg, JJ., joined. Stevens, J., filed an opinion concurring in part and dissenting in part, in which Breyer, J., joined as to Parts I and II. Souter, J., filed an opinion concurring in part and dissenting in part, in which Ginsburg, J., joined. Breyer, J., filed an opinion concurring in part and dissenting in part. Roberts, C. J., filed an opinion concurring in part, concurring in the judgment in part, and dissenting in part, in which Alito, J., joined. Scalia, J., filed an opinion concurring in the judgment in part and dissenting in part, in which Thomas, J., joined, and in which Roberts, C. J., and Alito, J., joined as to Part III.[4]

A new decisional paradigm or a recent decisional pathology? Legal historians might comment that the developmental shift from an even- to an odd-numbered Supreme Court made manifest "a changing assumption about whether deliberation on legal subjects by trained judges is likely to result in disagreement"—thereby justifying the need for a tie-breaking vote (Orth 2006, 16). The expectation and acceptance of disagreement over legal issues obviously predate the fractious Rehnquist Court. Indeed, Thomas Jefferson, "so exercised by the possibility of a decision 'by a majority of one' being presented as the opinion of the Court," argued for requiring the justices to announce their individual opinions publicly, serially, so that all would have to speak up and be accountable (Orth 2006, 19). Jefferson's prescription of 1820 has been fulfilled in the proliferating separate judicial opinions of the 1990s and 2000s.

There was nevertheless a proximate cause for the contemporary manifestation of the deeply rooted dissensus in American appellate judging: "O'Connorism," which previous chapters have explained as the *behavioral emphasis on and jurisprudential expression of the individual justice's creative preeminence* on the multimember, collegial decision-making body of the U.S. Supreme Court. The ways that O'Connor exercised influence as an associate justice and the legacies of those actions for the institution and its decisional output were her particular contribution to the judicial individualism of the contemporary era.

NAMING AND BLAMING: THE SOBRIQUET "O'CONNORISM"

The practice of the past two centuries of signed majority opinions "emphasize[d] the role and voice of the individual Justice," but "at the same time as the edicts of the Court's majority [were] being expressed" (Chemerinsky 2002, 2032). The Supreme Court as an institution does foreground the individual judicial voice—and, frequently, judge-made legal test—as its communicative device. But on the contemporary Court, fragmented, plural opinions became an ever more common pattern for communicating "the Court's" policy pronouncements. According to one study, these closely divided, finely parsed, and often criticized rulings coincided with a measurable loss of public opinion poll support for Rehnquist Court decisions (Marshall 2005, 180). The Rehnquist Court allegedly failed to move American public opinion through its choral and contextual-factor-oriented decision making (Sracic 2000).

Yet, conversely, the Rehnquist Court's judicial self-assertiveness also failed to galvanize a public reaction to the politicized nature of Supreme Court action—as the nonplussed public opinion in the wake of the politically charged decision in *Bush v. Gore* (2000) suggests (Gibson, Caldeira, and Spence 2003; Kritzer 2005; Nicholson and Howard 2003). Whatever the public backlash or lack thereof, the Rehnquist Court's hands-on approach to many issues of public policy, combined with its individual justices' vigorous doctrinal participation in these legal policy debates, marked a judicial body that took itself—and its selves—seriously.

That self-seriousness manifested itself methodologically. The Rehnquist Court honed to a finely tuned practice the careful retention of precedential standards through the creation of fact-based exceptions to them. The justices, of course, and especially the Court's centrists, were the ultimate arbiters of those exceptions. The circumspect doctrinal standards governing the Rehnquist Court's judicial intrusion into the policy arena employed and emphasized reasonableness balancing and the pluralism of judicial viewpoints. At times this approach occasioned confusing cross-referencing and quoting between justices in their separate opinions, and exemplified "the Court's response to complex legal issues in a system which place[d] no formal limit on the prerogative of each judge to speak out separately" (Ellington 1998, 823). The Court also fostered a decisional methodology that seemed restrained in particular cases, but in reality profoundly increased judicial power and discretion because doctrinal promulgation was a perpetually aggregative and additive process. Although this is, to some degree, the common law method, O'Connorism as a practice of constitutional interpretation takes the cumulative distillation of judge-made rules into precedent to new lengths—such that doctrine is never truly set, and so never really governs judicial choice.

O'Connorist jurisprudence, of course, only reinforced certain truths about judicial interpretation in a common law system: that "doctrinal unpredictability is critical to a developmental scheme valuing both adaptability and durability," and that "the definition of the Constitution is more a competitive than a conclusive exercise."[5] So the behavioral emphasis on and jurisprudential expression of individual justices' creative preeminence were not an entirely new decisional paradigm. Nor was the doctrinal methodology attached to it—which frequently smacked of judiciousness for its own sake—roundly condemned as recent or even pathological. At most, its detrimentally juricentric nature was critiqued, but its jurisprudential drawbacks were overshadowed by its ultimate political convenience. Indeed, the justices' arbitration of fact-based exceptions to malleable standards and their assuredness of purpose in doing so came to seem acceptable. No doubt the prudentialism of the results—the moderate compromises—O'Connor and the other Rehnquist justices produced in their judicial practice lent a certain credence to it.[6] Messy and invasive, O'Connorism was nevertheless made palatable by its very pluralistic flexibility, that is, the lack of bright-line commandments in this jurisprudence and the multiple opinions expressing it.

Despite public acquiescence, the rule-of-thumb balancing approach that so often characterized the opinions of Associate Justice Sandra Day O'Connor—hence, the doctrinal pronouncements of the Rehnquist Court—creates certain problems for the federal judiciary. The most obvious difficulty is that the Supreme Court either must revisit these issues constantly or be content to let crucial matters be decided by the lower courts. The latter may well have been the dynamic by default during the Rehnquist years, given the declining plenary docket and diminished supervisory role the High Court assumed (O'Brien 2005a). Yet even unsupervised, the federal appellate courts in fact may have carried out these instructions too well, for the decision-making style and jurisprudential approach that characterized the Rehnquist bench arguably have trickled down and effectively (1) changed opinion writing of lower federal courts and (2) empowered individual appellate judges. It is certainly the case that lower federal courts have grown accustomed to Supreme Court decisions that are more detailed and more divided into parts, and to reading them carefully to ascertain their meaning, such that plurality opinions are no different than majority opinions when it comes to treatment by or compliance on the part of lower courts (Corley 2007). Relatedly, separate opinion authorship is not uncommon on federal circuit courts, and both concurrence and dissent are clearly linked to identifiable policy and institutional goals of these judges (Hettinger, Lindquist, and Martinek 2003). Coping with or copying a common practice of split decisions and judicial chorality, federal appellate judges are no strangers to a declining norm of consensus.

Judicial individualism, multivocal decisions, and individual jurists' creative preeminence thus feed on one another, systemically, with the individualism of the contemporary Supreme Court reproducing itself in the lower federal courts. As the aforementioned studies of the decline of consensus in the courts of appeal demonstrate, lower federal judges are afflicted with "do as I do." Another problem specific to the rule-of-thumb doctrinal approach coincident with the Rehnquist Court's performance of judicial individualism involves, for want of a better term, the "rule of law." As one O'Connor critic has phrased it: "Open-ended balancing tests and flexible standards do not, by themselves, undermine the rule of law. But when the factors used in these tests are applied by judges mysteriously, and the weights assigned to the various elements used in the balancing tests are left unexplained, rule of law problems do emerge" (Segall 2006, 109). Those "rule of law problems" are that lower courts are handed doctrine difficult to understand and impossible to apply, and must themselves resort to O'Connoresque "exercises in deciding each case as if no other case matters" (Segall 2006, 136). In the best of situations, standards-based legal doctrines delegate decision-making authority to the judicial decision maker—of whatever level court—at the point of application, and thus require more information and decisional competence from rule appliers than rule creators (Vermeule 2006, 69). But even informed and competent judges who apply higher court directives in particular cases at a later time require some direction. Idiosyncratic judicial balancing tests in the hands of pluralists by temperament and/or political moderates (or judicial moderates with some practical political experience) may yield tolerable if constitutionally ineloquent political results. Those ineloquent results, however, of ad hoc decision making by higher court rule formulators yield "expensive, time consuming, and agonizing lower court litigation" (Segall 2006, 135) that is more conducive to legal inconsistency than legal transparency and predictability.

Taken to a logical extreme, O'Connorist rules of thumb fragment legal policy making by the federal judiciary to the point of total doctrinal implosion. Candidly speaking, the systemic consequences of judicial obfuscation at the highest level of doctrinal promulgation are confused and unstable expectations about the commandments of the law. One case at a time without any guidelines is not the rule of law at all, Solomonic though each discrete dispute resolution might be. O'Connorist doctrine approached this state of affairs in some policy areas, such as nondiscrimination in electoral districting. The circuit court case headnote with which this chapter began shows one result: each and every appellate judge must "know voting equality when he/she sees it"—and express it in the judicial chorus. How much disarray or at least delegation the legal and judicial system can stand before it collapses is as of yet an untested proposition of O'Connor-era decisional conventions.

A damning indictment, surely, of O'Connorism and the supreme judicial individualism that nurtures it. But what nurtured judicial individualism on the Rehnquist-era Supreme Court? Is the above bleak forecast an extended one?

As a High Court phenomenon, supreme judicial individualism stemmed from the coincidence of several specific things. One was the division among the Court's modern Republicans as to judicial activism and its place within "conservative" jurisprudence (Keck 2004; Tushnet 2006). Although none interpreted legal conservatism as judicial restraint, the Republican jurists nevertheless had singularly different messages to impart regarding the newly ascendant judicial ethos. O'Connor made an obvious contribution here: she was a player among those jurists, a centrist Republican and moderate jurist who endorsed most of the Supreme Court's active policy pronouncements—right and left—during her tenure. But her importance for the specter of "nine individuals pursuing distinctive variations" extended beyond her particular ideological niche among the justices to her approach to the influence and importance of the associate justice position.

That approach built upon and furthered the institutional decentralization in decision making gripping the modern Court. The withering of institutional norms of consensus was a second factor responsible for the rampant individualism dominating the Rehnquist Court. O'Connor alone did not exhibit Rehnquist-era judicial individualism, nor did she single-handedly drive a supremely individualist Court, but her contributions were specific and identifiable and shaped the Court on which she served. Hers was rule-of-thumb jurisprudence as active judicial engagement in deciding what policies are (constitutionally) reasonable and why, and hers was collaborative judicial engagement over reasonableness standards with its concomitant tendency to produce many individual refinements—that is, separate opinion statements.

O'Connor was not, of course, the first powerful associate justice in history, for the precedents of Van Devanter as the social leader of the Taft Court, Black as the intellectual giant of the early Warren Court, and Brennan as the majority maker of the late Warren and Burger Courts come to mind. Nor was O'Connor the first great judicial pragmatist and wielder of the separate opinion to enunciate "(juris)prudentialism" (Broughton 1999). That distinction belongs to the second Justice Harlan (Ellington 1998), to whom O'Connor has been compared for her precedent-oriented and conservative balancing approach to fundamental rights (Anders 1993).

The power and prominence of associate justices on the Supreme Court have long pedigrees, but attained a new institutional significance for intra-Court operations during Associate Justice O'Connor's tenure. It may seem ironic or somehow misplaced to call a "queen" an associate justice who by her actions helped further decentralization of decision-making power on the modern Supreme Court. Indeed, the regal metaphor rather implies more of a snipe at Rehnquist—his inability to wield the power of his realm—and the individualist disarray that ensued. Although former Rehnquist clerk Chief Justice Roberts has said that Rehnquist was a successful chief "because of his temperament," even he admitted that Rehnquist "cared somewhat about building consensus, but not all that much" (Rosen 2006, 231, 233). Famous for the apocryphal allusion to his job as "herding hogs on ice," perhaps Chief Justice Rehnquist's noted commitment to his critical but burdensome administrative duties as the third branch leader and advocate and presiding officer of the Judicial Conference of the United States (Hudson 2007; Wheeler 2005) left a leadership vacuum[7] the strategic centrist O'Connor was simply able to fill. This confluence of personal leadership styles, complementary for their decentralizing impact, was another factor presaging the judicial individualism of the Rehnquist Court period.

The diffused policy leadership, multivocal decision making, individual jurists' creative preeminence, and rule-of-thumb balancing jurisprudence—the elements of the contemporary Supreme Court—seem both reactive and learned. They are reactive to political and judicial conditions on the Court and, as I explored at the end of Chapter 5, to the expansive complexity of its modern agenda of legal and administrative issues. They are learned in that they constitute the institutional norms and practices of the contemporary appellate multimember court judicial process in which judges render decisions and make policy. As elements reactive to replicable or continuing conditions and learned on the job, there is no reason to expect their discontinuation on or confinement to the High Court. Long live O'Connorism indeed.

REMEMBERING THE "CONSTITUTIONAL" MONARCHY OF THE QUEEN'S COURT

Chief Justice Roberts has labeled the behavioral and methodological individualism of the contemporary period of the Supreme Court "the personalization of judicial politics" (Rosen 2007a, 106). For some, a "modest judiciary" would be the correction (Harnett 2006, 1758). For some—including the current chief justice—one possible correction is jurisprudential sparseness and judicial humility. In this he seems to be invoking all those court commentators who drew from the Rehnquist record the lesson of a return to restraint. But is saying little and doing little, even to produce univocality, necessarily a virtue? Not according to two Rehnquist Court veterans at this writing sitting on the Roberts bench. In a public debate with Justice Stephen Breyer on the new aspiration for narrowly based unanimity, Justice Scalia retorted, "lots of luck," and then went on to suggest that unanimity isn't all that it's cracked up to be (Mauro 2006). With Breyer concurring in the sentiment, Scalia remarked that any case can be reduced to a narrow, technical holding, although it serves neither the lower courts nor the country to do so (Lithwick 2007). This criticism of lack of doctrinal guidance from the highest court in the federal judicial system is the same one leveled at the rule-of-thumb balancing approach of O'Connorism.

Reforming an immodest judiciary could also come through Supreme Court use of clear doctrinal rules with unambiguous application and a constitutionally legitimate pedigree. The rules need not be narrow in scope,[8] but they would restrict or narrow an implementing court's compliance options. Their enunciation would reduce uncertainty in the legal system and contain judicial discretion—two problems endemic in the use of O'Connoresque standards for fact-sensitive balancing. Despite the surface appeal of such a remedy, rule-based judging necessitates satisfaction of several difficult conditions both empirically and theoretically. The first is identifying unambiguous, legitimately derived rules. What form do they take, what is their appropriate interpretive pedigree, and, equally important, what stance should courts take toward precedents that do not espouse such clear doctrinal rules? Is reconciliation or repudiation of the offending precedent the more "modest" course of action? A second difficulty is judges' reliance for rule-based decisions on judicial vision of correct principles and appropriate rules both in content and in source. These difficulties can only be resolved by an equally difficult maxim: "trust the judge" to create and identify "rules," to clear the doctrinal underbrush of directionless standards, to envision the principles of the constitutional polity. None of these targets of trust sound like particularly modest or restrained activities, and all would seem to require the same level of confidence in judicial wisdom on which O'Connorist jurisprudence depends.[9] If the Rehnquist Court commentators illustrated anything, it was diminished contemporary faith in judicial review of the constitutional order. To make such faith the centerpiece of a reconceptualized and corrected, albeit rule-governed, judicial function seems misguided or naive.

There is one other option for a modest judiciary to correct the excesses of judicial individualism: renounce the "judge-besotted constitutional culture" (Vermeule 2006, 12) and adopt the antijuricentric vision of certain Rehnquist Court commentators that I discussed in Chapter 4. The unhealthy preoccupation with what the Supreme Court says, and even more unhealthy pretense that what it says is "final" until it changes its mind, could be replaced entirely by an understanding of constitutional interpretation as a collaborative political process (Devins and Fisher 2004). A limited scope for judicial authority would remain, for statutory interpretation (governed by textual formalism) and obvious error correction (of statutes that transgressed clear and unambiguous constitutional language), but gone would be personalized judicial politics and pronouncements. Although attractively straightforward in its clarity of purpose, this anti–Supreme Court and judge-free constitutional review is clearly more than a correction of O'Connorism: it is a wholesale shift in systemic confidence. Leaving aside whether it is deserved or desirable, this populist remedy may be impracticable given the perennially high figures for "current" public dissatisfaction with the political branches, Congress, and the presidency, bodies that presumably would be central to the dialogue about constitutional norms.

Although these "neonarrowist" versions of a modest judiciary are fraught with conceptual and implementation complications, their deficiencies likely will not cloud the critical eye now trained on judicial power as a result of the era of supreme judicial individualism. A Roberts Court that carries on in the vein of its predecessor will mean that judicial restraint as jurisprudential humility, or at least univocal reticence, will continue to be a chimera or a sham. Never at a loss for words of criticism, Justice Scalia already lambasted the new Court for "faux judicial restraint," citing (in his own unrestrained concurring opinion) the cravenness of a Roberts majority's incremental, sophist weakening of a Rehnquist Court rule-of-thumb precedent.[10] We are seemingly no closer to a clear-eyed understanding of judicial restraint in the wake of the O'Connorist Rehnquist period, nor a forthright account of what this judicial role does and does not entail.

Yet the judicial dissembling Scalia skewered may provide a way toward that account by hinting at the real detrimental impact of O'Connor-style judicial pragmatism for the Supreme Court as an institution as part of the individualist legacy. The upshot is that preserving the rule of thumbs and rule-of-thumbism in the name of judicial restraintism is fundamentally dishonest—no matter how politically realistic or expedient it might be. To call O'Connorism restraintist, or to call a Court performing (or continuing) an O'Connorist role the best (or least worst) one can expect, all things considered, is to lay the groundwork for further compliance with a doctrinal approach that perpetuates idiosyncratic judicial balancing or "judgment" but not "fessing up" to it. As a general formula for judicial power, the decisional conventions of this judicial role have potentially distressing implications.

Decentralized, multivocal, and rule-of-thumb decision-making conventions certainly can be derided for the problems of efficacy in law-based governance they create. But they also present a critical problem of legitimacy. Taken to a politically calculative extreme, a rule-of-thumb approach masks ideological legal policy making as "judicious" balancing of interests and adapting of precedential guidelines. This is perhaps the greatest danger and the most worrisome legacy of the "model justice" as a judicial guide. The memory inures us to judicial power without frankly acknowledging it as such, and provides comfort and cover where none should exist for unaccountable and possibly unwarranted judicial decision making.

The queen's Court enshrined but also defanged the decisional conventions of the juridical role of supreme judicial individualism. The practical and pluralist-seeming methodology of O'Connorism during O'Connor's service papered over its dysfunctions with accommodation of divergent interests both among the Court's policy makers and in the polity at large. Its institutional and decisional practices of decentralized policy leadership and empowerment of judicial associates, choral communication of Court decisions that privileged multiple judicial voices, circumstantial balancing standards that required continuing appeals to individual judicial reason, and institutional confidence in judicial constitutional reasoning were not externally restraintist. They exerted and extended judicial influence and policy discretion. But they were internally pluralist. For the High Court, "O'Connor Court" internal power-sharing procedures were an important developmental benchmark. Yet political scientists who study the courts should not forget that pluralist institutions empower those interests best equipped to organize and bargain effectively.[11] On the Rehnquist Court, that was the strategic accommodationist O'Connor and her shifting centrist coalitional adherents. Under her sway, Court power was benevolently inclusive of centrist plural interests even as it was emphatically not institutionally limited or limiting. Her rule-of-thumb Court was moderate without being especially modest.

The limits observed by that "constitutional monarch," the queen's Court, depended less on structural guarantees (as is the case with most constitutional monarchies) than on sovereign self-effacement and disinclination toward extreme solutions. This personal or behavioral predilection arguably produces restrained, measured actions, as would a successor's continuation of rule-of-thumb-ism and other pluralist judicial practices. But the balancing approaches and empowered, pragmatic judicial pluralities easily can be put to work for more ambitious, less conciliatory accomplishments that are then, disconcertingly, rendered hard to criticize in terms of invalid juridical methods or ends. O'Connorism's wrapping dresses as it conceals the vagaries of judicial power.

This impression came about because the rule-of-thumb balancing approach seemed restrained for particular case outcomes. Methodologically, it eschewed bright-line solutions or extreme judicial exertions of influence. But with each usage, this jurisprudential approach validated and increased judicial discretionary power. Its incrementalist development of legal doctrine also incrementally developed judicial power, along with faith in both the wisdom and correctness of that power. The evolutionary implications of O'Connorist jurisprudential theory and individualist judicial practice are troubling not because they extol the expertise of the judicial technician but because they extol the political craft of negotiated policy compromise *as* an appropriate judicial craft. Lost is any notion that legal principle governs or restrains judging, because there is no referent external to the judge's view of what is reasonable. To some degree, of course, judicial interpretation in the American constitutional context was always founded, at bottom, in the "judicial reasonable person" and his or her view of constitutional and precedential rules. Judicial O'Connorism, however, renders judicial interpretation without any other foundation, limitation, or basis for critique. If judicial angels—or "models"—are to govern, all to the good, but if not, justices must be obliged to control themselves through more than noblesse oblige.

The Supreme Court of the Rehnquist period was never the juricentric monster some critics portrayed it to be. But the new devotion to restrained judging it engendered was misplaced when applied to its "first among equals" associate justice. O'Connor was admired as a "model" not because of her restraint but *despite* her lack of it. Her legacy, like her Court's, became confused in the process of remembrance. Rehnquist Court behavioral and jurisprudential legacy may be long-lived, as it is now probably institutionally and ideationally entrenched. But there is the potential for great mischief—even well intentioned—from its approach to judicial power, and this is the true risk of long-lived O'Connorism. Accepting and remembering the queen's Court as a constitutionally limited monarch misapprehends limits, and so becomes unable to see their transgression by an heir.

NOTES

INTRODUCTION: A SUPREMELY INDIVIDUALIST LEGACY

1. The chat site http://after-words.org and its "grim amusements" are illustrative here.

2. Senator Cornyn of Texas, a Republican, later picked up on Leahy's phrase in his questioning of nominee Judge Samuel Alito, arguing that he indeed measured up to "the model Supreme Court justice who is clearly in the mainstream."

3. Among the statements made during her extended resignation period was her reminder that she wished to be remembered simply as "a good judge," as she had commented during her confirmation hearings in 1981.

4. Nor was she the political scientists' justice in the sense of expeditiously bequeathing her judicial papers for academic attention. With the recent action by Justice Blackmun clearly in mind, O'Connor joined two of her fellow justices in a "Statement of Understanding about the Release of Court Working Papers" to then chief justice Rehnquist. They worried about untimely or premature disclosure of confidential views and the resultant harm to the vital and creative processes of the Court, suggesting a ten-year-minimum rule for public release of judicial papers (Blackmun Papers, Memo of June 17, 1993, Box 627, Folder 3). As I observe in note 3, O'Connor in many ways embraced—and cultivated—an apolitical image as a jurist.

5. He finishes the statement by adding, "Her judicial approach was indefensible in theory and impeccable in practice" (226). The Conclusion of this book takes up this matter.

CHAPTER 1. POLICY LEADERSHIP ON THE EARLY REHNQUIST COURT

1. O'Brien (2005) defines policy leadership by justices on the Court as "persuading others to vote in ways (in the short and long run) favorable to their policy goals" (252).

2. Johnson's (2004) research along with comments by certain sitting justices suggest that oral argument became such a forum for exerting influence over the group product. As Justice Kennedy observed, citing Justice Stevens in assent, "what is happening [in oral argument] is the Court having a conversation with itself through the intermediary of the attorney" (O'Brien 2005, 247).

3. Compare this figure with similar figures produced by Epstein and Knight (1998) using cases orally argued in the 1983 Burger Court term and landmark cases from 1969 to 1985: in 84 percent of cases examined, at least one substantive memorandum (suggesting revision or describing future action) was circulated; in more than two-thirds of the landmark cases, at least one justice tried to bargain with the majority

opinion writer; and in more than half of the cases (65 percent of landmark cases), a significant change occurred in the language of the opinion.

4. For Epstein and Knight's definition of a "substantive" memorandum, see page 10.

5. Tables detailing this descriptive information can be found in an appendix available from the author upon request.

6. Powell, Souter, and Kennedy were notable practitioners of this old-style bargaining and influence tool, in their exchanges with Blackmun. Since Blackmun's papers are the chapter's source, personal notes to Blackmun are the only hard evidence at hand. But presumably, the aforementioned justices used note-writing tactics with other colleagues with whom they had a rapport.

7. The case in question was *Stansburg v. California*.

8. The entire statement is as follows: "Barry Goldwater, during his 1964 run for the Presidency, was asked why he spent so much time campaigning in the South. His response was that 'You have to go hunting where the ducks are.' That is the position I find myself in in this case" (Memo of June 10, 1992, Box 646, Folder 6).

9. As Blackmun's clerk characterized the process in her June 2, 1994, memo to the justice, "If you *add your voice to the chorus*, [O'Connor] may have no choice but to reconsider her refusal to make the requested changes" (Box 647, Folder 5 [emphasis added]). Whether "choral" decision making exhibits individualistic or collective leadership is taken up in Chapter 2.

10. With the play on words, O'Connor is making a joke of the question of whether a taking had occurred, an issue that had divided the justices for a time in the case.

CHAPTER 2. THE CHORAL COURT OF SEPARATE VOICES

1. From Box 130b of the Lewis F. Powell, Jr. Papers (cited in Ward and Weiden 2006, 217).

2. There is a 1977 memo from Powell's outgoing administrative clerk to the justice's incoming clerk that likewise suggests proactive drafting within chambers of separate statements for potential circulation: "It is useful to offer the Justice a draft of the suggested changes [to the circulated opinion] or separate opinion as soon as possible. . . . This procedure not only improves your 'bargaining power,' but permits the Justice to see whether the suggested position will write before he decides how to vote" (Ward and Weiden 2006, 156).

3. The year 1964 was the first Court year in which cases with at least one concurring opinion topped 30 percent. A rate of 35–40 percent was sustained by the middle years of the Burger Court era, and has continued ever since.

4. They were also unwilling to support bright-line articulations of liberal doctrinal positions, as Kennedy demonstrated by his desertion of the *Planned Parenthood v.*

Casey (1992) coalition in the so-called partial-birth abortion decision, and O'Connor revealed in her dissent in the 2005 juvenile death penalty case of *Roper v. Simmons*.

5. As another study remarks, "Ginsburg's writings indicate that she values the power of the separate opinion, and . . . makes use of the dissent and concurrence with a precision and a purpose that parallels Harlan [II]" (Ellington 1998, 821).

6. Figures throughout this section, unless otherwise noted, are derived from the Benesh-Spaeth Database (2005), which goes up through the 2004 term, as first reported in Nancy Maveety, Charles C. Turner, and Lori Beth Way, "Changes in the Use of Concurrence: The Burger and Rehnquist Courts Compared," presented to the annual meeting of the American Political Science Association, Chicago, Illinois, September 2–5, 2004.

7. It is, therefore, an open question who the intended audiences are for concurring opinions by Supreme Court justices. Baum's audience-based perspective on judicial behavior (2006) argues that judicial self-presentation should be considered in any model of judicial decision making, but acknowledges the difficulty in identifying the constellations of audiences that affect any particular judge (171–174).

8. As reflected by mean ideology scores; see discussion in Maveety, Turner, and Way (2004), n. 11.

9. See Maveety (2003), 112, table 7.

10. "Statistics," *Harvard Law Review* 118, no. 1: 579, table 3.

11. A more recent, extreme example of this phenomenon of decision by a chorus of majority voices was the Court's ruling in *McConnell v. Federal Election Commission* (2003), upholding parts of the Bipartisan Campaign Reform Act of 2002 and finding some parts unconstitutional. The "opinion" of the Court was delivered in three separate installments by Stevens and O'Connor, by Rehnquist, and by Breyer. (Stevens and Rehnquist also filed dissenting opinions of their own.) Three justices filed partial concurrences/partial dissents: Scalia, Kennedy, and Thomas. The decision, like the statute it addressed, was complex and multifaceted and, needless to say, difficult to comprehend without a careful reading.

12. Memo of December 20, 1991, Blackmun Papers, Box 586, Folder 9.

13. Memo of April 15, 1992, Blackmun Papers, Box 586, Folder 6.

14. Memo of April 6, 1992, Blackmun Papers, Box 586, Folder 10 (emphasis added).

15. The marked judicial dissensus on the Roosevelt Courts also precipitated the behavioral revolution in the study of judging and the insistence that politics as much as law animated judicial decisions. Such views sparked ideologically oriented understandings of judicial decision making and the "attitudinal model" of judicial behavior.

16. The findings of Ward and Weiden (2006) challenge this unmediated ideological connection. "Because most clerks apply to every justice," they observe, "the process of achieving ideological congruence has been made more difficult and has resulted in increasing partisan differences among clerks who work for the same justice, which in turn has led to certain clerks being more influential than others" (108).

CHAPTER 3. ASSOCIATES' JUSTICE

1. To be fair, Sunstein singled out O'Connor as exemplifying "conservative minimalism" and Ruth Bader Ginsburg as exemplifying "liberal minimalism." But the most illustrative minimalist decisions from the modern Court were largely O'Connor's.

2. A term used to designate a variant of judicial supremacy. The significance of this encapsulation of the Rehnquist Court's exhibition of its judicial power for court commentators' construction of the judicial role in a constitutional democracy in general, and during the Rehnquist period in particular, is discussed in Chapter 4.

3. Vermeule (2006) remarks that legal pragmatism could be construed as "a form of consequentialism that rests upon a suppressed, implicit, but indispensable appeal to *convergence on particulars* across a range of value theories" (85).

4. Or, whether certain justices were privileged creative actors, the jurists largely responsible for adjusting the Court's judge-made balancing tests during readjudication of the constitutional issues—operating as a "queen's cabinet Court."

5. As something akin to a legal pragmatic methodology of judicial "sagacity." For further discussion of the Rehnquist justices' alleged commitment to individualized judicial earnestness as a role orientation, see Chapter 4.

6. Attitudinalists would not think so, expecting only that the pivotal or ideologically median justice would support the median outcome. The jurisprudential trappings of such judicial action would scarcely matter.

7. The exchange occurred on the LAWCOURTS listserv (LAWCOURTS-L@usc.edu) on September 15, 2006, and involved participants from law schools and political science departments.

8. She also dissented in *Gratz*, the companion case to *Grutter* in the Michigan litigation that split the difference on affirmative action policies for university admissions, but her approach governed the Court's overall compromise settlement of the issue.

9. Coincidentally (or not), this was an O'Connor majority opinion.

10. *U.S. v. Booker*, 543 U.S. 220 (2005), which invalidated mandatory federal sentencing guidelines as violating the Sixth Amendment, was certainly also consequential for criminal justice policy. But the cacophonous split of the Court rendered the decision more of a doctrinal first word than a "last word." Among the pressing issues

in federal sentencing that require follow-up analysis are what "advisory" guidelines mean and how much discretion federal judges actually have in imposing sentences shorter than the statutory minimum. The Roberts Court addressed both questions in cases it accepted for review in its 2006 term. See Linda Greenhouse's piece for the *New York Times* on November 4, 2006, "Supreme Court to Revisit Federal Sentencing Guidelines."

11. The case list does not include a single Fourth Amendment ruling. Although it is arguable that the Rehnquist Court made many significant contributions to policy on "reasonable" invasive, warrantless searches, its opinions did not articulate a jurisprudence distinctive from the Burger Court's totality-of-facts balancing approach for Fourth Amendment search-and-seizure questions. Certain Rehnquist Court decisions were rights-protective, such as *City of Indianapolis v. Edmund* (2000) and *Kyllo v. U.S.* (2001), but these were exceptions to the Court's general understanding of the limits on privacy interests in Americans' persons and effects.

Still, the Rehnquist Court's articulation of a "reasonableness" approach to the constitutionality of warrantless searches through a cumulative case-by-case methodology (see Bradley 2005b) illustrated the "explicit personalization of constitutional interpretation" that characterized its jurisprudential approach overall. That no single Fourth Amendment case was the decision of doctrinal consequence further epitomizes that Court era as one of individualized judicial application of rule-of-thumb balancing frameworks.

12. O'Connor wrote what might be considered the split-the-difference opinion in her concurrence in the judgment that preserved the *Bowers v. Hardwick* precedent (and thus escaped Scalia's withering comments about fidelity to stare decisis directed at the majority opinion) by grounding her holding against the Texas sodomy statute in the Equal Protection Clause.

13. In *Romer*, the Kennedy-led majority invalidated a Colorado constitutional amendment ballot initiative that prohibited the state or any of its subdivisions from providing gays, lesbians, and bisexuals with legal protection from the injuries caused by discrimination. Viewing the amendment as imposing a special disability upon homosexual persons alone, the Court held six to three that it was an invalid form of legislation lacking even a rational relationship to a legitimate state interest and "inexplicable by anything but animus toward the class that it affects."

14. The notion of heresthetic manipulation of the dimensions of choice in a collective decision-making situation is discussed by Shepsle (2003), and was developed by Riker (1986). It refers to the strategy of introducing a new issue dimension into a choice situation in order to convert a losing outcome into a winning one by producing

a new majority coalition. See the discussion in Chapter 1 elaborating on the *Casey* decision from the perspective of Stevens's maneuvers to capture the center, evidence of which is recorded in the memos and drafts exchanged between the justices found in the judicial papers of Justice Harry Blackmun at the Library of Congress. See also Greenburg (2007).

15. Even postviability abortion services were not absolutely impermissible, as the Court revealed in its 2000 decision of *Stenberg v. Carhart*, which invalidated the federal ban on certain late-term abortion procedures because there was no exception for the preservation of maternal health.

16. Rehnquist had been an advocate of constitutional states' rights federalism since his tenure as an associate justice. See his 1976 majority opinion in *National League of Cities v. Usery* (426 U.S. 833), and Maveety (1987). Thomas's 1995 dissent from the five-to-four ruling of *U.S. Term Limits v. Thornton* (514 U.S. 779) vigorously defended the powers reserved for the states under the Tenth Amendment, going so far as to characterize the Constitution as a compact of states. He was joined by Rehnquist and O'Connor as well as Scalia.

17. Joondeph (2007) questions whether a commitment to state autonomy was really the motivating force behind O'Connor's federalism jurisprudence. He argues that if the full universe of "federalism" decisions during her tenure is considered, O'Connor's more significant preference is revealed: to reduce government regulation in general.

18. Later in the opinion, O'Connor explained that the danger of racial classification and separation of voters by race, even when done to remedy racial vote dilution, is that "it reinforces racial stereotypes and threatens to undermine our system of representative democracy by signaling to elected officials that they represent a particular racial group rather than their constituency as a whole" (509 U.S. at 650). Legal analysts have argued that her *Shaw* ruling recognizes the "expressive harm" that occurs when the government appears to use race in the redistricting context in a way that subordinates all other relevant values, thus impermissibly endorsing too dominant a role for race. See Pildes and Niemi (1993).

19. In *U.S. v. Morrison* (2000) the same five-justice majority invalidated the Violence Against Women Act along similar lines of reasoning as *Lopez*: the regulated activity was neither economic nor sufficiently causally linked to interstate commerce to come under congressional jurisdiction. Thomas again concurred, to object to the "rootless and malleable standard" presented by the "substantially affects" test. In *Gonzales v. Raich* (2005) the Court condoned the reach of federal commerce power to the prohibition of marijuana manufacture and possession in the Controlled Substances Act as

applied to intrastate manufacture and possession for medical purposes under California law. In this case, however, several *Lopez* majority justices dissented from what they viewed as a violation of precedent as to the limits on Congress: O'Connor, speaking for Rehnquist and Thomas and applying the test Kennedy and she had framed for *Lopez*, objected to the Court's compliance in "extinguish[ing] California's experiment." Kennedy himself joined the opinion of the Court; Scalia concurred in the judgment, rejecting "substantial effects" analysis and supporting the federal regulation by relying on the Necessary and Proper Clause.

20. See the discussion in Chapter 4.

21. The Court's holding in *Smith* was not a rule-of-thumb, noncategorical jurisprudential approach.

22. For the Rehnquist Court decisions limiting congressional power under Section 5 of the Fourteenth Amendment, see *Board of Trustees of the University of Alabama v. Garrett* (2001), *Kimel v. Florida Board of Regents* (2000), and *Florida Prepaid Postsecondary Education Expense Board v. College Savings Bank* (1999).

23. Such authorizations were, rather, an impermissible attempt by Congress "to substantively redefine the States' legal obligations" (528 U.S. at 88).

24. Breyer's argument here resembled O'Connor's concurring opinion in the 2004 constitutional challenge to the "under God" reference in the Pledge of Allegiance in *Elk Grove Unified School District v. Newdow*, in which she noted that "the history of a given practice is all the more relevant when the practice has been employed pervasively without engendering significant controversy" (524 U.S. 1 [2004]). Both she and Breyer expressed concern that religious accommodations "cause no political divisiveness," and have found the latter relevant to the endorsement-of-religion question (ibid.).

25. These issues were among the first addressed by the Roberts Court in its own racial considerations in school admissions cases heard in the 2006 term.

26. In light of the Roberts Court's narrowing of the implications of the *Grutter* precedent in the 2006 ruling of *Parents Involved in Community Schools v. Seattle School District*.

27. Corley (2007) similarly finds that plurality opinions are no different from majority opinions when it comes to treatment by the lower federal courts: her study of all treatments of Supreme Court opinions from 1986 through 2003 concludes that the courts of appeal are no less likely to comply with a rule announced in a plurality opinion than with a precedent established by a majority. Corley surmises that this is because of lower courts having become accustomed to reading longer and more partitioned Supreme Court opinions carefully in order to ascertain their meaning (13).

28. Hansford and Spriggs's finding renders somewhat beside the point the claim of another recent study of the judicial process (Sunstein, Schkade, Elman, and Sawicki

2006), that although rulings in which the Supreme Court has spoken definitively are initially followed with unanimity, there is a slide toward judicial partisanship and doctrinal dissensus over time. In other words, legal questions are seldom easy (requiring only application of clear law) for long, so there is arguably little difference in the long run between the Supreme Court laying out a "clear" legal path and a discretion-laden, rule-of-thumb approach.

29. Although this is a supposition upon which Gillman (1993) relies to advance his argument about the demise of the laissez-faire framework with respect to economic regulation, and that Brandwein (2006) implicitly folds into her analysis of "legal idioms" and constitutional development.

CHAPTER 4. THE COMMENTATORS' COURT AND THE RETURN TO JUDICIAL RESTRAINT

1. Opening Statement, Senator Patrick Leahy, January 9, 2006, Judge Samuel Alito Confirmation Hearings.

2. Nor could skepticism of the effectiveness of Court-ordered reform by policy analysts such as Horowitz (1977) and Rosenberg (1991).

3. Kahn also speculates at the end of his 1994 treatise that "recent landmark decisions by the Rehnquist Court offer evidence that it has decided to view Supreme Court decision making in constitutive terms" (265).

4. Indeed, in certain areas such as abortion, affirmative action, and gender equality, the Burger Court's decisions expanded on its predecessor's in being progressively egalitarian.

5. Fowler and Jeon (2005) assert that the Warren Court was an aberration in another way: whereas the norm of stare decisis and pattern of precedent citation in opinions had taken hold on the Supreme Court by the turn of the twentieth century, the Warren Court's sharp decline in the number of citations per opinion strongly suggests a deviation from it. Though the citation rate recovered in the decades following the Warren years, the same study reports but does not comment upon a second fall in the citation rate by 2000, during the final years of the Rehnquist era (see Fowler and Jeon's Figure 3).

6. "Cause" in this sense may be dubious, especially in the face of arguments about a dialogue between the Supreme Court and the interpretive community (Kahn 1994, 212) and an interdependent or even "result-specific" relationship between the legal academy and the Court's decision making (Smith 2004). Without confessional data, it is impossible to know the degree to which justices are influenced by "scholarship as a medium for bestowing praise and blame" (ibid., 102)—or by the so-called Greenhouse

effect. But the behavior of the present Supreme Court is the causal fodder for constitutional theories and interpretations of American politics. If that behavior confounds or
challenges extant theory, then scholarly correction—in reaction—will ensue.

7. I borrow here a phrase from Powe (2000), who called the Warren Court the judicial "touchstone of determining what is right and wrong" (xiv). The Rehnquist Court
was a different and, arguably, more negative sort of touchstone.

8. The Rehnquist Court was also solicitous of judicial power in questions of
executive-judicial interbranch conflict, as O'Connor's plurality opinion for *Hamdi v.
Rumsfeld* (2004) makes quite clear. Only Thomas's dissent objected to the Court "balancing away" executive war powers.

9. Other studies of the time further questioned the Supreme Court's performance
of a countermajoritarian function, suggesting that this very role idea was based on
flawed assumptions about judicial independence and judges' principled, as opposed
to political, decision making. See Graber (1993) and Peretti (1999).

10. What would change, according to such a conceptualization, "is the justices'
attitudes and self-conceptions. . . . In effect—although the analogy is more suggestive than literal—Supreme Court justices would come to see themselves in relation
to the public somewhat as lower court judges now see themselves in relation to the
Supreme Court: responsible for interpreting the Constitution according to their best
judgment, but with an awareness that there is a higher authority out there with power
to overturn their decisions" (Kramer 2004b). That "higher authority" is popular political response.

11. And suggest that the current judicial era has occasioned the abdication of that
job, as legal scholar Laurence Tribe's recent "Open Letter" (2005) testifies.

12. Or what I characterized in Chapter 3 as the rule-of-thumb jurisprudential
approach.

13. Perhaps this trait is also related to what one observer suggested was the Rehnquist Court's disinclination to acknowledge error, as when the joint opinion in *Planned
Parenthood v. Casey* (1992) "grounded the policy of adhering to precedent in concerns
for the institution's rhetorical effectiveness." Whatever the justices think of the errors
of prior decisions, this same observer continued, "they must adhere to most of them
lest the public realize the epistemic shallowness of the body of constitutional law that
the Supreme Court has erected" (Posner 2004, 44–45).

14. Legal studies professor Robert Van Sickel has offered an unvarnished version
of this same point specifically with respect to Justice O'Connor. Responding on June
23, 2003, to a discussion thread from the LAWCOURTS listserv on the *Gratz* and *Grutter* rulings, Van Sickel said this: "I believe that this role orientation [of seeking the

'middle ground' in controversial cases] IS [O'Connor's] philosophy of the Constitution, not that it is a coherent philosophy of any sort. . . . Given that she has embarked on an ambitious book-writing campaign, I believe that her recent opinions are best understood as part of a campaign to increase her personal stature as a political/historical figure. I think she's starting to believe her own press clippings about being the most important justice of the last 20 years."

15. Preliminary commentary on the first term of the new Roberts Court suggested the continuation of "finely spun Court decisions" that allow the Court to appear wise—as syndicated columnist George Will wrote on July 3, 2006. "Kennedy Reigns Supreme on Court" was the headline of journalist Charles Lane's end-of-term commentary piece for the *Washington Post* on July 2, 2006. Quoting Georgetown law professor Richard Lazarus, Lane's piece implied that Kennedy relished the role of being a significant moderating force and viewed himself as "a major intellectual force" for balancing the real values in conflict in the Court's cases.

16. Judicial role orientation is notoriously difficult to discern from observable criteria, and its study is often dismissed as a subjective enterprise by contemporary behavioral law and court scholars. Nevertheless, in resurrecting the theory of judicial restraint, current Supreme Court scholarship reignites concerns about how Supreme Court justices interpret their institutional role.

17. Or "strategic action," as the many contemporary paeans to the strategic model of judicial behavior would have it.

CHAPTER 5. THE QUEEN REGENT'S COURT IN THE ROBERTS TRANSITION

1. Jeffrey Rosen's January–February 2007 portrait of the new chief justice in the *Atlantic* is representative of this dimension of Roberts's leadership plans.

2. The quotation finishes, "So understood, [the decisions] say little about where the Court may be going now that Justice Alito is in place" (Hartnett 2006, 1757).

3. The *Wall Street Journal* "Law Blog" posting by Peter Lattman can be accessed at http://blogs.wsj.com/law/2007/04/18/supreme-disharmony.

4. These included *Beard v. Banks*, in which Thomas joined by Scalia concurred in Breyer's majority opinion limiting inmates' access to secular newspapers and magazines; *Sanchez-Llamas v. Oregon*, in which Ginsburg concurred only in the judgment and agreed in part with the dissent regarding the rights international treaties provide to foreign criminal suspects; and *Washington v. Recuenco*, in which Kennedy concurred only in the judgment of the Thomas majority's rejection of the grounds for automatic reversal of convictions. For the story, see http://online.wsj.com/public/resources/documents/info-scotusdiary.html.

5. The Court granted certiorari to decide on the authority of the military commission convened to try Hamdan on November 7, 2005. On December 30, 2005, the DTA was signed into law.

6. Not to mention emphatic judicial correction to the expansion of executive power defended by the dissenting opinion of Justice Thomas. Stevens repeatedly refers to "the sources which the Government and Justice Thomas rely upon."

7. The Rehnquist Court had invalidated a similar statute from Nebraska that also lacked a mother's health exception to the ban of the procedure in Stenburg v. Carhart in 2003. Kennedy dissented from the five-to-four ruling. Alito, replacing O'Connor for the Gonzales case, created the new five-to-four lineup.

8. Judicial dissensus in the 1940s was, of course, the inspiration for C. Herman Pritchett's path-breaking and proto-attitudinalist analysis of the Roosevelt Court. See Baum (2003). But the emphasis here, and in subsequent ideological models of judging, was on explaining dissent, not judicial vocality per se.

9. That justice is Ruth Bader Ginsburg. See Ellington (1998, 822) as well as my discussion of Justice Ginsburg's views of separate opinion writing in Chapter 2.

10. Vermeule (2006, 286) calls judicial pragmatism and the reasonableness-based doctrinal standards it employs "consequentialism with no value theory" of what is "sensible" or "pragmatically best" (84), that is, too focused and too reliant on a "celebratory view" of the mental processes of judges (55–58).

CONCLUSION: LONG LIVE THE QUEEN'S COURT?

1. On popular culture depictions of judicial power, see Asimow and Mader (2004) and Pohlman and Kahn (2005).

Geyh (2006) notes that the American public "ha[s] been steeping in a culture of legal realism" for a long time (21), and even is "being fed a steady diet of messages, from a member of the Court, that judges . . . impos[e] their political will rather than interpret the law" (277). The member of whom Geyh speaks is Justice Scalia. For another illustration of Scalia's candor as to judicial power, see note 11 and the accompanying discussion in text. A more encompassing j'accuse comes from Vermeule (2006), who suggests that self-interested motivations of "misguided idealism" on the part of judges and legal academics promote ambitious renderings of the judicial interpretation project (286–287) and of judicial power in general.

2. But see Gerber (1998), who comments that the lionization of Chief Justice Marshall and his belief that "the Supreme Court's power and prestige would be enhanced if it spoke with a single voice" has distorted and eclipsed the contributions of the seriatim opinion style of the early Court (20).

3. Thanks to Professor Richard Briffault of Columbia Law School for pointing out the reference to *Hayden v. Pataki* (decided May 4, 2006).

4. The case is *League of United Latin American Citizens v. Perry* (decided June 28, 2006). See my discussion of the decision in Chapter 5.

5. The quoted phrases come from Lively (1992, xiv and 162).

6. Granted, some bemoaned the judicial triumphalism the approach entailed. In Chapter 4, I discussed the paradox of the Rehnquist-era ideational legacy with respect to judicial power. The "model justice" (of the Rehnquist Court) characterization eclipsed the image of the "juricentric court" (of the Rehnquist era), as O'Connor's constitutional pragmatism came to seem, in retrospect, less threatening—or, perhaps, politically convenient. See Whittington (2007) for a developmental perspective on this latter point about judicial supremacy.

7. Hudson (2007) also challenges this interpretation, quoting law professor Thomas Baker: "The Rehnquist Court really was the court of William Rehnquist in style and substance" (147). Unfortunately, Hudson does not elaborate upon or attempt to elucidate this claim.

8. Although Vermeule (2006) thinks that only a limited purview for rule-bound judging is appropriate to the institutional capacity and informational constraints on courts. "Judges deciding constitutional cases should confine themselves to enforcement of the sort of clear coordinating rules as to which settlement is more important than content," he urges, with control over the incremental updating of the Constitution shifted from courts to legislatures (278). As such, he fits within the neorestraintist, late Rehnquist-era legal commentary on judicial power. Indeed, he calls his position "neo-Thayerian" (12).

9. Although shifting that faith to higher court rule formulators and away from those courts and judges who apply higher court directives in particular cases at a later time. Rules "require more information and decisional competence . . . at the time the rule-formulators decide what the content of the rule should be. . . . It follows that one important consideration in the choice between rules and standards is *whether rule-creators or rule-appliers have better information and superior competence to translate information into sound legal policy*" (Vermeule 2006, 69 [emphasis added]). O'Connoresque rule-of-thumb "standards" delegate decision-making authority—and presume competence—to the judicial decision maker at the point of application.

10. The occasion was the Roberts Court ruling in *Federal Election Commission (FEC) v. Wisconsin Right to Life* (2007), which limited the restrictions upheld when the McCain-Feingold campaign finance law first came to the Court in 2003. The Roberts Court decision was splintered five to four; it nominally upheld the precedent and its affirmation

of restrictions on television advertising but created a broad fact-based exception to the provision (Greenhouse and Kirkpatrick 2007). Scalia presumably felt that "true" judicial restraint mandated a different course of action—although his objection to the McConnell v. FEC precedent probably had less to do with restoring restraintist judging than with promoting the policy of political expenditures as protected speech. The presence of "judicial restraint" seems often to turn more on satisfying decisional content than on satisfactory institutional exercise. This was the case with those who beheld it in O'Connor, and is arguably also true of Scalia in his 2007 accusation.

11. "Pluralism" consists of four basic premises or key assertions: political power is distributed in multiple, competing centers of power; policy making is reactive rather than proactive; political leaders are tolerant coalition builders; and the outcome of this process is gradual, moderate, political reform. Pluralism as such fits the definition of "legitimizing discourse" in that it supports the claims the politically prominent typically make to justify their power (see Merelman 2003, 18–19).

BIBLIOGRAPHY

Ackerman, Bruce, ed. 2002. Bush v. Gore: The Question of Legitimacy. New Haven, CT: Yale University Press.

Anders, David B. 1993. "Justices Harlan and Black Revisited: The Emerging Dispute between Justice O'Connor and Justice Scalia over Unenumerated Fundamental Rights." Fordham Law Review 61: 895–933.

Asimow, Michael, and Shannon Mader. 2004. Law and Popular Culture. New York: Peter Lang.

Baker, Lynn A. 1996. "Interdisciplinary Due Diligence: The Case for Common Sense in the Search for the Swing Justice." Southern California Law Review 70: 187.

Banks, Christopher P., David B. Cohen, and John Clifford Green, eds. 2005. The Final Arbiter: The Consequences of Bush v. Gore for Law and Politics. Albany: State University of New York Press.

Barnes, Robert. 2006. "New Justices Take the Podium, Putting Personalities on Display." Washington Post, November 20, A15.

———. 2007a. "Court Was Once Cloistered; Now Its Chief Does Nightline." Washington Post, January 6, A3.

———. 2007b. "Roberts Supports Court's Shrinking Docket." Washington Post, February 2, A6.

———. 2007c. "Roberts Court Moves Right, But with a Measured Step." Washington Post, April 20, A3.

Barnett, Randy E. 2003. "Kennedy's Libertarian Revolution." National Review Online (July 10).

———. 2005. Restoring the Lost Constitution. Princeton, NJ: Princeton University Press.

Barnhart, Rebecca, and Deborah Zalesne. 2004. "Celebrating the Jurisprudence of Justice Ruth Bader Ginsburg: Twin Pillars of Judicial Philosophy—The Impact of the Ginsburg Collegiality and Gender Discrimination Principles on Her Separate Opinions Involving Gender Discrimination." New York City Law Review 7: 275–314.

Baum, Lawrence. 1999. "Recruitment and Motivations of Supreme Court Justices." In H. Gillman and C. Clayton, eds., The Supreme Court in American Politics: New Institutionalist Interpretations. Lawrence: University Press of Kansas.

———. 2003. "C. Herman Pritchett: Innovator with an Ambiguous Legacy." In N. Maveety, ed., The Pioneers of Judicial Behavior. Ann Arbor: University of Michigan Press.

———. 2006. Judges and Their Audiences: A Perspective on Judicial Behavior. Princeton, NJ: Princeton University Press.

Belsky, Martin H., ed. 2002. *The Rehnquist Court: A Retrospective.* New York: Oxford University Press.

Benesh, Sara C., and Harold J. Spaeth. 2005. "The Supreme Court Justice–Centered Judicial Databases: The Warren, Burger, and Rehnquist Courts (1953–2004 Terms)—Documentation." Program for Law and Judicial Politics, Michigan State University.

Berger, Raoul. 1977. *Government by Judiciary: The Transformation of the Fourteenth Amendment.* Cambridge, MA: Harvard University Press.

Best, Bradley J. 2002. *Law Clerks, Support Personnel, and the Decline of Consensual Norms on the United States Supreme Court, 1935–1995.* New York: LFB Scholarly Publishing.

Bickel, Alexander. 1961. "Forward: The Passive Virtues." *Harvard Law Review* 75: 40–79.

———. 1962. *The Least Dangerous Branch: The Supreme Court at the Bar of Politics.* Indianapolis, IN: Bobbs-Merrill.

Biskupic, Joan. 2005. *Sandra Day O'Connor: How the First Woman on the Supreme Court Became Its Most Influential Justice.* New York: HarperCollins.

Blackmun Papers. Library of Congress Archives, Manuscript Division (Madison Building).

Blasi, Vincent, ed. 1983. *The Burger Court: The Counter-Revolution That Wasn't.* New Haven, CT: Yale University Press.

Bork, Robert. 1989. *The Tempting of America: The Political Seduction of the Law.* New York: Free Press.

Bradley, Craig M. 2005a. "Introduction." In C. Bradley, ed., *The Rehnquist Legacy.* New York: Cambridge University Press.

———. 2005b. "The Fourth Amendment: Be Reasonable." In C. Bradley, ed., *The Rehnquist Legacy.* New York: Cambridge University Press.

Bradley, Gerard V. 2004. "Is the Constitution Whatever the Winners Say It Is?" In C. Wolfe, ed., *That Eminent Tribunal: Judicial Supremacy and the Constitution.* Princeton, NJ: Princeton University Press.

Brandwein, Pamela. 2006. "The *Civil Rights Cases* and the Lost Language of State Neglect." In R. Kahn and K. Kersch, eds., *The Supreme Court and American Political Development.* Lawrence: University Press of Kansas.

Breyer, Stephen. 2005. *Active Liberty: Interpreting Our Democratic Constitution.* New York: Alfred A. Knopf.

Brigham, John. 2005. "Let's Not Call It 'the Rehnquist Court.'" *Law and Courts Newsletter* 15: 24–26.

Broughton, J. Richard. 1999. "Unforgettable, Too: The (Juris) Prudential Legacy of the Second Justice Harlan." *Seton Hall Constitutional Law Journal* 10: 57–109.

Brust, Richard. 2003. "The Man in the Middle: Justice Kennedy's Opinion in the Gay Rights Case Underlines His Growing Influence." *American Bar Association Journal* 2003: 89.

Caldeira, Gregory A., and Christopher J. W. Zorn. 1998. "Of Time and Consensual Norms in the Supreme Court." *American Journal of Political Science* 42: 874–902.

Chemerinsky, Erwin. 2002. "The Rhetoric of Constitutional Law." *Michigan Law Review* 100: 2008–2035.

Choper, Jesse. 1980. *Judicial Review and the National Political Process: A Functional Reconsideration of the Supreme Court*. Chicago: University of Chicago Press.

Corley, Pamela C. 2007a. "Lower Court Response to Supreme Court Plurality Opinions." Paper presented at the annual meeting of the Southern Political Science Association, New Orleans, Louisiana, January 4–7.

———. 2007b. "Bargaining and Accommodation on the U.S. Supreme Court: Insight from Justice Blackmun." *Judicature* 90, no. 4 (January–February): 157–165.

Cramton, Roger C., and Paul D. Carrington, eds. 2006. *Reforming the Court: Term Limits for Supreme Court Justices*. Durham, NC: Carolina Academic Press.

Crowe, Justin. 2007. "The Forging of Judicial Autonomy: Political Entrepreneurship and the Reforms of William Howard Taft." *Journal of Politics* 69: 73–87.

Danelski, David J. 1960. "The Influence of the Chief Justice in the Decisional Process of the Supreme Court." In S. Goldman and A. Sarat, eds., *American Court Systems: Readings in Judicial Process and Behavior*. Reprint, San Francisco: W. H. Freeman, 1978.

Davis, Sue. 1999. "The Chief Justice and Judicial Decision Making: The Institutional Basis for Leadership on the Supreme Court." In C. Clayton and H. Gillman, eds., *Supreme Court Decision Making: New Institutionalist Approaches*. Chicago: University of Chicago Press.

Devins, Neal, and Louis Fisher. 2004. *The Democratic Constitution*. New York: Oxford University Press.

Ditslear, Corey, and Lawrence Baum. 2001. "Selection of Law Clerks and Polarization in the U.S. Supreme Court." *Journal of Politics* 63: 869–885.

Dworkin, R. M., ed. 2002. *A Badly Flawed Election: Debating Bush v. Gore, the Supreme Court, and American Democracy*. New York: New Press.

Edelman, Paul H., and Jim Chen. 1996. "The Most Dangerous Justice: The Supreme Court at the Bar of Mathematics." *Southern California Law Review* 70: 63–96.

———. 2001. "The Most Dangerous Justice Rides Again: Revisiting the Power Pageant of the Justices." *Minnesota Law Review* 86: 131.

Eisgruber, Christopher L. 2007. "Umpires, Ideologues, and Justices: How to Evaluate Supreme Court Nominees." Paper presented at the Program in Law and Public Affairs, Woodrow Wilson School, Princeton University, April 2.

Ellington, Toni J. 1998. "Ruth Bader Ginsburg and John Marshall Harlan: A Justice and Her Hero." *University of Hawai'i Law Review* 20: 797–834.

Ely, John Hart. 1980. *Democracy and Distrust: A Theory of Judicial Review.* Cambridge, MA: Harvard University Press.

Epstein, Lee, and Jack Knight. 1998. *The Choices Justices Make.* Washington, DC: Congressional Quarterly Press.

Epstein, Lee, Jeffrey A. Segal, and Harold J. Spaeth. 2001. "The Norm of Consensus on the U.S. Supreme Court." *American Journal of Political Science* 45: 362–377.

Epstein, Lee, Jeffrey A. Segal, Harold J. Spaeth, and Thomas G. Walker. 2003. *The Supreme Court Compendium: Data, Decisions, and Developments.* 3rd ed. Washington, DC: Congressional Quarterly Press.

Epstein, Lee, Thomas Walker, and William Dixon. 1988. "On the Mysterious Demise of Consensual Norms in the U.S. Supreme Court." *Journal of Politics* 50: 361–389.

Fiss, Owen. 1979. "Forward: The Forms of Justice." *Harvard Law Review* 93: 1.

Fowler, James H., and Sangick Jeon. 2005. "The Authority of Supreme Court Precedent: A Network Analysis." Working paper, University of California–Davis.

France, Steve. 1999. "Opinions with Style." *American Bar Association Journal* (September).

Franck, Matthew J. 1996. *Against the Imperial Judiciary: The Supreme Court vs. the Sovereignty of the People.* Lawrence: University Press of Kansas.

Friedelbaum, Stanley H. 1994. *The Rehnquist Court: In Pursuit of Judicial Conservatism.* Westport, CT: Greenwood Press.

Friedman, Barry. 2004. "The Cycles of Constitutional Theory." *Law and Contemporary Problems* 67: 149–174.

Friedman, Lawrence M. 2002. "The Rehnquist Court: Some More or Less Historical Comments." In M. Belsky, ed., *The Rehnquist Court: A Retrospective.* New York: Oxford University Press.

Garrow, David. 2002. "William H. Rehnquist in the Mirror of Justices." In M. Belsky, ed., *The Rehnquist Court: A Retrospective.* New York: Oxford University Press.

Gerber, Scott Douglas. 1998. "Introduction: The Supreme Court before John Marshall." In S. Gerber, ed., *Seriatim: The Supreme Court before John Marshall.* New York: New York University Press.

Gerber, Scott D., and Keeok Park. 1997. "The Quixotic Search for Consensus on the U.S. Supreme Court: A Cross-Judicial Empirical Analysis of the Rehnquist Court Justices." *American Political Science Review* 91: 390–408.

Gerhardt, Michael J. 2001. "Norm Theory and the Future of the Federal Appointments Process." *Duke Law Journal* 50: 1687–1715.

Geyh, Charles Gardner. 2006. *When Courts and Congress Collide: The Struggle for Control of America's Judicial System*. Ann Arbor: University of Michigan Press.

Gibbons, John J. 1998. "The Legacy of the Burger Court." In B. Schwartz, ed., *The Burger Court: Counter-Revolution or Confirmation?* New York: Oxford University Press.

Gibson, James L., Gregory A. Caldeira, and Lester Kenyatta Spence. 2003. "The Supreme Court and the U.S. Presidential Election of 2000: Wounds, Self-Inflicted or Otherwise?" *British Journal of Political Science* 33: 535–556.

Gillman, Howard. 1993. *The Constitution Besieged: The Rise and Demise of Lochner Era Police Powers Jurisprudence*. Durham, NC: Duke University Press.

Ginsburg, Ruth Bader. 1990. "Remarks on Writing Separately." *Washington Law Review* 65: 133–150.

———. 1992. "Speaking in a Judicial Voice." *New York University Law Review* 67: 1185–1209.

Gottlieb, Stephen E. 2001. *Morality Imposed: The Rehnquist Court and Liberty in America*. New York: New York University Press.

Graber, Mark. 1993. "The Nonmajoritarian Difficulty: Legislative Deference to the Judiciary." *Studies in American Political Development* 7: 35–73.

———. 2005. "Constructing Judicial Review." *Annual Review of Political Science* 8: 425–451.

Greenburg, Jan Crawford. 2007. *Supreme Conflict: The Inside Story of the Struggle for Control of the United States Supreme Court*. New York: Penguin.

Greenhouse, Linda. 2005a. *Becoming Justice Blackmun: Harry Blackmun's Supreme Court Journey*. New York: Times Books/Henry Holt.

———. 2005b. "Forward: The Third Rehnquist Court." In C. Bradley, ed., *The Rehnquist Legacy*. New York: Cambridge University Press.

———. 2006a. "Roberts Dissent Reveals Strain beneath Court's Placid Surface." *New York Times*, March 22.

———. 2006b. "Roberts Is at Court's Helm, but He Isn't Yet in Control." *New York Times*, July 1.

Greenhouse, Linda, and David D. Kirkpatrick. 2007. "Justices Loosen Ad Restrictions in Campaign Finance Law." *New York Times*, June 26.

Grey, Thomas C. 1989. "Holmes and Legal Pragmatism." *Stanford Law Review* 41: 787.

Griffin, Stephen M. 1996. *American Constitutionalism*. Princeton, NJ: Princeton University Press.

Grofman, Bernard. 2006. "Operationalizing the Section 5 Retrogression Standard of the Voting Rights Act in Light of *Georgia v. Ashcroft*: Social Science Perspectives on

Minority Influence, Opportunity, and Control." Paper presented at the Program in Law and Public Affairs, Woodrow Wilson School, Princeton University, March 13.

Hand, Learned. 1958. *The Bill of Rights: The Oliver Wendell Holmes Lectures, 1958.* Cambridge, MA: Harvard University Press.

Hansford, Thomas G., and James F. Spriggs. 2006. *The Politics of Precedent on the U.S. Supreme Court.* Princeton, NJ: Princeton University Press.

Harriger, Katy J. 2004. "The Limits of Presidential Immunity: *Clinton v. Jones.*" In G. Ivers and K. McGuire, eds., *Creating Constitutional Change.* Charlottesville: University of Virginia Press.

Hartnett, Edward A. 2006. "Modest Hope for a Modest Roberts Court: Deference, Facial Challenges, and the Comparative Competence of Courts." *Southern Methodist University Law Review* 59: 1735–1760.

Haynie, Stacia. 1992. "Leadership and Consensus on the U.S. Supreme Court." *Journal of Politics* 54: 1158–1169.

Henry, Robert. 1998. "The Players and the Play." In B. Schwartz, ed., *The Burger Court: Counter-Revolution or Confirmation?* New York: Oxford University Press.

Hettinger, Virginia A., Stefanie A. Lindquist, and Wendy L. Martinek. 2003. "Separate Writing on the United States Courts of Appeals." *American Politics Research* 31: 215–250.

Horowitz, Donald L. 1977. *The Courts and Social Policy.* Washington, DC: Brookings Institution.

Hudson, David L. 2007. *The Rehnquist Court: Understanding Its Impact and Legacy.* Westport, CT: Praeger.

Irons, Peter. 1994. *Brennan vs. Rehnquist: The Battle for the Constitution.* New York: Alfred A. Knopf.

Issacharoff, Samuel, Pamela S. Karlan, and Richard H. Pildes. 1998. *The Law of Democracy: Legal Structure of the Political Process.* Westbury, NY: Foundation Press.

Jackson, Robert H. 1941. *The Struggle for Judicial Supremacy: A Study of a Crisis in American Power Politics.* New York: Alfred A. Knopf.

Johnsen, Dawn E. 2004. "Functional Departmentalism and Nonjudicial Interpretation: Who Determines Constitutional Meaning?" *Law and Contemporary Problems* 67: 105–147.

Johnson, Timothy K. 2004. *Oral Arguments and Decision Making on the United States Supreme Court.* Albany: State University of New York Press.

Joondeph, Bradley W. 2007. "The Deregulatory Valence of Justice O'Connor's Federalism." Paper presented at the annual meeting of the Western Political Science Association, Las Vegas, Nevada, March 8–10.

Kahn, Ronald. 1994. *The Supreme Court and Constitutional Theory*. Lawrence: University Press of Kansas.

———. 2006. "Social Constructions, Supreme Court Reversals, and American Political Development: *Lochner, Plessy, Bowers*, but Not *Roe*." In R. Kahn and K. Kersch, eds., *The Supreme Court and American Political Development*. Lawrence: University Press of Kansas.

Kahn, Ronald, and Ken I. Kersch. 2006. "Introduction." In R. Kahn and K. Kersch, eds., *The Supreme Court and American Political Development*. Lawrence: University Press of Kansas.

Kalman, Laura. 1996. *The Strange Career of Legal Liberalism*. New Haven, CT: Yale University Press.

Karlan, Pamela S. 1996. "Still Hazy after All These Years: Voting Rights in the Post-Shaw Era." *Cumberland Law Review* 26: 287.

Karst, Kenneth L. 2003. "Justice O'Connor and the Substance of Equal Citizenship." *Supreme Court Review* 2003: 357–458.

Keck, Tom. 2004. *The Most Activist Supreme Court in History: The Road to Modern Judicial Conservatism*. Chicago: University of Chicago Press.

Kersch, Ken I. 2006. "The New Deal Triumph as the End of History? The Judicial Negotiation of Labor Rights and Civil Rights." In R. Kahn and K. Kersch, eds., *The Supreme Court and American Political Development*. Lawrence: University Press of Kansas.

Kilgore, Carrol D. 1977. *Judicial Tyranny*. Nashville, TN: Thomas Nelson.

Klein, David E. 2002. *Making Law in the United States Courts of Appeals*. New York: Cambridge University Press.

Kramer, Larry D. 2004a. *The People Themselves: Popular Constitutionalism and Judicial Review*. New York: Oxford University Press.

———. 2004b. "We the People: Who Has the Last Word on the Constitution?" *Boston Review* (February–March).

Kritzer, Herbert M. 2005. "The American Public's Assessment of the Rehnquist Court." *Judicature* 89: 168–176.

Lamb, Charles M., and Stephen C. Halpern. 1991. *The Burger Court: Political and Judicial Profiles*. Urbana: University of Illinois Press.

Lane, Charles. 2006. "Kennedy Reigns Supreme on Court." *Washington Post*, July 2.

Lasser, William. 1988. *The Limits of Judicial Power: The Supreme Court in American Politics*. Chapel Hill: University of North Carolina Press.

Lazarus, Edward. 1999. *Closed Chambers: The Rise, Fall, and Future of the Modern Supreme Court*. New York: Penguin Putnam.

———. 2004. "Why the Scales Won't Tip." *Washington Post*, November 7, B3.

Levin, Mark R. 2005. *Men in Black: How the Supreme Court Is Destroying America*. Washington, DC: Regnery.

Levinson, Sanford. 2006. *Our Undemocratic Constitution: Where the Constitution Goes Wrong (and How We the People Can Correct It)*. New York: Oxford University Press.

Liptak, Adam. 2007. "The New 5–4 Supreme Court." *New York Times*, April 22.

Lithwick, Dalia. 2007. "Why Are the Justices Popping Up All over the Tube?" *American Lawyer* (February 28).

Lively, Donald E. 1992. *Foreshadows of the Law: Supreme Court Dissents and Constitutional Development*. Westport, CT: Praeger.

Lovell, George. 2003. *Legislative Deferrals: Statutory Ambiguity, Judicial Power, and American Democracy*. New York: Cambridge University Press.

Maltz, Earl M. 2003. "Introduction." In E. Maltz, ed., *Rehnquist Justice: Understanding the Court Dynamic*. Lawrence: University Press of Kansas.

Maltzman, Forrest, James F. Spriggs II, and Paul J. Wahlbeck. 2000. *Crafting Law on the Supreme Court: The Collegial Game*. New York: Cambridge University Press.

Margolick, David. 2007. "Meet the Supremes." *New York Times Book Review* (September 23).

Marshall, Thomas R. 2005. "American Public Opinion and the Rehnquist Court." *Judicature* 89: 177–180.

Mauro, Tony. 2006. "Scalia, Breyer Debate Unanimity on the High Court." *Legal Times*, December 13.

Maveety, Nancy. 1987. "The Populist of the Adversary Society: The Jurisprudence of Justice Rehnquist." *Journal of Contemporary Law* 13: 221–247.

———. 1996. *Justice Sandra Day O'Connor: Strategist on the Supreme Court*. Lanham, MD: Rowman & Littlefield.

———. 2003. "Justice Sandra Day O'Connor: Accommodationism and Conservatism." In E. Maltz, ed., *Rehnquist Justice: Understanding the Court Dynamic*. Lawrence: University Press of Kansas.

———. 2005. "The Era of the Choral Court." *Judicature* 89: 138–145.

Maveety, Nancy, Charles C. Turner, and Lori Beth Way. 2004. "Changes in the Use of Concurrence: The Burger and Rehnquist Courts Compared." Paper presented at the annual meeting of the American Political Science Association, Chicago, Illinois, September 2–5.

———. 2007. "Beginning to Write Separately: The Origins and Development of Concurring Judicial Opinions." Paper presented at the annual meeting of the Western Political Science Association, Las Vegas, Nevada, March 8–10.

McCloskey, Robert G. 2000 [1960]. *The American Supreme Court.* 3rd ed. Chicago: University of Chicago Press.

McConnell, Michael W. 2004. "Toward a More Balanced History of the Supreme Court." In C. Wolfe, ed., *That Eminent Tribunal: Judicial Supremacy and the Constitution.* Princeton, NJ: Princeton University Press.

McFeatters, Ann Carey. 2005. *Sandra Day O'Connor: Justice in the Balance.* Albuquerque: University of New Mexico Press.

Meese, Edwin III. 1985. "Speech before the D.C. Chapter of the Federalist Society Lawyers Division." Washington, DC, November 15.

Merrill, Thomas W. 2003. "The Making of the Second Rehnquist Court: A Preliminary Analysis." *St. Louis University Law Journal* 47: 569–658.

Miller, R. K. 1999. "Presidential Sanctuaries after the Clinton Sex Scandals." *Harvard Journal of Law and Public Policy* 22: 647–734.

Molot, Jonathan T. 2004. "Principled Minimalism: Restriking the Balance between Judicial Minimalism and Neutral Principles." *Virginia Law Review* 90: 1753–1847.

Murphy, Walter F. 1964. *The Elements of Judicial Strategy.* Chicago: University of Chicago Press.

Murphy, Walter F., C. Herman Pritchett, and Lee Epstein. 2002. *Courts, Judges, and Politics.* Boston: McGraw Hill.

Nagel, Robert F. 2004. "Nationhood and Judicial Supremacy." In C. Wolfe, ed., *That Eminent Tribunal: Judicial Supremacy and the Constitution.* Princeton, NJ: Princeton University Press.

Nicholson, Stephen P., and Robert M. Howard. 2003. "Framing Support for the Supreme Court in the Aftermath of *Bush v. Gore.*" *Journal of Politics* 65: 676–695.

Norton, Anne. 1993. *Republic of Signs: Liberal Theory and American Popular Culture.* Chicago: University of Chicago Press.

O'Brien, David M. 2005a. "A Diminished Plenary Docket: A Legacy of the Rehnquist Court." *Judicature* 89: 134–137, 182.

———. 2005b. *Storm Center: The Supreme Court in American Politics.* 7th ed. New York: W. W. Norton.

O'Connor, Sandra Day. 2003. *The Majesty of the Law: Reflections of a Supreme Court Justice.* New York: Random House.

O'Hara, James B. 1998. "Introduction." In B. Schwartz, ed., *The Burger Court: Counter-Revolution or Confirmation?* New York: Oxford University Press.

Orth, John V. 2006. *How Many Judges Does It Take to Make a Supreme Court? And Other Essays on Law and the Constitution.* Lawrence: University Press of Kansas.

Parshall, Lisa K. 2004. "The Evolution of Justice Kennedy? A Judicial Conservative's

Support for Gay Rights." Paper presented at the annual meeting of the Midwest Political Science Association, Chicago, Illinois, April 15–18.

Peppers, Todd C. 2006. *Courtiers of the Marble Palace: The Rise and Influence of the Supreme Court Law Clerk.* Palo Alto, CA: Stanford University Press.

Peretti, Terri Jennings. 1999. *In Defense of a Political Court.* Princeton, NJ: Princeton University Press.

Perry, Michael J. 1982. *The Constitution, the Courts, and Human Rights.* New Haven, CT: Yale University Press.

———. 1994. "The Constitution, the Courts, and the Question of Minimalism." *Northwestern University Law Review* 88: 84.

Peters, Christopher D., and Neal Devins. 2005. "Alexander Bickel and the New Judicial Minimalism." In K. Ward and C. Castillo, eds., *The Judiciary and American Democracy: Alexander Bickel, the Countermajoritarian Difficulty, and Contemporary Constitutional Theory.* Albany: State University of New York Press.

Pildes, Richard, and Richard Niemi. 1993. "Expressive Harms, 'Bizarre Districts,' and Voting Rights: Evaluating Election-District Appearances after *Shaw v. Reno.*" *Michigan Law Review* 92: 483.

Pohlman, H. L., and Michael A. Kahn. 2005. *May It Amuse the Court: Editorial Cartoons of the Supreme Court and Constitution.* Athens, GA: Hill Street Press.

Posner, Richard A. 2004. "The People's Court." *New Republic* (July 19).

Post, Robert C., and Reva B. Siegel. 2000. "Equal Protection by Law: Federal Antidiscrimination Legislation after Morrison and Kimel." *Yale Law Journal* 110: 441.

———. 2003. "Protecting the Constitution from the People: Juricentric Restrictions on Section Five Power." *Indiana Law Journal* 78: 1–45.

Powe, Lucas A., Jr. 2000. *The Warren Court and American Politics.* Cambridge, MA: Belknap Press of Harvard University Press.

———. 2003. "The Politics of American Judicial Review: Reflections on the Marshall, Warren, and Rehnquist Courts." *Wake Forest Law Review* 38: 697–732.

Rappaport, Michael. 2004. "It's the O'Connor Court." *Northwestern University Law Review* 99: 369.

Ray, Laura Krugman. 1990. "The Justices Write Separately: Uses of Concurrence by the Rehnquist Court." *University of California–Davis Law Review* 23: 777–831.

———. 2003. "Justice Ginsburg and the Middle Way." *Brooklyn Law Review* 68: 629–682.

Richards, Mark J., and Herbert M. Kritzer. 2002. "Jurisprudential Regimes in Supreme Court Decision Making." *American Political Science Review* 96: 305–320.

Richey, Warren. 2004. "The Quiet Ascent of Justice Stevens." *Christian Science Monitor*, July 9, 1–3.

Riker, William H. 1986. *The Art of Political Manipulation.* New Haven, CT: Yale University Press.

Rosen, Jeffrey. 1996. "Two Cheers for the Rehnquist Court." *Nexus: A Journal of Opinion* 1: 37–44.

———. 1999. "The Age of Mixed Results." *New Republic* (June 28): 43–51.

———. 2001. "A Majority of One." *New York Times*, June 3, 32.

———. 2005a. "Two Kinds of Pragmatist." *Los Angeles Times Book Review* (October 23): R3–R4.

———. 2005b. "Rehnquist the Great?" *Atlantic Monthly* (April).

———. 2006. *The Supreme Court: The Personalities and Rivalries That Defined America.* New York: Times Books/Henry Holt.

———. 2007a. "Roberts's Rules," *Atlantic* 299 (January–February): 104–113.

———. 2007b. "The Dissenter." *New York Times Magazine* (September 23).

Rosenberg, Debra. 2007. "Justice: Bench Player." *Newsweek* (February 12).

Rosenberg, Gerald N. 1991. *The Hollow Hope: Can Courts Bring about Social Change?* Chicago: University of Chicago Press.

Rostow, Eugene V. 1962. *The Sovereign Prerogative: The Supreme Court and the Quest for Law.* New Haven, CT: Yale University Press.

Savage, David G. 1993. *Turning Right: The Making of the Rehnquist Court.* New York: Wiley.

———. 2006. "Roberts Leading Court onto Unusually Common Ground." *Los Angeles Times*, March 9.

Scalia, Antonin. 1994. "The Dissenting Opinion." *Journal of Supreme Court History* 1994: 33–44.

Schwartz, Herman, ed. 1987. *The Burger Years: Rights and Wrongs in the Supreme Court, 1969–1986.* New York: Penguin.

———. 1998. *The Burger Court: Counter-Revolution or Confirmation?* New York: Oxford University Press.

———. 2002. *The Rehnquist Court: Judicial Activism on the Right.* New York: Hill and Wang.

Segal, Jeffrey A., and Harold J. Spaeth. 1993. *The Supreme Court and the Attitudinal Model.* New York: Cambridge University Press.

Segall, Eric J. 2006. "Justice O'Connor and the Rule of Law." *Florida Journal of Law and Public Policy* 17: 107–137.

Shapiro, Martin. 1983. "Fathers and Sons: The Court, the Commentators, and the Search for Values." In V. Blasi, ed., *The Burger Court: The Counter-Revolution That Wasn't.* New Haven, CT: Yale University Press.

Shepsle, Kenneth A. 2003. "Losers in Politics (and How They Sometimes Become Winners): William Riker's Heresthetic." *Perspectives on Politics* 1: 307–316.

Siegel, Andrew M. 2006. "The Court against the Courts: Hostility to Litigation as an Organizing Theme in the Rehnquist Court's Jurisprudence." *Texas Law Review* 84: 1097–1202.

Silverstein, Mark. 1994. *Judicious Choices: The New Politics of Supreme Court Confirmations.* New York: W. W. Norton.

Simon, James F. 1995. *The Center Holds: The Power Struggle inside the Rehnquist Court.* New York: Simon and Schuster.

Smith, Christopher E., and Kimberly A. Beuger. 1993. "Clouds in the Crystal Ball: Presidential Expectations and the Unpredictable Behavior of Supreme Court Appointees." *Akron Law Review* 27: 115.

Smith, Christopher E., and Thomas R. Hensley. 1994. "Unfulfilled Aspirations: The Court-Packing Efforts of Presidents Reagan and Bush." *Albany Law Review:* 1111.

Smith, Steven D. 2004. "The Academy, the Courts, and the Culture of Rationalism." In C. Wolfe, ed., *That Eminent Tribunal: Judicial Supremacy and the Constitution.* Princeton, NJ: Princeton University Press.

Somin, Ilya. 2007. "Controlling the Grasping Hand: Economic Development Takings after *Kelo.*" *Supreme Court Economic Review* 15: 183.

Spaeth, Harold J., and Michael F. Altfeld. 1984. "Measuring Influence on the U.S. Supreme Court." *Jurimetrics* 24: 236–247.

———. 1985. "Influence Relationships within the Supreme Court: A Comparison of the Warren and Burger Courts." *Western Political Quarterly* 38: 70–83.

Sracic, Paul A. 2000. "Once upon a Time, There Was Clarity." *Washington Post,* December 17, B2.

Starr, Kenneth W. 2002. *First among Equals: The Supreme Court in American Life.* New York: Warner Books.

Sunstein, Cass R. 1999. *One Case at a Time: Judicial Minimalism on the Supreme Court.* Cambridge, MA: Harvard University Press.

———. 2005. *Radicals in Robes: Why Extreme Right-Wing Courts Are Wrong for America.* New York: Basic Books.

———. 2006. "Symposium Article: Problems with Minimalism." *Stanford Law Review* 58: *Symposium: Looking Backward, Looking Forward: The Legacy of Chief Justice Rehnquist and Justice O'Connor:* 1899–1918.

Sunstein, Cass, Davide Schkade, Lisa M. Ellman, and Andres Sawiki. 2006. *Are Judges Political? An Empirical Analysis of the Federal Judiciary.* Washington, DC: Brookings Institution.

Teles, Steven. 2008. *Parallel Paths: The Evolution of the Conservative Legal Movement.* Princeton, NJ: Princeton University Press.

Toobin, Jeffrey. 2007. *The Nine: Inside the Secret World of the Supreme Court*. New York: Doubleday.

Tribe, Laurence H. 2005. "An Open Letter to Interested Readers of *American Constitutional Law*." April 29, 2005.

Tushnet, Mark. 1999. *Taking the Constitution away from the Courts*. Princeton, NJ: Princeton University Press.

———. 2003. *The New Constitutional Order*. Princeton, NJ: Princeton University Press.

———. 2005. *A Court Divided: The Rehnquist Court and the Future of Constitutional Law*. New York: W. W. Norton.

———. 2006. *A Court Divided: The Rehnquist Court and the Future of Constitutional Law (with an Epilogue)*. New York: W. W. Norton.

Tushnet, Mark, ed. 1993. *The Warren Court in Historical and Political Perspective*. Charlottesville: University of Virginia Press.

Vanberg, Georg. 2001. "Legislative-Judicial Relations: A Game-Theoretic Approach to Constitutional Review." *American Journal of Political Science* 45: 346–361.

Vermeule, Adrian. 2006. *Judging under Uncertainty: An Institutional Theory of Legal Interpretation*. Cambridge, MA: Harvard University Press.

Ward, Artemus. 2004. "The Gay Rights Jurisprudence of Anthony Kennedy: An Institutional Analysis." Paper presented at the annual meeting of the Midwest Political Science Association, Chicago, Illinois, April 15–18.

———. 2007. "Review of *The Political Thought of Antonin Scalia*, by James B. Staab." *Law and Politics Book Review* 17, no. 2: 96–100.

Ward, Artemus, and David Weiden. 2006. *Sorcerers' Apprentices: 100 Years of Law Clerks at the United States Supreme Court*. New York: New York University Press.

Way, Lori Beth, and Charles C. Turner. 2006. "Disagreement on the Rehnquist Court: The Dynamics of Supreme Court Concurrence." *American Politics Research* 34: 293–318.

Way, Lori Beth, Charles C. Turner, and Nancy Maveety. 2007. "Separate Opinions in the Early Twentieth Century: An Examination of Concurrence on the Taft Court." Paper presented at the annual meeting of the American Political Science Association, Chicago, Illinois, August 29–September 2.

Wheeler, Russell R. 2005. "Chief Justice Rehnquist as Third Branch Leader." *Judicature* 89: 116–122.

Whittington, Keith E. 2003. "William H. Rehnquist: Nixon's Strict Constructionist, Reagan's Chief Justice." In E. Maltz, ed., *Rehnquist Justice: Understanding the Court Dynamic*. Lawrence: University Press of Kansas.

———. 2004. "The *Casey* Five versus the Federalism Five: Supreme Legislator or

Prudent Umpire?" In C. Wolfe, ed., *That Eminent Tribunal: Judicial Supremacy and the Constitution*. Princeton, NJ: Princeton University Press.

———. 2005. "Interpose Your Friendly Hand: Political Supports for the Exercise of Judicial Review by the United States Supreme Court." *American Political Science Review* 99: 583–596.

———. 2007. *Political Foundations of Judicial Supremacy: The Presidency, the Supreme Court, and Constitutional Leadership in U.S. History*. Princeton, NJ: Princeton University Press.

Wilkinson, J. Harvie, III. 2006. "Symposium Article: The Rehnquist Court at Twilight—The Lures and Perils of Split-the-Difference Jurisprudence." *Stanford Law Review* 58: *Symposium: Looking Backward, Looking Forward: The Legacy of Chief Justice Rehnquist and Justice O'Connor, 1969–1996*.

Wolfe, Christopher. 2004. "The Rehnquist Court and 'Conservative Judicial Activism.'" In C. Wolfe, ed., *That Eminent Tribunal: Judicial Supremacy and the Constitution*. Princeton, NJ: Princeton University Press.

Wood, Sandra L. 1998. "Bargaining on the Burger Court: Of Memos, Changes, and Endorsements." Paper presented at the annual meeting of the Midwest Political Science Association, Chicago, Illinois, May 23–25.

Yen, Hope. 2006. "Narrower High Court Decisions Urged." Associated Press, May 22.

Yoo, John. 2006. "Courts at War." *Cornell University Law Review* 91: 573–602.